NEW YORK

AND ITS ENVIRONS

BY

GUSTAV KOBBÉ

AUTHOR OF "JERSEY COAST AND PINES" ETC.

WITH MAPS AND ILLUSTRATIONS

NEW YORK

HARPER & BROTHERS, FRANKLIN SQUARE

TO

EDWARD D. ADAMS,

IN A SUGGESTION FROM WHOSE FERTILE MIND THE AUTHOR'S FIRST GUIDE-BOOK HAD ITS ORIGIN.

ILLUSTRATIONS.

MAPS AND PLANS.

CONTENTS.

CHAPTER VII.

CITY HALL PARK TO MADISON SQUARE.

CHAPTER VIII.

FIFTH AVENUE.

CHAPTER IX.

CHAPTER X.

CENTRAL PARK.

CHAPTER XI.

EAST OF CENTRAL PARK.

CHAPTER XII.

PUBLIC CHARITIES AND CORRECTION.

CHAPTER XIII.

ENVIRONS.

PREFACE.

This aims to be a work worthy of the great city to which it is a guide. It is not intended to usurp the functions of a directory; but to point out and describe such features of New York City and its varied life, as an intelligent and cultured stranger might be interested in seeing, care having been taken to discriminate between what is of interest to New Yorkers only and what a visitor to the city would find worthy of attention. There is much in New York which must be familiar to those who have long resided in it or have been enterprising enough to explore it, which can have no place in a guide, if only because too many details would tend to confuse rather than enlighten a stranger. Yet the author believes that many New Yorkers who consider themselves familiar with their city may first learn from this book what a really wonderful and attractive place they live in. Considerable historical matter has been introduced in the description of what may, by comparison, be called the ancient part of the city—that portion of it which lies below Canal street—for only in this way could an adequate idea be conveyed of the developement of the little Dutch trading post of New Amsterdam into the stately metropolis of the New World. The stockade erected along the present line of Wall street as a means of defense against Indian attacks; the skiff which constituted the ferry to Brooklyn, starting from what is now the corner of Exchange place and Broad street, down the ditch which ran through the latter street; cattle grazing on the common pasture where City Hall Park now is;

anglers casting their lines in the Fresh Water Pond or Collect where the Tombs now stands;—such historical data will, it is hoped, serve to emphasize the contrast between the New York of to-day and the New York of the past.

The main portion of the book is arranged in the form of an itinerary. This is preceded by an Introduction giving general information regarding the city's topography and history; routes of travel, hotels, restaurants, shops, postal and telegraph facilities and similar matters. The itinerary begins at the southern end of the city. The islands in the harbor are first described. Then, starting at the Battery, the stranger is conducted up Whitehall street to Bowling Green; from there up Broadway to Madison square and thence up Fifth avenue to Central Park, detours being made to points of interest east and west of the main thoroughfares. The Metropolitan Museum of Art, the Lenox Library and the American Museum of Natural History are then described, and a chapter on Central Park follows, the itinerary concluding with a description of those parts of the city east, west and north of the Park. A chapter is then devoted to points of interest in the environs of New York. The author will consider it a favor if any one discovering mistakes of commission or omission will call his attention to them.

GUSTAV KOBBÉ.

SHORT HILLS,
ESSEX COUNTY, NEW JERSEY.

INTRODUCTORY.

TOPOGRAPHY AND STATISTICS.

TOPOGRAPHY.—New York City is situated: latitude, 40°, 42″ 40′ north; longitude, 74°, 0″ 3′ west, at the mouth of the Hudson river, 18 miles from the Atlantic ocean, 190 miles southwest of Boston, 205 miles northeast of Washington, and 715 miles east of Chicago. It comprises the Island of Manhattan, Governor's Island, the most southerly point in the bay, occupied, however, by the United States Government; Blackwell's, Ward's and Randall's Islands in the East river, and so much of the mainland north of the Harlem river which is bounded north by the city of Yonkers, west by the Hudson river and east by the Bronx river. Its greatest length from the Battery to its most northerly point is 16 miles; its greatest width, from the mouth of the Bronx to the Hudson river, 4½ miles; its area, 41½ square miles (26,500 acres).

The most important part of the City is the Island of Manhattan, 13½ miles long and 2½ miles wide at its widest point, at Fourteenth street, being very much narrower both below and above this line, especially at the Battery and above One Hundred and Sixtieth street, where it narrows to a strip between the Harlem and the Hudson rivers. Its area is 22 square miles (14,000 acres). Its boundaries are: North, Spuyten Duyvil creek and the Harlem river; west, the Hudson river; east, the East river; south, New York bay. The highest point, 238 feet above tide water, is at Washington Heights, and the extreme northern point is the termination of the bold bluff which rises between the Hudson and Harlem rivers. Various sections of the City have local names. Yorkville begins at Eighty-sixth street on the East side and runs to Harlem, which extends from about One Hundred and Tenth street north and northeast of Central Park to One Hundred and Fifty-ninth street, embracing the section east of Eighth avenue. Bloomingdale, Manhattanville, Carmansville and Washington Heights. The last named, with Fort Washington, are on the west side of the upper part of the Island of

Manhattan. (See large map of City.) So much of the City as lies on the mainland is called the "Annexed District." Here are, among other localities, all shown on the map of the City, Morrisania, West Farms, Tremont, Fordham, Williamsbridge and Woodlawn.

Population and Structures.—The total number of structures of all kinds in New York City has been enumerated at about 107,000, of which some 71,000 are below Fifty-ninth street, 75,000 being used wholly or in part for dwellings. The population of New York City is a matter of dispute between the Federal Census Bureau and the City authorities, the Federal census placing it at 1,513,501, and the census made under the supervision of the City authorities at 1,710,715. When, as is the case with London, not only the City itself, but what might properly be called the Metropolitan District, the suburbs lying within a radius of twenty miles of New York, is considered, the population is very much larger, probably approaching 3,000,000.

Food Supply.—The annual food supply for this population has been computed as follows: Beef, 423,056,500 lbs.; Veal, 367,105,000 lbs.; Mutton and Lamb, 78,749,000 lbs.; Pork, 244,465,300 lbs. Total, 1,113,758,000 lbs. Fish, 54,750,000 lbs.; Oysters, about 15,000,000 a day during the season, from September 1st to May 1st; Poultry, 73,436,000 lbs.; Eggs, 66,862,400; Butter, 84,671,400 lbs.; Vegetables, 8,000 barrels a day. For Wines see *Commercial Statistics* below.

Croton Aqueducts.—New York's water supply is derived from the Croton water-shed, the Croton river being a stream in Westchester County, about 40 miles from New York and emptying into the Hudson. The various lakes and streams which make up this water-shed are carefully guarded against pollution. The first Croton aqueduct was built in 1842. Its capacity for the last 16 years has been 94,744,742 gallons per day, the water flowing into it from Croton Lake, artificially formed by a dam at the head of the aqueduct, which raised the Croton river 40 feet. There are also storage reservoirs. From Croton Lake the old aqueduct runs southwest, crossing the Harlem river by High Bridge, where there is a reservoir and a water-tower for supplying the upper part of the city; another tower being at

Ninth avenue, Ninety-seventh and Ninety-eighth streets. The main reservoirs are those in Central Park, which are respectively a retaining and a receiving reservoir, the former, the more northerly, having a capacity of 1,000,000,000 gallons and the receiving reservoir of 150,000,000; the high-service reservoir at High Bridge having a capacity of 11,000,000 gallons. The supply not proving adequate, on account of the remarkable growth of the city, an act for the construction of a new aqueduct and the incidental reservoirs and dams was passed in 1883. This new aqueduct has been in operation since June, 1890, although a complete system of reservoirs and dams has not yet been constructed. The new aqueduct also taps the Croton water-shed at a point near the present Croton Lake, and runs to a gate-house at One Hundred and Thirty-fifth street and Convent avenue and thence through pipes to various points, including the reservoirs in Central Park. It is considered a great work of engineering. It was constructed horse-shoe shape at an average depth of 170 feet below the surface, tunneling through solid rock being resorted to wherever it was found practicable. Instead of being led across the Harlem river on a bridge, as the old aqueduct was across High Bridge, it runs 307 feet below the river bed through solid rock, rising perpendicularly to the established grade from the south shore of the river. The following are some of the statistics of the new aqueduct: Length, 33⅛ miles; height of inside horse-shoe, 13.53′ at greatest height, and 13.60′ at greatest breadth to the Harlem river; beneath the Harlem river a well 10½ feet in diameter; capacity 250,000,000 gallons per day. Cost so far about $22,000,000. Changes are contemplated in the original plans for storage reservoirs in the Croton water-shed, so that information concerning these cannot yet be given, nor can the full cost of the work be estimated until plans are finally adopted.

Street Plan.—According to the last Quarterly Report of the Department of Public Works the total length of paved streets in New York City is 361.19 miles; of sewers, 436.58 miles; and there are in use 26,981 gas lamps, 881 electric lights, and 138 naphtha lamps.

From the Battery to Fourteenth street, a distance of 2½ miles, the streets are irregularly laid out, following, especially in the lower part of this section, the lines of old thoroughfares. Above Fourteenth street the city is laid out into avenues—1 to 12, and A, B, C, D east of First avenue, where the broadening of the city necessitates; with Lexington and Madison avenues above Twenty-third street, and Park avenue built over Fourth avenue from Thirty-fourth street to Forty-second street, the Fourth avenue horse-cars running under it through a tunnel, Fourth avenue continuing again above the Grand Central Depot. So much of the city as lies on the mainland is not, however, regularily laid out as yet; nor in the northwest and extreme northerly part of the Island is the division of avenues and streets characteristic of the street plan from Fourteenth to Fifty-ninth street exactly carried out. In this regular street plan the avenues are mostly 100 feet and the streets 60 feet wide, with the exception of important thoroughfares like Fourteenth, Twenty-third, Thirty-fourth, Forty-second, Fifty-seventh, and other streets in the upper part of the city, which are 100 feet wide. There are twenty blocks to a mile. The house numbers run from Fifth avenue east and west, the odd numbers being on the upper side, the even numbers on the south side of the streets, and respectively on the west and east sides of the avenues. The street numbers are so divided as to give 100 to a block, from 1 to 100 west or east being found on the first block west or east of Fifth avenue, and so on. Broadway, which below Fourteenth street is the main artery of the city's commerce, is only 80 feet broad. Beginning at Bowling Green it runs in a straight line to Tenth street, where it deflects towards the west and continues on the line of the old Bloomingdale road to a point at Fifty-ninth street where it crosses Eighth avenue. The Boulevard, which continues Broadway to Inwood, near the end of the Island, is 150 feet wide and is a well laid-out thoroughfare, as is also St. Nicholas avenue, which leaves Central Park at Lenox avenue and One Hundred and Tenth street and runs to One Hundred and Sixty-second street, at which point it joins the old Kingsbridge road. Wall street, in some respects the most important street in the United States, being the financial centre of the whole country, is a narrow cañon less than half a mile long.

Political Divisions.—The City is divided into twenty-four Wards—the Twenty-third and Twenty-fourth being on the mainland—but for purposes of representation in Congress, the State Senate and the State Assembly is also divided into Congressional, Senatorial and Assembly districts. These larger divisions are in turn subdivided into election districts.

Commerce.—New York is the most important port of the United States, about 65 per cent. of the entire foreign commerce of this country being carried on through it. As a port of entry it embraces all the towns and cities and other settlements on New York Bay, the Hudson and East rivers, including the important cities of Brooklyn and Jersey City. Some interesting statistics of the City's entries and clearances of vessels will be found under CUSTOM HOUSE. Other commercial statistics, obtained from the Chamber of Commerce and showing the relative commercial importance of New York and the rest of the United States, are as follows: The total foreign commerce of the United States for 1889, latest statistics accessible, was $1,613,137,633, of which $876,808,110 fell to New York. Sugar and molasses, New York $44,367,704; the rest of the United States only about $5,000,000 in all. Coffee, New York $58,860,319; the rest of the United States only about $16,000,000, all told. Tea, New York $9,643,514; the rest of the United States only about $3,000,000, all told. Wool, New York $41,048,679 as against about $11,500,000. Silk, New York $31,129,113 as against about $6,225,000. Champagne, New York $3,672,752 as against about $750,000. Still Wines in casks, $1,502,208 as against about five-eighths of a million; in bottles, New York $975,861 as against about $350,000. About 75 per cent, of the immigration into the United States passes through New York.

Water Front.—The Island of Manhattan alone has 24¾ miles of water front, all but 2½ miles of which, on the Harlem River is available for deep sea vessels, and a ship canal, now in course of construction by the United States Government, will make the Harlem River front equally available, besides affording a route from Long Island Sound independent of the passage through Hell Gate. At present most of the shipping is accommodated below Fourteenth street on the North River and on the East River below Grand street. From the Battery to these points there is a perfect forest of masts, ships of all nations, among them many steamers being moored here. A great improvement and extension of New York's water front is in contemplation, but at present this important feature of the city is picturesque chiefly through its dirty surroundings and its irregularity. The large map of the city in the front of the book shows the various ferries and steamship lines. The Battery is given up chiefly to ferries. From here the tour of the East River lies along South street. To Coenties slip the piers are lined with small sailing vessels, Coenties slip being the center for canal-boats; and beyond, between Wall and Fulton street ferries, are large and small sailing vessels, many of them fruiterers, and several steamship lines. The piers near Fulton Market derive a local color from the fishing smacks that cluster near the wholesale fish-market under the shadow of the great East River Bridge. Above Catherine street are the dry docks, and beyond these iron foundries, lumber-yards and gas-works. Pier A, to the north of the Battery, is used as headquarters for the Department of Docks and for the River Police. Pier 1 is the Iron Steamboat Company's pier. At Fulton and Vesey streets is Washington Market, and in its vicinity the great produce-distributing district of the city, the piers here being used for ferries and for various vessels tributary to this business. At Warren and Murray streets are the great Boston boats, the Providence and Fall River lines, and from here to Twenty-third street a succession of foreign and domestic steamship companies. The great European steamships have piers in the neighborhood of Christopher street, and just above this is the floating oyster-market, a series of moored barges.

Approaches by Water.—The approaches to New York from the Atlantic ocean are most beautiful. The lighthouse on Fire Island beach on the Long Island coast is usually the first point sighted by incoming European vessels. From here vessels are signaled by telegraph to New York City. The most conspicuous picture on the Jersey coast, which soon afterwards looms up, are the twin lights on the Highlands of Navesink, back of Sandy Hook beach. The steamers in entering the Lower bay approach so near Sandy Hook that the details of its shore—a waste of sand, stunted cedars and scrub oak, with a light-house and two beacons, a telegraph tower from which vessels are also signalled, an unfinished fort, and various apparatus of the United States Ordnance Corps—are discernible. Between Sandy Hook, which is part of a sandy peninsula and the mainland, is Sandy Hook bay. To the north and northwest is Staten Island. Between its south shore and the New Jersey shore is Raritan bay, into which the Raritan river empties, and on the west Staten Island is separated from New Jersey by the narrow Staten Island Sound, which joins the Kill von Kull—the latter separating the Island on the north from the mainland and entering New York bay. The broad sheet of water lying between Sandy Hook and the Narrows is known as Lower New York bay, of which Raritan bay and Sandy Hook bay may be considered parts. Across from Sandy Hook, on the Long Island shore, are Coney Island and Rockaway Beach, the former with its numerous large caravansaries, its Observatory and huge wooden elephant, while to the north the Staten Island and Long Island shores, approaching each other, form the Narrows, the gateway into New York bay—the almost land-locked, secluded, yet vast harbor of New York. The first station under the jurisdiction of the Commissioners of Quarantine is the ship *Illinois*, anchored from May 1st to November 1st, three miles below Swinburne Island. From this ship all vessels arriving from infected ports are boarded. Three miles above this are Swinburne and Hoffman Islands, artificially made upon a reef, and respectively seven and eight miles south of New York City; the hospital for contagious diseases being located on Swinburne Island, and quarters for well persons from infected vessels on Hoffman Island. Vessels from non-infected ports are boarded from Clifton, Staten Island, just inside the Narrows, where also the Custom House Inspector usually boards vessels from foreign ports. On the Staten Island shore of the Narrows is Fort Wadsworth; on the Long Island shore, Fort Hamilton; a little off the shore, the circular Fort Lafayette, built in 1812, where during the Civil War political suspects were imprisoned. Once through the Narrows, New York City lies straight ahead—to the right Brooklyn, to the left Staten Island, and further up the harbor Bergen Neck and Jersey City. The Statue of Liberty on Bedloe's Island (p. 69), and the East River Bridge (p.138), become next to the city the most conspicuous features in the view. Governor's Island, with its picturesque fortifications lies but a thousand yards south of the Battery, the southernmost point of the Island of Manhattan, and Ellis Island, where is the official funnel through which three-fourths of the immigration pours into the United States lies between Bedloe's Island and the Jersey shore. At the Battery the harbor sweeps around on the east into the East river (the local name for Long Island Sound), and on the west into the Hudson, to which the local name of North river is given. The great European steamship lines have their piers on the North river, the English lines on the New York side, the German, Dutch and Belgian on the New Jersey side, the North German Lloyd (Bremen) and Hamburgh piers being at Hoboken. The East river runs between New York City and Brooklyn, broadening out after sweeping to the east from the Island of Manhattan into the beautiful expanse of Long Island Sound, 110 miles long and from three to twenty miles wide, with Long Island on the east and New York and Connecticut on the west. On Throgg's Neck, about twenty miles from the Battery, and on Willet's Point, on the opposite shore, are fortifications, those on the former being Fort Schuyler. On the East river are Blackwell's, Ward's and Randall's Islands, which are described under Public Charities and Correction.

Hell Gate lies in the narrow bend in the East river, just north of Blackwell's Island, between Astoria and Ward's Island. Navigation of it was made dangerous not only by the sharp and narrow turn of the river and the resulting rush of tide, but also by a ledge of rocks projecting from the Long Island shore for a considerable distance and rising at various intervals almost to the surface, causing numerous dangerous currents and eddies. From 1870 to 1876, under the United States Government, Gen. Newton directed a series of operations, drilling the principal rocks and charging them with nitro-glycerine, which was exploded during the summer of 1876. October 10, 1885, Flood Rock, which was even larger than the rock blown up in 1876, was removed by similar operations.

HISTORY.

The Island of Manhattan was discovered by Henry Hudson, after whom the Hudson river is named, in September, 1609. Though the Dutch, in whose service Hudson's expedition was undertaken, dispatched trading vessels to this region, the first settlement on the island appears to have been made in 1623, and it was not until 1624 that a governor, Cornelis Jacobson May, was installed. In 1625 May was succeeded by William Verhulst, and he in turn, in 1626, by Peter Minuit, under whose administration Fort Amsterdam, on ground now just south of Bowling Green, was erected (p. 84). The purchase of Manhattan Island from the Indians was effected by Minuit, the price paid being goods to the value of $24. In 1644 the fortifications were extended to what is now the line of Wall street, and ran from the East to the North river. They consisted of a ditch and palisaded breastwork, these being completed in 1653. Meanwhile Peter Stuyvesant, who was governor for seventeen years and under whom the rule of the Dutch virtually terminated, although there was a brief interregnum in 1673, had arrived in 1647. March 12, 1664, Charles II granted the entire territory to his brother, the Duke of York, and the latter's representative, Col. Richard Nichols, arriving before New Amsterdam with a small fleet, the city was surrendered without an attempt to resist the superior force. New Amsterdam was changed to New York, Col. Nichols assuming the governorship. In July, 1673, Capt. Manning, being in command of the city, surrendered ignominiously to a Dutch force, but the Dutch remained in possession only until November 10, 1674, being ousted by the treaty of peace between England and the States General. Events of importance prior to the rupture of the colonies from Great Britain were: In 1689, a rebellion headed by Jacob Leisler, the leader of the progressive party, who chose these forcible means to settle a disputed election, the rebellion ending in his trial and death; in 1696, the building of the first Trinity Church; in 1702 a fatal epidemic; in 1735, the Zenger trial, which established the freedom of the press in America, Zenger in his *New York Weekly Journal*, having opposed Gov. Cosby's claim to half the salary of his predecessor, and having been therefor imprisoned for libel, but eventually acquitted on a trial by jury; in 1741, the negro plot, information on the part of a negress leading to the hanging of some and burning of other negroes, who were supposed to be in a conspiracy to attack the whites and sack the city, although there seems but little doubt that the girl's testimony was perjured. The dissatisfaction which led to the Revolution and the final separation of the colonies from Great Britain first vented itself in New York in 1765, a congress of delegates from nine colonies meeting here and adopting a bill of rights, which asserted the sole power of taxation to be vested in the colonies. The Sons of Liberty were organized to oppose the Stamp Act, and in 1770 a meeting of 3,000 citizens resolved to oppose all oppressive measures. The Colonial Assembly terminated April 3, 1775, delegates to the Continental Congress being elected July 25th of that year, and the twenty-one pieces of cannon, all that were mounted on the city forts, were removed. After the battle of Long Island, September 15, 1776, the British crossed to Manhattan Island, and after Washington had withdrawn from Harlem Heights the city remained in the possession of the British until the close of the war, the final evacuation taking place November 25, 1783. During the Revolution there were two disastrous fires, in the first of which, September 21, 1776, Trinity Church was destroyed. The British had used all the churches excepting the Episcopal for prisons, riding-schools and barracks, leaving them nearly destroyed or in a state ill adapted for religious uses, and had wrought other depredations. Both under the Dutch and English colonial governors the city had been the seat of government. From 1785 to 1790, it was the seat of government of the United States, Washington being inaugurated April 30, 1789, and from 1784 to 1797 it was the State capital. In 1788 the Hospital Riot, caused by one of the students in the New York Hospital (p. 60), who was operating in the dissecting-room, waving an arm from the cadaver at some boys who peeped in at him through the window, a mob gathering and attacking the building. In 1791, 1795 and 1798, the city was visited by yellow fever. During the last ten years of the last century the city began to extend a little beyond the present City Hall Park. The corner-stone of the City Hall was laid in 1803, the structure being finished in 1812. The city's growth from the beginning of the century has been very rapid. By 1805 it had extended beyond the Collect and Marsh, respectively at the site of the present Tombs and the line of Canal street; the Collect being filled in at this time and Canal street laid out. There were disastrous fires in 1804, and in 1811. By this latter year the city had grown to such proportions that a commission was appointed to survey and lay out the island north of Houston street, a work which was completed in 1821. A further expansion was caused by the yellow fever epidemics of 1819, 1822 and 1823, which drove people to the upper part of the island. Gas was generally introduced in 1825, and in this same year the completion of the Erie Canal further stimulated the city's growth. The Harlem Railroad was incorporated in 1831. Notwithstanding the cholera epidemics of 1832 and 1834, the great fire of December 16, 1835—which destroyed 648 of the finest commercial structures in the city, east of Broadway, below Wall street—and the great financial panic of 1837, the city continued to progress. The first Croton Aqueduct was built in 1842. July 19, 1845, there was another great fire, which destroyed $5,000,000 worth of property in the district bounded by Broadway, Exchange place, Broad and Stone streets. The Astor place riots, which grew out of the rivalry between Macready and Forrest, the actors, occurred in May, 1849, and resulted in the loss of several lives. A cholera epidemic in the summer of 1849 carried off over 5,000 persons. July 14, 1853, an industrial exhibition was opened in the Crystal Palace, a fine building in the form of a Greek cross. It was burned in 1858. Meanwhile there had been another cholera epidemic in 1855. In 1857 the Metropolitan Police was established, and the resistance to the act of the Legislature by Fernando Wood, then Mayor, resulted in what are known as the Police Riots. During the Civil War, New York furnished 116,382 men to the Federal armies. July 13, 1863, the most serious riot from which New York has ever suffered broke out in opposition to the draft, the mob holding possession of the city for three days, the riot being finally quelled on the 17th. There were several collisions between the rioters and the troops, and it is estimated that over 1,000 persons were killed, among them several negroes, against whom the mob's fury seemed especially directed. July 12, 1871, 62 persons were killed in a riot which grew out of a procession of Orangemen in celebration of the Battle of the Boyne. Trouble having been apprehended, the paraders were provided with a militia escort, which was compelled to fire upon those who attacked the procession. In 1871, it was discovered that a ring, known as the Tweed ring, and consisting of several of the most prominent officials of the city, had been robbing the treasury, and in the ensuing election in November, the opponents of the ring were elected, and the leader of the ring, William M. Tweed, and several of the conspirators were convicted and imprisoned, Tweed dying in prison. A portion of Westchester county was annexed in 1873, and a great stimulus to the growth of the city has been given by the elevated railroads, the first of which was built in 1868.

ROUTES OF TRAVEL.*

STEAMSHIPS BETWEEN NEW YORK AND FOREIGN AND DOMESTIC PORTS.

Ports.	From	Agent and Location of Office.	Line.
Alexandria, Va.	Foot Beach street.	Old Dominion S. S. Co., 235 West st.	Old Dominion.
Amsterdam	Fifth st., Hoboken.	Funch, Edye & Co., 27 S. William st.	Royal Neth.
Antwerp	Sussex street, J. C.	Peter Wright & Sons, 6 Bowling Gr.	Red Star.
Antwerp	Fourth st., Hob'kn	Funch, Edye & Co., 27 S. William st.	White Cross.
Aux Cayes	West 25th street	Pim, Forwood & Co., 24 State st.	Atlas.
Baltimore	Rector street, N.R.	H. C. Foster, Pier 7, North River	
Bangor and Belfast, Maine	Pier 49, East River.	F. H. Smith & Co., 19 William street.	N. Y., Me. & N. B.
Barbadoes	West Tenth street.	A.E.Outerbridge & Co.,39 Broadway	Quebec S. S. Co.
Bermuda (Hamilton)	West Tenth street.	A.E.Outerbridge & Co.,39 Broadway	Bermuda.
Bordeaux	†Prentice Stores	Funch, Edye & Co., 27 S. William st.	Bordeaux.
Brazil, *via Newport News*	†Roberts' Stores	P. F. Gerhard & Co., 19 Whitehall st.	U. S. & Brazil.
Brazil, *via Baltimore*	†Martin's Stores	Shipton Green, 112 Pearl street	Red Cross.
Brazil, *Para, Maranham, Ceara* Brazil, *Para and Manaos*	†Martin's Stores, Brooklyn.	Booth & Co., 15 Frankfort street.	Booth.
Brazil, *Rio Janeiro and Santos*	†Roberts' Stores	Funch, Edye & Co., 27 S. William st.	Sloman.
Bremen, *via Southampton*	Second st., Hob'kn.	Oelrichs & Co., 2 Bowling Green	N. German Lloyd.
Bristol, England	West 26th street	James Arkell & Co., 25 Whitehall st.	Bristol City.
Brunswick, Ga	Burling Slip	C. H. Mallory & Co., Pier 20, E. R.	Mallory's.
Bucksport, Me	Pier 49, East River.	F. H. Smith & Co., 19 William street.	N. Y., Me. & N. B.
Buenos Ayres and Rosario	Pier 49, East River.	John Norton & Sons, 90 Wall street.	River Plate.
Charleston, S. C.	Pier 29, East River.	W. P. Clyde & Co., 5 Bowling Green.	Charleston.
City Point	Beach street, N. R.	Old Dominion S. S. Co., 235 West st.	Old Dominion.
Copenhagen	Fourth st., Hob'kn.	Funch, Edye & Co., 27 S. William st.	Thingvalla.
Colon	Canal street, N. R.	Pacific Mail S. S. Co., foot Canal st.	Pacific Mail.
Colon	Pier 41, North River	J. M. Ceballos & Co., 80 Wall street.	C. T. Espanola.
Curacoa	Pier 36, East River.	Boulton, Bliss & Dallett, 71 Wall st.	Red D.
Demarara	Pier 15, East River.	George Christall, 45 Exchange pl.	Trinidad.
Dominica	West Tenth street.	A.E.Outerbridge & Co.,39 Broadway	Quebec S. S. Co.
Eastport, Me	Pier 49, East River.	F. H. Smith & Co., 19 William street.	N. Y., Me. & N. B.

ROUTES OF TRAVEL—Continued.

Ports.	From	Agent and Location of Office.	Line.
Fernandina, Fla.	Burling Slip	C. H. Mallory & Co., Pier 20, E. R.	Mallory's.
Galveston, Texas	N. Moore st., N. R.	J. T. Vansickle, foot N. Moore st.	Morgan's.
Galveston, Texas	Burling Slip	C. H. Mallory & Co., Pier 20, E. R.	Mallory's.
Glasgow, *via Londonderry*	†Columbia Stores.	Austin Baldwin & Co., 53 Broadway.	State.
Glasgow, "	Leroy street, N. R.	Henderson Bros., 7 Bowling Green	Anchor.
Halifax, N. S.	†Robinson's Stores	Bowring & Archibald, 18 Broadway.	Red Cross.
Hamburg	Newark st., Hob'kn	C. B. Richard & Co., 61 Broadway, or R. J. Cortis, 37 Broadway.	Hamburg.
Havana, Cuba	Wall st., East River	J. M. Ceballos & Co., 80 Wall street.	C. T. E.
Havana, Cuba	Pier 41, North River	J. E. Ward & Co., 113 Wall st.	N. Y. & Cuba.
Havre, France	Morton st., N. R.	A. Forget, 3 Bowling Green	C. G. T.
North Hayti	West 25th street	Pim, Forwood & Co., 24 State st.	Atlas.
Hayti	Pier 15, East River.	W. P. Clyde & Co., 5 Bowling Green.	Clyde's.
Hull	Second st., Hob'kn	Sanderson & Son, 22 State street	Wilson's.
Jacksonville, Fla.	Pier 29, East River.	W. P. Clyde & Co., 5 Bowling Green.	Clyde's.
Key West, Fla	Burling Slip	C. H. Mallory & Co., Pier 20, E. R.	Mallory's.
Kingston, Jamaica	West 25th street	Pim, Forwood & Co., 24 State st.	Atlas.
Kingston, Jamaica	†Atlantic Dock	Williams & Rankine, 19 Whitehall st.	H. & C. A. Co.
Liverpool, *via Queenstown*	King street, N. R.	A. M. Underhill & Co., 35 Broadway	Guion.
Liverpool, "	Christopherst., N.R	J. Bruce Ismay, 41 Broadway	White Star.
Liverpool, "	Christopherst., N.R	Peter Wright & Sons, 6 Bowling Gr	Inman.
Liverpool, "	Clarkson st., N. R.	V. H, Brown & Co., 4 Bowling Green	Cunard.
Liverpool	Houston st., N. R.	F. W. J. Hurst, 27 State street	National.
London, Eng.	Houston st., N. R.	F. W. J. Hurst, 27 State street	National.
London, Eng.	†Prentice Stores	Henderson Bros., 7 Bowling Green.	Hill.
Maracaibo, *via Curacoa*	Pier 36, East River.	Boulton, Bliss & Dallett, 71 Wall st.	Red D.
Martinique	West Tenth street.	A. E. Outerbridge & Co., 39 Broadway	Quebec S. S. Co.
Matanzas	Wall street, E. R.	J. E. Ward & Co., 113 Wall street	N. Y. & Cuba.
Mediterranean Ports	†Prentice Stores	Henderson Bros., 7 Bowling Green	Anchor.
Mediterranean Ports	†Wall street Stores	Phelps Bros. & Co., 33 Broadway	M. & N. Y.
Mediterranean Ports	Second st., Hob'kn	Oelrichs & Co., 2 Bowling Green	N. German Lloyd.

Mexico	Pier 41, North River	J. M. Ceballos & Co., 80 Wall st.	C. T. E.
Nassau	Pine street, E. R.	James E. Ward & Co., 113 Wall st.	Nassau.
New Orleans, La	N. Moore st., N. R.	J. T. Vansickle, foot N. Moore st.	Morgan's.
New Orleans, La	Pier 9, North River	Samuel H. Seaman, Pier 9 N. R.	Cromwell.
Norfolk, Va	Beach street, N. R.	Old Dominion S. S. Co., 235 West st.	Old Dominion.
Philadelphia, Pa	Pier 33½, E. R.	W. P. Clyde & Co., Pier 33½ E. R.	Clyde's.
Portland, Me	Market st., E. R.	Horatio Hall, Pier 38 East River	Maine S. S. Co.
Porto Rico	†Atlantic Basin	Miller, Bull & Co., 76 Beaver street.	N. Y. & P. R.
Port Royal, S. C	Burling Slip	C. H. Mallory & Co., Pier 20 E. R.	Mallory's.
Richmond, Va	Beach street, N. R.	Old Dominion S. S. Co., 235 West st.	Old Dominion.
Rockland, Me	Pier 49, East River.	F. H. Smith & Co., 19 William st.	N. Y., Me. & N. B.
Rockport, Me	Pier 49, East River.	F. H. Smith & Co., 19 William st.	N. Y., Me. & N. B.
Rotterdam	Fifth st., Hoboken.	Funch, Edye & Co., 27 S. William st.	N. S. N. Co.
St. John, N. B	Pier 49, East River.	F. H. Smith & Co., 19 William st.	N. Y., Me. & N. B.
St. Johns, N. F	†Robinson's Stores	Bowring & Archibald, 18 Broadway.	Red Cross.
St. Kitts and St. Lucia	West Tenth street.	A.E. Outerbridge & Co., 39 Broadway	Quebec S. S. Co.
St. Thomas	†Roberts' Stores	P. F. Gerhard & Co., 19 Whitehall st.	N. S. & B.
San Francisco, Cal	Canal street, N. R.	Pacific Mail S. S. Co., Pier 42 N. R.	Pacific Mail.
Santiago de Cuba	Pine street, E. R.	J. E. Ward & Co., 113 Wall street.	Ward's.
Santiago de Cuba	Pier 41, N. R.	J. M. Ceballos & Co., 80 Wall st.	C. T. E.
Savannah, Ga	Spring street, N. R.	R. L. Walker, agent on Pier, or W. H. Rhett, 317 Broadway.	Ocean.
Southampton, Eng	Second st., Hob'kn	Oelrichs & Co., 9 Bowling Green.	N. German Lloyd.
Stettin	Fourth st., Hob'kn	Funch, Edye & Co., 27 S. William st.	Thingvalla.
Trinidad	West Tenth street.	A.E. Outerbridge & Co., 39 Broadway	Quebec S. S. Co.
Turk's Island	Pier 15, East River.	W. P. Clyde & Co., 5 Bowling Green.	Clyde's.
Vera Cruz	Wall street, E. R.	James E. Ward & Co., 113 Wall st.	N. Y. & Cuba.
Vera Cruz	Pier 41, North River	J. M. Ceballos & Co., 80 Wall st.	C. T. E.
Washington, D. C	Beach street, N. R.	Old Dominion S. S. Co., 235 West st.	Old Dominion.
West Point, Va	Beach street, N. R.	Old Dominion S. S. Co., 235 West st.	Old Dominion.
Wilmington, N. C	Pier 29, East River,	W. P. Clyde & Co., 5 Bowling Green	N.Y. & Wilmington.
Windward Islands	West Tenth street.	A.E. Outerbridge & Co., 39 Broadway	Quebec S. S. Co.

* For details see Mackey's A B C Guide or Bullinger's Counting-House Monitor. † Brooklyn.

RAILROADS.*

FROM GRAND CENTRAL DEPOT, FORTY-SECOND STREET AND FOURTH AVENUE.

New York Central and Hudson River Railroad.—To all points on east shore of the Hudson River, connecting at Albany for Saratoga, Lake George, both shores of Lake Champlain, the Adirondacks and Montreal. Fast vestibuled car service for Buffalo and Niagara Falls via Utica, Syracuse and Rochester, and from Buffalo in connection with the Lake Shore Line and "Big Fou " Lines to Chicago, Cincinnati, Indianapolis and St. Louis. Connection also for Detroit.

New York and Harlem Railroad.—Lake Mahopac and Berkshire Hills, besides many of the Westchester County suburbs.

New York, New Haven and Hartford Railroad.—For Stamford, South Norwalk (connection for Ridgefield and Litchfield), Bridgeport (connection for Stockbridge and Lenox), New Haven, Hartford, Springfield, and Boston. Also for *Quebec.*

New York and Boston Shore Line.—Runs on the tracks of the New York, New Haven and Hartford to New Haven; to Boston via the shore of Long Island Sound (New London and Stonington) and Providence.

New York and New England Railroad.—Runs on the tracks of the New York, New Haven and Hartford Railroad to New Haven, and then via Willimantic to Boston.

FROM OTHER DEPOTS.

Baltimore and Ohio Railroad.—Ferry from foot of Liberty street. Depot, Jersey City (Central Railroad of New Jersey). Fast vestibuled Pullman car service to Philadelphia, Baltimore, Washington, Pittsburgh,

*Foreigners will find the service on the great railroads of the United States most admirable, everything being done to secure speed with safety, and every consideration being paid to the comfort of the passenger Baggage to a reasonable amount (say a trunk and portmanteau to each passenger) is carried free, the passenger receiving a check for it at the baggage office. The fares are also reasonable—in the author's experience lower than those in England or on the Continent. Tickets can generally be purchased at any of the large hotels.

Cleveland, Chicago, Cincinnati and St. Louis, and all points west. To Philadelphia the service is over the Royal Blue Line, composed of the Central Railroad of New Jersey, Philadelphia and Reading Railroad and Baltimore and Ohio Railroad.

Brooklyn, Bath and West End Railroad.—Ferry foot of Whitehall street to Thirty-ninth street, Brooklyn.

Central Railroad of New Jersey.—Ferry from foot of Liberty street. Newark, Elizabeth, Plainfield, Bound Brook, Easton, Allentown and the Pennsylvania coal region (Wilkesbarre, Scranton, Reading and Harrisburg), and via Philadelphia and Reading Railroad to Trenton and Philadelphia. See also New Jersey Southern Railroad and New York and Long Branch Railroad.

Delaware, Lackawanna and Western Railroad.—Ferry from foot of Barclay or Christopher streets. Depot, Hoboken, N. J. Paterson, Lake Hopatcong, Schooley Mountain, Delaware Watergap, Wilkesbarre, Scranton, Richfield Springs, Utica, Syracuse, Oswego, Ithaca and Buffalo (connects for the West). Morris and Essex Division to Newark, Orange, Summit and Morristown. Also branches to Montclair and Bernardsville.

Long Island Railroad.—Ferry from East Thirty-fourth street and James Slip. Depot at Hunter's Point (Long Island City). For Manhattan Beach, Long Beach, Babylon, Shinnecock Hills, Southampton and points on Long Island generally.

Manhattan Beach and Coney Island Railroad.—Same ferries and depot as Long Island Railroad.

New York and Greenwood Lake Railroad.—See New York, Lake Erie and Western Railroad.

New Jersey Southern Railroad.—Finely appointed twin screw steamers from foot of Rector street. Depot at Atlantic Highlands, N. J. To Jersey Coast Resorts.

New York and Northern.—Connects at One Hundred and Fifty-fifth street with Sixth and Ninth avenue L Railroad. Croton Lake, Lake Mahopac and intermediate points.

New York and Sea Beach Railroad.—For Coney Island. Ferry foot of Whitehall street to Bay Ridge.

Northern Railroad of New Jersey.—Same ferry and depot as New York, Lake Erie and Western. Piermont and Nyack.

New York, Lake Erie and Western Railroad.—Ferry foot of Chambers street or West Twenty-third street. Depot, Jersey City. Fast vestibuled Pullman car service to the Pennsylvania coal regions; Elmira, Watkin's Glen, Rochester, Buffalo, Niagara Falls, Detroit, Cleveland, Chicago, Cincinnati, Louisville and St. Louis.

Pennsylvania Railroad.—Ferry foot of Desbrosses street or Cortlandt street. Depot, Jersey City. Fast vestibuled Pullman car service to Philadelphia, Wilmington, Baltimore, Washington and points South, Southwest and West, the Pennsylvania Railroad system being the most extensive in America.

New York and Long Branch Railroad.—Owned by the Central Railroad of New Jersey. Operated by the Central Railroad of New Jersey and the Pennsylvania Railroad. For points on the Jersey Coast to Point Pleasant.

New York, Ontario and Western Railroad.—Ferry foot of Jay street or West Forty-second street. Depot, Weehawken. Utica, Rome, Oswego, Cape Vincent, (Thousand Islands), Buffalo (connection for the West), and Suspension Bridge (Niagara Falls).

West Shore Railroad.—Ferry and depot same as New York, Ontario and Western Railroad. Runs along the west shore of the Hudson River to West Point, Newburgh, Kingston (Catskill Mountains) and Albany, and thence to Buffalo and Niagara Falls via Utica, Oswego and Rochester.

Staten Island Rapid Transit Company.—Ferry foot of Whitehall street. Depot, St. George, Staten Island. Points on Staten Island.

Montreal to New York.—"New Canada Short Line," Grand Trunk Railroad, Delaware and Hudson Canal Company's Railroad (west shore of Lake Champlain); Hudson River Railroad. Central Vermont Railroad (east shore of Lake Champlain) and Hudson River Railroad.

Ottawa to New York.—Canada Atlantic Railroad via Delaware and Hudson Canal Company's Railroad or Central Vermont Railroad.

Quebec to New York.—Quebec Central via Central Vermont and New York, New Haven and Hartford Railroad.

BAGGAGE INSPECTION.

The Customs officer usually boards foreign vessels from Clifton, S. I., and distributes blank forms upon which the passenger designates articles subject to duty in his baggage. In case of a family, the senior member can make the statement on one form, and swear to it. Should any one trunk or package in the baggage contain dutiable articles of a value exceeding $500, or should its contents be so numerous or varied as to forbid a thorough examination on the vessel or wharf, it is sent to the public stores for appraisement. On landing at the wharf, the baggage when discharged is examined, and any attempt at smuggling is punished by confiscation of the article whose concealment has been attempted. The Customs officers of the United States will be found attentive and polite and liberal in their interpretation of the Customs laws, especially where no attempt at smuggling is made, the rule applicable being that a passenger is allowed to bring into the country articles for personal use as numerous and as good in quality as is consistent with his station in life.

STEAMBOATS

To Principal Landings on the Hudson River.

LANDINGS.	Pier foot of street.	FARES. Regular.	FARES. Excursion.	Miles.
Albany, by day.	Desbrosses...	$2 00	$3 50	145
Albany, People's Line (night)	Canal.	1 50	2 50	145
Albany, Citizens' Line (night)	Christopher..	1 50	2 50	145
Catskill (Albany Day Line)..	Desbrosses...	1 50	....	115
Cornwall (by Mary Powell)..	Desbrosses...	75	1 00	56
Fishkill Landing...........	Franklin.	55	....	60
Fort Lee	W. 13th......	15	25	.10
Fort Lee	W. 125th.....	10	....	10
Hudson (Albany Day Line)..	Desbrosses...	1 50	....	120
Hyde Park (by Mary Powell)	Desbrosses...	1 00	1 50	81
Milton (by Mary Powell).....	Desbrosses...	75	1 25	72
Newburg (Albany Day Line)	Desbrosses...	75	1 00	60
Newburg (by Mary Powell)..	Desbrosses...	75	1 00	60
New Hamburg (Mary Powell)	Desbrosses...	75	1 25	67
New Hamburg	Franklin.	75	1 25	67
Nyack.......................	Spring........	30	50	28
Peekskill....................	Spring........	40	50	48
Poughkeepsie (Alb'y D'y Li'e)	Desbrosses...	1 00	1 50	76
Poughkeepsie (Mary Powell).	Desbrosses...	75	1 25	76
Rhinebeck (Alb'ny Day Line)	Desbrosses...	1 25	....	90
Rondout (Albany Day Line)..	Desbrosses...	....	....	95
Rondout (by Mary Powell)...	Desbrosses...	1 00	1 50	95
Sing Sing....................	Franklin.	25	....	35
Tarrytown	Spring........	40	75	28
Tivoli.......................	W. 11th.	1 00	....	100
Troy (Albany Day Line).....	Desbrosses...	2 15	....	151
Troy (Citizens' Line).... ...	W. 10th......	1 50	2 50	151
West Point (Alb'ny Day Line)	Desbrosses...	75	1 00	53
West Point (by Mary Powell)	Desbrosses...	75	1 00	53
Yonkers.....................	Spring.......	15	25	17

Steamboats to Landings not on the Hudson River.

LANDINGS.	Pier foot of street.	FARES. Regu-lar.	FARES. Excur-sion.	Miles.
Atlantic Highlands..........	Rector........	$0 60	$1 00	20
Bedloe's Island..............	Battery Park.	....	25	...
Blackwell's Island...........	26th st., E. R.	20	....	...
Boston, boat, *via* Fall River.	Murray.......	3 00	....	240
Boston, by boat, *via* Norwich	Watts........	3 00	....	240
Boston, boat, *via* Providence	Warren.......	3 00	....	225
Boston, boat, *via* Stonington	Spring........	3 00	....	215
Bridgeport	Catherine	50	75	65
Coney Island................	Pier 1, N. R..	....	....	...
Glencove....................	*Peck slip....	35	50	23
Governor's Island...........	Pier 3, E. R..	Gov't boat	....	...
Great Neck..................	*Peck slip....	35	50	16
Greenport...................	Beekman.....	1 25	....	125
Hartford	Peck slip.....	1 50	2 25	150
New Brunswick, N. J...	Morris........	50	80	35
New Haven..................	Peck slip.....	75	1 25	76
New Haven..................	Cortlandt	75	1 25	76
New London................	Watts........	1 40	....	120
Newport....................	Murray.......	2 00	....	170
New Rochelle...............	Pike..........	25	....	20
Orient......................	Beekman	1 25	....	120
Perth Amboy...............	Morris........	25	40	24
Portchester.................	Pike........ .	25	....	27
Providence..................	Warren.......	2 25	....	180
Red Bank...................	Franklin.....	50	80	35
Rockaway Beach............	West 23d.....	....	50	...
Roslyn......................	*Peck slip....	35	50	30
Rossville....................	Morris........	25	40	21
Sag Harbor..................	Beekman.....	1 25	....	140
Sand's Point	*Peck slip....	35	50	26
Saybrook....................	Peck slip.....	1 50	2 25	100
Seabright....................	Jane.	25	40	30
Sea Cliff.....................	*Peck Slip....	35	50	28
Shelter Island...............	Beekman.....	1 25	....	130
South Amboy................	Morris........	30	50	27
South Norwalk..............	*Beekman....	40	60	48
Southold....................	Beekman.....	1 25	....	135
Stamford....................	Pike..........	35	50	40
Stonington..................	Spring........	1 75	....	120
Willet's Point...........	Pier 3, E. R..	Gov't boat	....	14

* Land also at foot of East Thirty-first street.

FERRIES.

FERRY.	Fare	FROM NEW YORK TO
Astoria........ ...	3	92d st., E. R., to Astoria.
"	7	Beekman st. E. R. to Astoria.
Bay Ridge.......	10	Whitehall st. to Bay Ridge.
Blackwell's Island	20	26th st. E. R. to Blackw'l's Isl'd.
" "	25	52d st. E. R. to Blackw'l's Isl'd.
Brooklyn........	2	Catherine st. to Main st. B'klyn
"	2	Fulton st. N. Y. to Fulton st. Brooklyn.
"	2	Whiteh'l st. to Atlantic st. B'k'n
"	2	Whitehall st. to Hamilton av. Brooklyn.
"	5	Whitehall to 39th st. So. B'klyn
"	2	Wall st. to Montague st. B'klyn
Brooklyn, E. D..	2	Grand st. E. R. to Grand st. B'k'n
" ".....	2	Houston st. to Grand st. B'klyn
" ".....	2	Grand st. to Broadway, E. D.
" ".....	3	Roosevelt st. to Broadw'y, E. D.
" ".....	3	E. 23d st. to B'dw'y, B'k'n, E. D.
College Point. ...	10	99th st. E. R. to College Point
Fort Lee.........	10	130th street to Fort Lee.
" "	15	W. 13th st.
Governor's Island	Pass	Pier 3, E. R., to Governor's Isl'd
Green Point......	3	10th st. E. R. to Greenpoint av.
" "	3	23d st. E. R. to Greenpoint av.
Hart's Island	40	26th st. E. R. to Hart's Island
Hoboken	3	Barclay st. to Newark and Ferry sts., Hoboken.
"	3	Christopher st. to Newark and Ferry sts., Hoboken.
"	3	14th st. N. R. to 14th st. Hob'k'n
Hunter's Point...	6	*See Long Island City.*
Jersey City	3	Desbrosses st. to Montgomery st., Jersey City.
" "	3	Cortl'dt st. to M'ntg'm'y st. J. C.
" "	3	West 34th st. N. R. to Montgomery st. Jersey City.
" "	3	Liberty st. to Cen. R. R. of N. J. Dock.

FERRIES—Continued.

FERRY.	Fare	FROM NEW YORK TO
Jersey City	3	Chambers st. to Pavonia Ferry, Erie R. R. Dock.
" "	3	23d st. N. R. to Pavonia Ferry, Erie R. R. Dock.
Long Island City.	6	James' Slip to Long Island City
" " " ..	3	34th st. E. R. to Long Isl'nd City
Morrisania........	10	Pier 22 E. R. to Morrisania.
Randall's Island..	25	26th st. E. R. to Randalls Isl'nd
" " ..	25	116 or 120th st. E. R. to Randall's Island.
" " ..	25	122d st. E. R. to Randall's Isl.
Staten Island.....	10	Whitehall st. to Staten Island.
Ward's Island....	20	26th st. E. R. to Ward's Island
" "	20	115th st. East River.
Weehawken	5	42d st. N. R. to R. R. Slip.
"	5	42d st. N. R. to Old Ferry Slip
"	5	Jay st. N. R. to R. R. Slip.

CAB AND COACH FARES.

Regulated by city ordinance. Complaints made to the Mayor's Marshal, Room 1, City Hall. It is the duty of every cab or coachman to hand to the passenger a card, giving rates, and to have the card conspicuously posted in his vehicle under penalty of a fine. The rates are in full for from 1 to 4 persons in a coach and 1 or 2 persons in a cab or hansom. It is well for a passenger to make a bargain before entering.

Cab and Hansom Rates.—50 cents first mile or part thereof; 25 cents each additional mile. 25 cents for stops over 5 to 15 minutes. By the hour, going from place to place with stops at the passenger's option, $1.00 for first hour or part thereof, and 50 cents for each succeeding half hour or part thereof.

Coach Rates.—$1.00 for first mile or part thereof; 40 cents each additional half mile or part thereof. Stops over 5 to 15 minutes 38 cents. By the hour $1.50; 75 cents each succeeding half hour.

MAIN STREET CAR LINES.*

New York City is pretty well gridironed with horse and cable railroads (usual fare 5 cents). The stranger will generally find the elevated railroads most convenient, especially between distant points. Therefore only street railways most important from the visitor's point of view are given.

SOUTH AND NORTH.

Broadway Line.—From Central Park througn Seventh avenue and Broadway to the Battery. Transfers at Barclay street to University place branch, and at Park place to Seventh avenue branch and *vice versa.*

Bleecker Street and Fulton Ferry Line.—From Fulton Ferry to Twenty-third Street Ferry, *via* Broadway, Bleecker, Hudson, Fourteenth streets and Ninth avenue to Twenty-third Street. Branch from East River Bridge.

"*Belt Lines.*"—Run along or near the water front of both the East and North rivers crossing the city through Fifty-ninth street.

---

* Tramways.

Eighth Avenue Line.—From Broadway and Vesey street, *via* West Broadway, Hudson street to Eighth avenue, Fifty-ninth street (Central Park).

From Broadway and Canal street, to Eighth avenue and One Hundred and Fifty-fourth street.

Fourth Avenue Line.—From Broadway and Post Office (lower end), through Park row, to Centre street, Grand street, Bowery, Fourth avenue, Grand Central depot. Transfer cars at Thirty-second street, to Thirty-fourth street or Hunter's Point Ferry (Long Island Railroad).

Madison Avenue Line.—Same route as Fourth Avenue Line to Grand Central Depot, to Vanderbilt avenue, Forty-fourth street, Madison avenue to bridge over Harlem River, to One Hundred and Thirty-eighth street (Mott Haven).

Sixth Avenue Line. — From Broadway and Vesey street, *via* West Broadway, Canal, Varick, Carmine streets to Sixth avenue, Fifty-ninth street (Central Park).

Third Avenue Line.—From Broadway and Park row, through Park row to Chatham square, Bowery, Third avenue, Harlem, connecting with the following lines: *Harlem, Morrisania, Tremont, and Fordham; Harlem, Morrisania, and West Farms; Harlem and Port Morris.*

Harlem and Manhattanville (*High Bridge Branch*).—From One Hundred and Twenty-fifth street, East River, to New Amsterdam avenue, to One Hundred and Eightieth street (cable).

EAST AND WEST.

Christopher and Tenth Street Line.—From Christopher Street Ferry to Ferry foot East Tenth street.

Central Cross-Town Railroad.—From Twenty-third street, East River Ferry, through Avenue A, to Eighteenth street, Broadway, Fourteenth street to Christopher Street Ferry.

Desbrosses, Vestry, and Grand Street Line.— From Grand Street Ferry, through Grand street to Desbrosses Street Ferry.

Fourteenth Street and Union Square Line.—Christopher Street Ferry to Fourteenth street and Fourth avenue. Connection by branch at Ninth avenue and Fourteenth street with ferry foot of West Fourteenth street.

Chambers Street. — From the Erie Ferry, foot of Chambers street, to Duane, Chambers, New Chambers street, James Slip.

Grand Street Branch.—From foot of Grand street to Erie Ferry.

Harlem and Manhattanville.—From East river at One Hundred and Twenty-fifth street, through One Hundred and Twenty-fifth street to Manhattanville. Transfers at New Amsterdam avenue for cable road up New Amsterdam avenue to One Hundred and Eighty-seventh street.

Twenty-third Street and Erie Ferry.—From foot of West Twenty-third street to foot of East Twenty-third street. Branch to Thirty-fourth Street Ferry.

Forty-second Street and Boulevard Line. — From Thirty-fourth Street Ferry, East River, *via* First avenue, Forty-second street, Seventh avenue, Broadway, to Boulevard at Seventy-second street, to Fort Lee Ferry. Branch from Thirty-fourth Street Ferry to Forty-second street, to West Shore Ferry, West Forty-second street. Branch from First avenue and One Hundred and Tenth street to Fort Lee Ferry.

Fifth Avenue Stage Line.—From South Fifth avenue and Bleecker street, through Washington square, through Fifth avenue to Eighty-sixth street.

MANHATTAN ELEVATED RAILWAY.

DAILY, INCLUDING SUNDAYS.

This is the most rapid and convenient local transportation route. It has stations convenient to all important points on the east side, and to all important points below One Hundred and Fifty-fifth street on the west side of the city. The accompanying map shows more clearly than any description the various branches of this important system which has contributed largely to the growth of the upper part of the city. Fare 5 cents. Children under 5 years of age free. Passengers deposit ticket in the gate-box before entering train. Below are further particulars with a list of stations. An asterisk * after a station denotes that cross-town car lines pass the station. The first elevated railway in New York City, part of the present Ninth avenue branch,

ELEVATED RAILROAD.

began running in 1868. The present Sixth avenue branch was next opened in June, 1878.

SECOND AVENUE LINE.

This line is open from 5.30 A. M. to 11.58 P. M.

Passengers for Thirty-fourth Street Ferry, East River, change cars at Thirty-fourth Street Station and take branch train for ferry. No extra charge.

Passengers to or from City Hall change cars and cross the Bridge at Chatham Square Station.

Passengers to or from Suburban Rapid Transit Railway change cars at One Hundred and Twenty-ninth street.

STATIONS.

South Ferry, Hanover square, Fulton street,* Franklin square, Chatham square, Canal street,* Grand street,* Rivington street, First street, Eighth street,* Fourteenth street,* Nineteenth street, Twenty-third street,* Thirty-fourth street,* Forty-second street,* Fiftieth street, Fifty-seventh street, Sixty-fifth street, Seventieth street, Eightieth street, Eighty-sixth street, Ninety-second street, Ninety-ninth street, One Hundred and Eleventh street, One Hundred and Seventeenth street, One Hundred and Twenty-first street, One Hundred and Twenty-seventh street, One Hundred and Twenty-ninth street.

THIRD AVENUE LINE.

This line, including City Hall Branch, is open at all hours of the day and night.

City Hall passengers, to or from Second Avenue Line change cars and cross the Bridge at Chatham Square Station. Direct connection made at City Hall Station, without going to the street, with trains crossing Brooklyn Bridge.

Passengers for Grand Central Depot change cars at Forty-second Street Station and take branch train, which is run from 6.00 A. M. to 12.00 midnight. No extra charge.

---

* Cross-town car lines.

Passengers for Thirty-fourth Street Ferry, East River, change cars at Thirty-fourth Street Station and take branch train, which is run from 5.30 A.M. to 12 midnight.

STATIONS.

South Ferry, Hanover square, Fulton street,* Franklin square, City Hall, Chatham square, Canal street,* Grand street,* Houston street,* Ninth street,* Fourteenth street,* Eighteenth street,* Twenty-third street,* Twenty-eighth street, Thirty-fourth street,* Thirty-fourth Street Ferry, Forty-second street,* Grand Central,* Forty-seventh street, Fifty-third street, Fifty-ninth street,* Sixty-seventh street, Seventy-sixth street, Eighty-fourth street, Eighty-ninth street, Ninety-ninth street, One Hundred and Sixth street, One Hundred and Sixteenth street, One Hundred and Twenty-fifth street,* One Hundred and Twenty-ninth street.

SIXTH AVENUE LINE.

This line is open at all hours of the day and night.

Passengers for Grand Central Depot leave train at Forty-second Street Station. Crosstown cars run between Station and Depot. Fare 5 cents.

New York and Northern Railway Connection.—Trains connecting with the New York and Northern Railway through trains carry a blue disc on the forward part of the engine.

Passengers for stations on Ninth Avenue Line change cars at Fifty-ninth Street Station. No extra charge.

STATIONS.

South Ferry, Battery place, Rector street, Cortlandt street, Park place, Chambers street,* Franklin street, Grand street,* Bleecker street,* Eighth street,* Fourteenth street,* Eighteenth street, Twenty-third street,* Twenty-eighth street, Thirty-third street,* Forty-second street,* Fiftieth street, Fifty-eighth street, Fifty-third street and Eighth avenue, Fifty-ninth street and Ninth avenue,* Sixty-sixth street, Seventy-second street, Eighty-first street, Ninety-third street, One Hundred and Fourth street, One Hundred and Sixteenth street and Eighth avenue, One Hundred and Twenty-fifth

* Cross-town car lines.

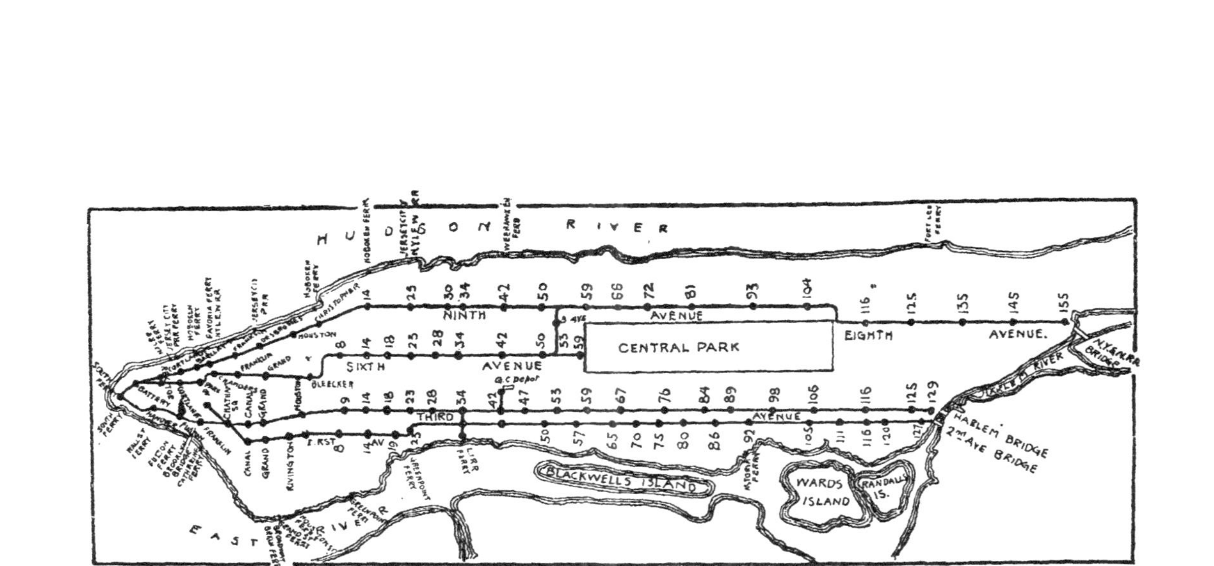

MAP OF THE ELEVATED RAILROADS.

street,* One Hundred and Thirty-fifth street, One Hundred and Forty-fifth street, One Hundred and Fifty-fifth street.

NINTH AVENUE LINE.

This line is open from 5.30 A. M. to 7.57 P. M.

Passengers for Sixty-sixth street, Seventy-second street, Eighty-first street, Ninety-third street, One Hundred and Fourth street, One Hundred and Sixteenth street, One Hundred and Twenty-fifth street (Harlem), One Hundred and Thirty-fifth street, One Hundred and Forty-fifth street, One Hundred and Fifty-fifth street, Fort Washington, High Bridge and the New York and Northern Railway, change cars at Fifty-ninth street. No extra charge.

STATIONS.

South Ferry, Battery place, Rector street, Cortlandt street, Barclay street, Warren street, Franklin street, Desbrosses street,* Houston street,* Christopher street,* Fourteenth street,* Twenty-third street,* Thirtieth street, Thirty-fourth street,* Forty-second street,* Fiftieth street, Fifty-ninth street.*

HOTELS.

It is presumed that readers of this Guide will not care to patronize any but absolutely unexceptionable hotels. Therefore only such are given. Should a reader discover any reason for finding fault with the service at any of these hotels he will confer a favor on the author by communicating the facts to him. Lodgings, in the sense in which the English use that term, are not to be had in New York. For boarding-houses reference must be had to the advertisements in the daily newspapers.

The New York hotels, like those of other large cities of the United States, are conducted on the American or European plan, or on both. In the American plan the charge includes both room and meals; in the European plan the charge is for room only, the guest being at liberty to take his meals either at the hotel restaurant or elsewhere. Several hotels combine both plans. For a

*Cross-town car lines.

visitor whose business or pleasure takes him about the city, the European plan is preferable, as it renders him independent of his hotel during the day time. Excellent rooms in hotels on the European plan can be had at $2 a day, the price running from $1 to $3, the last figure being for double rooms. Suites with sitting, bed and bath room, can be had at from $25 to $50 a week. Among the best known hotels are:

EUROPEAN PLAN—*Astor House*, in the heart of the down town business district on Broadway, between Vesey and Barclay streets, opposite the Post Office; *Brevoort*, 11 Fifth avenue, with a large English patronage; *Buckingham*, Fifth avenue and Fiftieth street (one of the most exclusive in the city); *Everett*, Fourth avenue and Seventeenth street, overlooking Union square; *Gilsey*, Broadway and Twenty-ninth street; *Grand*, Broadway and Thirty-first street; *Hoffman*, 1111 Broadway (on Madison square); *Hotel Brunswick*, 225 Fifth avenue, on Madison square; *Hotel Dam*, 104 East Fifteenth street (near Union square); *Hotel Imperial*, Thirty-second street and Broadway; *Hotel Normandie*, Thirty-eighth street and Broadway; *Langham*, Fifth avenue and Fifty-second street (an excellent family hotel); *Plaza*, Fifth avenue and Fifty-ninth street (the main entrance to Central Park); *St. James*, 1133 Broadway (near Madison square); *Union Square*, 16 Union square; *Albemarle*, Broadway and Twenty-fourth street.

AMERICAN PLAN—*Clarendon*, 219 Fourth avenue (near Union square) with a large English patronage; *Fifth Avenue*, in a fine situation at Fifth avenue and Twenty-third street (Madison square), in the centre of the shopping and amusement district—one of the best known hotels in the United States; *Grand Central*, 671 Broadway; *Metropolitan*, 584 Broadway (convenient to the wholesale dry goods district); *Murray Hill*, Park avenue and Forty-first street (convenient to the Grand Central Depot); *New York Hotel*, 721 Broadway (a favorite hotel with Southerners); *Sturtevant*, 1186 Broadway; *Victoria*, Twenty-seventh street, Broadway, and Fifth avenue (near Madison square); *Westminster*, Irving place and Sixteenth street (a quiet neighborhood near Union square); *Windsor*, Fifth avenue and Forty-sixth street —one of the best known hotels in the United States.

The *Clarendon* and *Sturtevant* (see above) give their guests the choice of the European or American plan. William Waldorf Astor is building two hotels, which will undoubtedly be unexceptionable. They are respectively at Fifth avenue and Thirty-third street (North-west corner) and Fifth avenue and Fifty-ninth street (North-east corner), overlooking the Plaza and Central Park. A first-class hotel is also building on the South-east corner of Fifth avenue and Fifty-ninth street.

RESTAURANTS, CHOP-HOUSES AND OYSTER SALOONS.

RESTAURANTS.—The most noted restaurant in New York City, in fact in the United States, is Delmonico's, 2 South William street (the site of the first restaurant bearing the now famous name); 22 Broad street, near the Stock Exchange, and south-west corner of Fifth avenue and Twenty-sixth street, near Madison square. The charges at these restaurants are high, but not out of proportion to the excellence of the cooking and service. Here, as at nearly all American restaurants, "one portion" is enough for two persons, so that a meal for two persons will not cost them more than each would have to pay if dining alone. Therefore, an even numbered party can luxuriate at Delmonico's and other first-class high-priced restaurants (such as the Savarin and the Hoffman House) at a comparatively small cost to each member of the party. For from $3.00 to $5.00 between them, two persons can secure a plain but admirably cooked and served dinner at such restaurants. *Table d'hôte* breakfasts, lunches and dinners can be had at various establishments, which usually serve also à la carte, the dinners costing from 75 cents to $1.50, generally including a pint of *vin ordinaire* (breakfast and lunches at proportionately less expense). Following is a list of reliable restaurants from downtown upwards; nearly all the restaurants have cafés attached. An asterisk implies special excellence, in the author's opinion. Specialties are bracketed. Braguglias-Carreno, 13 Broadway [Spanish dishes]; *Hoffman Café, 7 Beaver street; *Delmonico, 2 S. William street; *Delmonico, 22

Broad street; Kolb, 164 Pearl street; *Savarin, 120 Broadway; Cable, Bailey & Co., 130 Broadway; *Hoffman Café, 60 Broadway; J. A. P. Fisk, 76 Broad street; Sutherland, 64 Liberty street; Heckman, 122 William street, *table d'hôte* (in the oldest building in New York); Mouquin, 149 Fulton street; *Astor House, Broadway and Vesey street; Racky, 21 Frankfort street [German—German wines]; "Rathskeller," 2 Tryon Row, *table d'hôte* [German—imported beers]; Holtz & Freystedt, 349 Broadway [German—German wines]; Metropolitan Hotel, 584 Broadway; Filippini, 337 Broadway; Vienna Bakery, Broadway and Tenth street [Vienna rolls, coffee, tea and chocolate]; St. Denis Hotel, Broadway and Eleventh street; Hotel Hungaria, 4 Union square, East, *table d'hôte* [Hungarian wines]; Union Square Hotel, 16 Union square; Riccadonna, 42 Union square, East [Italian]; Everett House, Fourth avenue and Seventeenth street; Pursell, 910 Broadway, *table d'hôte;* Martinelli, 136 Fifth avenue, *table d'hôte* [Italian]; Moretti, 12 East Twenty-first street, *table d'hôte* [Italian]; Clark, N., 22 West Twenty-third street; Albemarle Hotel, Broadway and Twenty-fourth street; *Hoffman House, Broadway and Twenty-fifth street; *Hotel Brunswick, Fifth avenue and Twenty-fifth street, *table d'hôte;* *Delmonico, Fifth avenue and Twenty-sixth street; St. James Hotel, Broadway and Twenty-sixth street; Coleman House, Broadway and Twenty-seventh street; Heim, 29 West Twenty-seventh street [German wines]; Drentel, 9 West Twenty-eighth street, *table d'hôte;* Gilsey House, Broadway and Twenty-ninth street; Parker's, 1,297 Broadway (largely patronized by sportsmen); Murray Hill, Park avenue and Forty-first street; Grand Union Hotel, Fourth avenue and Forty-second street.

Chop-Houses.—"Old Tom's," Thames street (rear of Trinity Church); Farrish, 64 John street; Eschbach, Fourth avenue, between Twentieth and Twenty-first streets; "Studio," Sixth avenue, between Twentieth and Twenty-first streets; Browne, 31 West Twenty-seventh street.

Oyster Saloons.—Oyster saloons are scattered all over the city, and the character of the cooking and service can generally be judged of by appearances. Oysters are served at nearly all good restaurants in New York. Specially well-known oyster saloons are A. & P. Dorlon, Fulton Market; O'Neill, 358 Sixth avenue; Burns, 783 and 904 Sixth avenue.

BILLIARDS.

Nearly all the large hotels have well equipped billiard rooms. Best known among other billiard rooms are the "Columbia," 948 Broadway, and Sexton's, 1,292 Broadway.

LIBRARIES.

Apprentices', 18 East Sixteenth street (8 A. M.—9 P. M.); Astor, Lafayette Place (9 A. M.—5 P. M.; 4.30 P. M. in winter); City, City Hall (10 A. M.—4 P. M.); Columbia College, Forty-ninth street and Madison avenue (8 A. M.—10 P. M.); Cooper Union, Seventh street and Fourth avenue (8 A. M.—10 P. M.); Harlem, 2238 Third avenue (9 A. M.—9 P. M.); Lenox, Fifth avenue and Seventieth street (11 A. M.—4 P. M.); Mercantile, Astor Place (8 A. M.—9 P. M.); New York Hospital, 8 West Sixteenth street (10 A. M.—5 P. M.); New York Society, 67 University Place (8 A. M.—6 P. M.).

NEWSPAPERS AND PERIODICALS.

The principal daily newspapers are: MORNING—*Morning Advertiser*, Independent, 29 Park Row; *Herald*, Independent, Broadway and Ann street, Fifth avenue and Twenty-third street; *Morning Journal*, Independent, 162 Nassau street; *Press*, Republican, Park Row (Potter Building); *Sun*, Independent, Printing House Square; *Times*, Independent, Printing House Square; *Tribune*, Republican, Printing House Square; *World*, Democratic, Pulitzer Building (adjoining East River Bridge). German—*Staats Zeitung*, Democratic, Tryon Row. French—*Courier des Etats Unis*, Democratic, 19 Barclay street. Commercial—*Commercial Bulletin* (except Sunday), 32 Broadway; *Journal of Commerce* (except Sunday), 76 Beaver street. EVENING (except Sunday)—*Commercial Advertiser*, Republican, 29 Park Row; *Mail and Express*, Republican, 23 Park Row;

Evening Post, Independent, Broadway and Fulton street; *Evening Telegram*, Independent, Broadway and Ann street; *Evening Sun*, Independent, Printing House Square; *Evening World*, Democratic, Pulitzer Building. WEEKLY.—*Frank Leslie's Illustrated Newspaper*, 110 Fifth avenue (also German); *Harper's Bazar* (the leading weekly for women); *Harper's Weekly* (the leading weekly of the United States), Franklin Square; *Illustrated American*, Bible House; *Nation* (the leading political weekly of the United States), 210 Broadway. COMIC—*Life*, 28 West Twenty-third street; *Puck*, 39 East Houston street; *Judge*, 110 Fifth avenue. MONTHLY (illustrated)—*Century*, 33 East Seventeenth street; *Cosmopolitan*, Twenty-sixth street and Fifth avenue; *Harper's New Monthly Magazine*, Franklin Square; *Scribner's Magazine*, 743 Broadway.

THEATRES.

The most desirable seats in New York theatres are, except private boxes, in the parquet (also orchestra or dress circle). These cost $1.50 each, though at the "popular" theatres prices range much lower. Opera glasses may be hired in the lobby. Programmes free. The leading theatres, stock companies marked *, are :

Academy of Music, East Fourteenth street, corner of Irving place; Amberg's Theatre, Fifteenth street and Irving place; Bijou Theatre, Broadway and Thirtieth street; Broadway Theatre, Forty-first street and Broadway; Casino, Broadway and Thirty-ninth street (light opera); *Daly's Theatre, Broadway and Thirtieth street; Fifth Avenue Theatre, Twenty-eighth street and Broadway; Fourteenth Street Theatre, Fourteenth street and Sixth avenue; Garden Theatre, Madison avenue and Twenty-seventh street; Grand Opera House, Eighth avenue and Twenty-third street; Hammerstein's Columbus Theatre, One Hundred and Twenty-fifth street and Lexington avenue; Hammerstein's Harlem Opera House, One Hundred and Twenty-fifth street and Seventh avenue; *Harrigan's Theatre, Thirty-fifth street, east of Sixth avenue; Herrmann's Theatre, Broadway and Twenty-ninth street; *Lyceum Theatre, Fourth avenue and Twenty-third and Twenty-fourth streets; Madison

Square Garden, Twenty-sixth and Twenty-seventh streets, and Fourth and Madison avenues; *Madison Square Theatre, Twenty-fourth street, near Fifth Avenue Hotel; Metropolitan Opera House, Broadway and Thirty-ninth street; New Park Theatre, Thirty-fifth street and Broadway; Niblo's Garden Theatre, 522 Broadway; Palmer's Theatre, Broadway and Thirtieth street; Proctor's Theatre, Twenty-third street, between Sixth and Seventh avenues; Standard Theatre, Sixth avenue, Broadway and Thirty-third street; Star Theatre, Broadway and Thirteenth street; Tony Pastor's Theatre (Variety), Tammany Hall, Fourteenth street, near Third avenue; Union Square Theatre, Union square and Broadway.

CONCERTS.

The principal concerts to which the public is admitted are given at the Music Hall, Seventh avenue and Fifty-seventh street, by the Philharmonic, Symphony and Oratorio (choral) societies. Parquet, $1.50.

CONCERT-VARIETY PERFORMANCES.

Koster & Bials, Twenty-third street, between Sixth and Seventh avenues.

WAXWORKS.

Eden Musée, Twenty-third street, between Fifth and Sixth avenues.

MUSEUMS.

American Museum Natural History, Manhattan square.

Metropolitan Museum of Art, Central Park, near Eighty-first street and Fifth avenue entrance.

New York Historical Society, 170 Second avenue.

PICTURE EXHIBITIONS.

City Hall, City Hall Park.

Lenox Library, Fifth avenue and Seventieth street.

Metropolitan Museum of Art, Central Park, near Eighty-first street and Fifth avenue entrance.

See also *Art Stores, Academy of Design* and *Art Students' League.*

TURKISH AND RUSSIAN BATHS.

Produce Exchange, 8 Broadway; Hoffman House, 7 West Twenty-fourth street; Windsor Hotel, 7 East Forty-sixth street; 18 Lafayette Place.

CYCLORAMA.

Falls of Niagara, Nineteenth street and Fourth avenue.

DIVINE SERVICE.

Trow's Directory contains a complete list of churches of all denominations with the pastors' names. The best known churches in New York are:

Baptist.—Adoniram Judson Memorial, Thompson street and Washington Square, Edward Judson; Calvary, Fifty-seventh street, between Sixth and Seventh avenues, R. S. McArthur; Fifth Avenue, 6 West Forty-sixth street, W. H. P. Faunce.

Congregational.—Broadway Tabernacle, Broadway and Thirty-fourth street, Wm. M. Taylor.

Methodist Episcopal.—St. Andrew's, Calvary, Washington Square; John Street, 44 John street; Madison Avenue, Sixtieth street and Madison avenue.

Presbyterian.—Brick, 410 Fifth avenue, Henry J. Van Dyke; Church of the Covenant, 28 Park avenue, J. H. McElvaine; Fifth Avenue, 708 Fifth avenue, John Hall; Fourth Avenue, 286 Fourth avenue; University Place, George Alexander; West, 31 West Forty-second street, John R. Paxton. There are about 65 Presbyterian churches in the city.

Protestant Episcopal.—Trinity, the most noted church in New York City, Broadway and Rector streets, Morgan Dix; St. Paul's (Trinity Parish), Broadway and Vesey streets, James Mulcahey ; St. Augustine's Chapel (Trinity Parish), 107 East Houston street, A. C. Kimber. Other well-known congregations among the 90 odd of this denomination are: All Souls, Sixty-sixth street and Madison avenue, R. Heber Newton; Grace, Broadway, near Tenth street, W. R. Huntington; Heavenly Rest, 551 Fifth avenue, D. Parker Morgan; St. Ann's, 7 West Eighteenth street, Thomas Gallaudet; St. Bartholomew's, 348 Madison avenue, David H. Greer; St. George's, 7 Rutherford place, Wm. S. Rainsford; St. Ignatius (ritualistic), 56 West Fortieth street, A. Ritchie; St. Mark's, Stuyvesant street and Second avenue, J. H. Rylance; St. Mary, the Virgin (ritualistic), 228 West Forty-fifth street, T. McK. Brown; St. Thomas's, Fifth avenue and Fifty-third street, John W. Brown; Transfiguration, 5 East Twenty-ninth street, George H. Houghton; Bishop, Henry C. Potter, Diocesan House, 29 Lafayette place. A Protestant Episcopal Cathedral is to be built on the site of the old Leake & Watts Orphan Asylum building, on high ground, just northwest of Central Park. There is also a Protestant Episcopal City Mission, 68 Bleecker street, an interesting ministration of which is the City Prison Mission, Brockholst Morgan, missionary.

Reformed Dutch.—Collegiate Middle Church, 14 Lafayette place, Talbot W. Chambers; Fifth Avenue, Forty-eighth street and Fifth avenue, Edward B. Coe; Madison Avenue, Fifty-seventh street and Madison avenue, A. E. Kittredge; South Twenty-first street and Fifth Avenue, Roderick Terry.

Roman Catholic.—St. Patrick's Cathedral, the finest church structure in America, Fiftieth and Fifty-first streets, and Fifth avenue, Archbishop Corrigan; St. Francis Xavier, David A. Merrick; St. Paul, the Apostle, Fifty-ninth street and Ninth avenue, John McQuirk. There are 75 churches of this denomination.

Unitarian.—All Souls (formerly Dr. Bellows') 245 Fourth avenue, T. C. Williams; Messiah, 61 East Thirty-fourth street, Robert Collyer.

Universalist.—Divine Paternity (formerly Dr. Chapin's), 538 Fifth avenue, C. H. Eaton.

Synagogues.—Temple Emanu-El, 521 Fifth avenue, Gustav Gottheil, Beth-El, Fifth avenue and seventy-sixth street, Dr. Kohler; Ahavash Chesed, 652 Lexington avenue, Dr. Kohut; Shearith Israel, 5 West Nineteenth street.

FOREIGN CONSULS.

Argentine Republic—C. Carranza, 60 Wall street.
Austria-Hungary—T. A. Havemeyer, 33 Broadway.
Belgium—Chas. Mali, 329 Broadway.
Bolivia—Melchor Obarrio, 126 Liberty street.
Brazil—A. T. de Macedo, 23 State street.
Chili—F. A. Beelen, 15 Cortlandt street.
China—Shen Woon, 26 West Ninth street.
Colombia—Climaco Calderon, 24 State street.
Costa Rica—A. C. Flint, 142 Pearl street.
Denmark—Henri M. Bræm, 69 Wall street.
Dominican Republic—E. Vasquez, 31 Broadway.
Ecuador—Domingo L. Ruiz, 51 Liberty street.
France—Vicomte Paul d'Abzac, 4 Bowling Green.
German Empire—August Feigel, 2 Bowling Green.
Great Britain—Wm. Lane Booker, 24 State street.
Greece—D. N. Botassi, 115 Pearl street.
Guatemala—Jacob Baiz, 102 Front street.
Hayti—John Haustedt, 101 Pearl street.
Hawaiian Islands—E. H. Allen, 51 Leonard street.
Honduras—Jacob Baiz, 102 Front street.
Italy—G. Paolo Riva, 22 State street.
Japan—S. Fujii, 7 Warren street.
Korea—Everett Frazer, 124 Water street.
Liberia—Joseph W. Yates, 19 William street.
Mexico—Juan N. Navarro, 35 Broadway.
Monaco—James Dupas, 4 Bowling Green.
Netherlands—J. R. Planten, 19 William street.
Nicaragua—Alexander I. Cotheal, 140 Pearl street.
Norway—Christopher Ravn, 41 Broad street.
Peru—Juan Quintana, 19 Whitehall street.
Portugal—Baron d'Alnierium, 102 Broad street.
Russia—A. Olarovsky, 22 State street.
Siam—Isaac T. Smith, 115 Broadway.
Spain—A. B. Torese, 30 Broadway.
Sweden—Christopher Ravn, 41 Broad street.
Switzerland—J. Bertschmann, 69 Beaver street.
St. Domingo—E. Vasquez, 31 Broadway.
Turkey—Baltazzi Effendi, 132 Broadway.
Uruguay—Estrazulas, 120 Front street.
Venezuela—Dr. Rafael Villavicencio, 18 Broadway.

BANKERS.

BANKERS.—August Belmont & Co., 120 Broadway; Brown Bros. & Co., 59 Wall street; Cheque Bank, 2 Wall street; Drexel, Morgan & Co., 23 Wall street; A. Iselin & Co., 36 Wall street; Eugene Kelly & Co., 45 Exchange place; Kessler & Co., 54 Wall street; Kidder, Peabody & Co., 15 Wall street; Knauth, Nachod & Kuhne, 5 S. William street; Kountze Bros., 120 Broadway; Morton, Bliss & Co., 28 Nassau street; Post, Martin & Co., 45 Wall street; Roosevelt & Son, 33 Wall street; J. & W. Seligman & Co., 21 Broad street; Winslow, Lanier & Co., 17 Nassau street and 120 Broadway.

BANKS.

Following are the principal banks of the city. *National:* Bank of Commerce, 27 Nassau street; Bank of New York, 48 Wall street; Chemical, 270 Broadway; City, 52 Wall street; First, 2 Wall street; Importers and Traders, 247 Broadway; Mechanics, 33 Wall street; Park, 214 and 216 Broadway. *State:* Bank of America, 46 Wall street; Bank of the Metropolis, 29 Union square; Bank of the State of New York, 33 William street; Fifth Avenue, 531 Fifth avenue; German-American, 50 Wall street; Manhattan Company, 40 Wall street; Pacific, 470 Broadway. *Savings Banks:* Bank for Savings, 64 Bleecker street; Dry Dock, 343 Bowery; Emigrant and Industrial, 51 Chambers street; German, 157 Fourth avenue; Manhattan Savings Institution, 644 Broadway; Seamen's, 74 Wall street; Union Dime, 54 West Thirty-second street.

POSTAL INFORMATION.

General Post Office, Broadway and Park Row. There are eighteen branch P. O. Stations and twenty-one sub-stations, the latter in drug stores. Hotel guests can mail their letters and parcels at their hotel. There are no deliveries on Sunday. Closing of foreign mails is advertised in the newspapers. The following is condensed from the *New York Post Office Guide,* copies of which can be obtained at the General Post Office. Prepayment of postage is necessary. The rates for first, second and third class matter apply also to mail matter for Canada and Mexico.

RATES OF POSTAGE.

First class: Letters weighing one ounce or less, 2 cents; 2 cents additional for every extra ounce; postal cards, 1 cent. *Second class:* Newspapers or periodicals when sent by publisher or news agents, 1 cent a pound, or fraction thereof; otherwise, 1 cent for every 4 ounces, or fraction thereof. *Third class:* Printed matter unsealed, including books, circulars, handbills, engravings, music, magazines, pamphlets, newspapers, proof-sheets and manuscripts accompanying same, 1 cent each 2 ounces, or fraction thereof; limit of weight, 4 lbs., except for a single book, which may be more. *Fourth class:* All mailable matter not included in preceding classes, prepared for mailing so as to be easily withdrawn and examined, 1 cent per ounce, or fraction thereof; but seeds, plants, cuttings, bulbs, roots and scions, are 1 cent for each 2 ounces. *Foreign Postage:* 5 cents for a single letter to all the countries belonging to the Postal Union; postal cards, 2 cents. To countries not belonging to the union the rates vary. *Unmailable:* Poisons, fresh fruits and vegetables, live animals, explosives, and other dangerous articles or substances.

MONEY-ORDERS.

Domestic.—Obtained at the General Post Office, and at any of the branch or sub-stations, between the hours of 10 A. M. and 6 P. M. Applicant must fill up a blank form giving the amount he desires to send, the place at which it is to be paid, the name of the payee, and his own name. Fees: On orders not exceeding $5, 5 cents; over $5 and not exceeding $10, 8 cents; over $10 and not exceeding $15, 10 cents; over $15 and not exceeding $30, 15 cents; over $30 and not exceeding $40, 20 cents; over $40 and not exceeding $50, 25 cents; over $50 and not exceeding $60, 30 cents; over $60 and not exceeding $70, 35 cents; over $70 and not exceeding $80, 40 cents; over $80 and not exceeding $100, 45 cents. *International.*—International money-orders payable in the following countries: Great Britain and Ireland, Canada, Germany, France, Italy, Belgium, Switzerland, Sweden, Norway, Denmark, Portugal, Netherlands, Luxemburg,

Austro-Hungary, New South Wales, Queensland, Victoria, New Zealand, South Australia, West Australia, Tasmania, British India, Japan, Hawaii, Jamaica, Cape Colony, Egypt, Constantinople, Hong Kong, Bermuda, Gibraltar, Iceland, Natal, Windward Islands, Leeward Islands, Ceylon, Falkland Islands, Straits Settlements (Singapore, Penang and Malacca), Gambia, Mauritius, St. Helena, Trinidad, Malta, Tangier, Beyrout, Salonica, Azores and Madeira Islands. Fees: On orders not exceeding $10, 10 cents; over $10 and not exceeding $20, 20 cents; over $20 and not exceeding $30, 30 cents; over $30 and not exceeding $40, 40 cents; over $40 and not exceeding $50, 50 cents; over $50 and not exceeding $60, 60 cents; over $60 and not exceeding $70, 70 cents; over $70 and not exceeding $80, 80 cents; over $80 and not exceeding $90, 90 cents; over $90 and not exceeding $100, $1. Obtainable at the General Post Office and all branch offices, except M, S and T.

POSTAL NOTES.

Postal Notes, good for three months, are issued for any sum from one cent to four dollars and ninety-nine cents ($4.99) inclusive, but not for any fractional part of a cent, at a uniform fee of three cents.

They can be purchased at the General Post Office or at any branch station or sub-station, and are payable at any money-order office in the United States, including branch stations and sub-stations in New York. They are payable to bearer, and no identification is required.

PARCELS POST.

Under conditions, which may be ascertained at the General Post Office, branch or sub-stations, unsealed parcels of merchandise not over 11 pounds may be sent by parcels post to Jamaica, Barbadoes, Bahamas, British Honduras, Mexico, Sandwich Islands, Leeward Islands, Colombia, Costa Rica, and Salvador.

REGISTRATION.

Domestic and foreign letters and parcels may be registered at a fee of ten cents in postage stamps.

POSTE RESTANTE.

Advertised Domestic Mail Matter.—All domestic (except local) letters, book packets, and packages of merchandise (also those from Great Britain, Ireland or British Colonies) which have remained undelivered for two weeks and which do not bear the names and addresses of the senders (except those addressed to street and number, which are advertised as soon as they are returned by carrier as being undeliverable) are advertised at New York twice a week. The advertised lists of such matter are also displayed in the lobbies of the General Post Office. Undelivered local letters are not advertised, but remain at the *Poste Restante* for thirty days awaiting call, and if then unclaimed are sent to the Dead Letter Office, Washington.

Advertised Foreign Mail Matter.—All letters, book packets, and packages, of apparent value, arriving from foreign countries and found to be undeliverable through the ordinary methods, are treated as follows: 1. If addressed "*Poste Restante,*" or "*to be called for,*" they are retained, awaiting call, for two months, before being advertised. 2. If addressed to street and number, but found undeliverable, they are advertised as soon as returned by carriers. 3. If addressed "*Post Office*" only, they are retained fifteen days and then are advertised. All are retained awaiting call for four weeks after being advertised, and all then unclaimed are sent to the Dead Letter Office. Mail matter of foreign origin (except that from Great Britain, Ireland and British Colonies) remaining uncalled for at the New York Office is advertised in newspapers printed in the languages of the countries in which such matter originates.

Fee for Advertising.—A charge of *one cent* is made on the delivery of each article of advertised mail matter, to cover the cost of advertising.

SPECIAL DELIVERY.

Letters and packages are delivered by special messenger if, in addition to the regular postage, a 10 cent special delivery stamp is affixed.

TELEPHONE.

New York and its suburbs are served by the Metropolitan Telephone and Telegraph Company, which has numerous offices. There is, also, a long-distance telephone service.

MESSENGER SERVICE.

Messenger service is maintained by the American District Telegraph Company and the Mutual District Messenger Company. These companies have numerous offices, and messengers can be summoned from most of the hotels.

EXPRESS SERVICE.

Domestic and Railway Expresses can be ordered at most of the hotels, the companies calling for the baggage or parcels. Foreign express matter should be delivered at the offices of the following:

American Express Co., 65 Broadway; *American European Express* (Baldwin Brothers & Co.), office, 53 Broadway; *Bermuda and New York Express*, 15 Murray street; *Contanseau's Rapid Foreign Express Co.*, 71 Broadway and 653 Sixth avenue; *Cutajar & Co.'s Express*, 55 and 57 Beaver street; *Davies, Turner & Co., American, Foreign and European Express Co.*, 40 Broadway; *E. Losee's European Express*, 111 Broadway, basement; *Foreign Express Co.* (Limited), 15 Murray street; *Hampton Jr. & Co. Express*, 40 Exchange place; *Hensel, Bruckman & Lorbacher*, 25 William street; *Langes European Express*, 49 Exchange place; *Morris European & American Express Co.*, 18 Broadway; *R. F. Dowing & Co.'s Foreign Express*, 20 Exchange place and 65 Beaver street; *Pitt & Scott's Foreign Express*, 35 and 37 Broadway; *Scott's Foreign Delivery*, 157 Broadway; *Steglich & Baese* (European Parcel), 76 William street; *The International Express*, 47 Broadway; *The Transatlantic Express* (J. Terkuile), 31 and 33 Broadway; *United Foreign Express Co.*, 71 Broadway and 659 Sixth avenue; *United States Express Co.*, 49 Broadway; *Universal Express*, J. Metzger & Co., 30 Broadway; *Wells, Fargo & Co.'s European Express*, 63 Broadway.

The American Express Co., United States Express Co. and Wells, Fargo & Co., have branches in various parts of the city.

TELEGRAPH AND CABLE RATES.

Telegraph and cable rates are apt to vary, but will generally be found at or near the rates given below, which are those now in force. These give a good general idea of the cost of telegraphing in New York, and from New York to other points in the United States and Canada, and other foreign countries. Except in cable messages the "place from," date, address and signature are not charged for. In cable messages every word written by the sender is charged for.

The Western Union, which is the largest telegraph company in the United States, has its main office at Broadway and Dey street. The principal branch offices, Fifth avenue and Twenty-third street and 16 Broad street, are connected by pneumatic tubes with the main office. There are branch offices in the principal hotels, exchanges, the post-office and railway stations, and at many other points in the city. Day and night offices: Broadway and Dey street; 599 Broadway (near Houston street); 854 Broadway (near Fourteenth street): Fifth avenue and Twenty-third street; Broadway and Twenty-ninth street; Sixth avenue and Forty-seventh street; 134 East One Hundred and Twenty-fifth street.

Telegraph Rates.—Rates for messages of ten words or under (numbers must be spelled out): Local, 20 cents; to Baltimore, Md., 25 cents; Boston, Mass., 25 cents; Chicago, Ill., 40 cents; Cincinnati, O., 40 cents; Galveston, Texas, 75 cents; Montreal and Quebec, 40 cents; New Orleans, La., 60 cents; Omaha, Neb., 50 cents; Philadelphia, 20 cents; Pittsburg, Pa., 25 cents; St. Louis, Mo., 40 cents; Salt Lake City, Utah, 75 cents; San Francisco, Cal., $1; Washington, D. C., 25 cents. Words in excess of ten are charged at considerably lower rates, as are also night messages.

Cable Rates.—Cable messages can be sent from the main offices and branches of the Western Union and other cable companies at the following rates *per word:*

Great Britain, Ireland, France, Germany, 25 cents; Bermudas, 81 cents; Belgium, 31 cents; Denmark, 35 cents; Holland, 33 cents; Sweden, 39 cents; Norway, 35 cents; Switzerland, 31 cents; Hungary, 36 cents; Italy, 34 cents; Russia, 43 cents; Egypt—Alexandria, 58 cents; Cape Colony, $2.43; Japan, $2.11; Australia, $2.54 to $2.68; India, $1.31; South America: Ecuador, $1.84; Peru, $1.82 to $2.66; Chili, $2.25; Argentine Republic, $1.82 to $2.13; Uruguay, $2; Brazil, $1.69

to $2.13; Colon and Panama, 97 cents; Havana, 40; St. Thomas, $1.96.

STORES.

ANTIQUITIES AND BRIC-A-BRAC.—Sypher & Co., 246 Fifth avenue; A. A. Vantine & Co. (Oriental), 879 Broadway.

BOOKSELLERS.—Baker & Taylor Co., 740 Broadway; J. W. Bouton, 706 Broadway and 8 West Twenty-eighth street; Brentano's, 5 Union Square (also large dealers in periodicals); F. W. Christern, 254 Fifth avenue (French); C. T. Dillingham, 720 Broadway; Dodd, Mead & Co., 5 East Nineteenth street (also large dealers in rare books); E. P. Dutton & Co., 31 West Twenty-third street; David G. Francis, 12 East Fifteenth street; W. M. Goldthwaite, 107 Nassau street (maps and guides); Hunt & Eaton, 150 Fifth avenue; Ivison, Blakeman & Co., 806 Broadway; W. R. Jenkins, 851 Sixth avenue; Leggat Bros., 81 Chambers street; S. B. Luyster, 98 Nassau street; Henry Miller, 65 Nassau street; G. P. Putnam's Sons, 27 West Twenty-third street; Rand, McNally & Co., 323 Broadway; A. D. F. Randolph & Co., 182 Fifth avenue; Chas. Scribner's Sons, 745 Broadway; Gustav E. Stechert, 828 Broadway (German); E. Steiger & Co., 25 Park place (German); F. A. Stokes & Co., 182 Fifth avenue; B. Westermann & Co., 812 Broadway (German); Worthington Co., 747 Broadway. Harper & Bros., Franklin square, and D. Appleton & Co., Bond street, near Broadway, deal only in their own publications.

BOOTS AND SHOES.—W. Arnold, 44 West Twenty-third street; A. J. Cammeyer, 167 Sixth avenue; G. Cantrell, 25 West Twenty-third street; W. McClenahan, 58 East Twenty-third street; J. & J. Slater, 1185 Broadway.

CANES.—See *Men's Furnishing Goods.*

CARPETS AND RUGS.—W. & J. Sloane, 884 Broadway; A. A. Vantine & Co. (Oriental), 879 Broadway.

CHILDREN'S OUTFITS.—Best & Co., West Twenty-third street.

CHINA AND GLASS.—Bawo & Dotter, 30 Barclay; Davis Collamore, 921 Broadway and 151 Fifth avenue; Gilman Collamore, 284 Fifth avenue; Frank Haviland, 14 Barclay; Wilhelm & Graef, 1141 Broadway; A. A. Vantine & Co. (Oriental), 879 Broadway.

Cigars and Tobacco.—Cigars can be purchased at hotels, cafés and restaurants, and at the large groceries. Tobacco may be purchased at the large groceries. Cigar and tobacco stores are numerons.

Art Stores.—S. P. Avery, Jr., 368 Fifth avenue; Boussod, Valadon & Co.; Knoedler & Co. (Goupil's), 170 Fifth avenue; Reichard & Co., 226 Fifth avenue; William Schauss, 204 Fifth avenue. *Engravings and Etchings.*—F. Keppel & Co., 20 East Sixteenth street; C. Klackner, 5 East Seventeenth street; H. Wunderlich & Co., 868 Broadway.

Confectioners.—Huyler, 150 and 863 Broadway and 21 West Forty-second street; Maillard, 120, 178 and 1097 Broadway.

Dressmakers.—B. Altman & Co., 301 Sixth avenue; Arnold, Constable & Co., Broadway and Nineteenth street; Donovan, 282 Madison avenue; Everall Bros., 236 Fifth avenue (tailor-made); Ghormley, 45 East Nineteenth street; Krakauer, 391 Fifth avenue; Redfern, 210 Fifth avenue; Stern Bros., 32 W. Twenty-third street.

Dry Goods.—B. Altman & Co., 301 Sixth avenue; Aitken, Son & Co., 873 Broadway; Arnold, Constable & Co., Broadway and Nineteenth streets: Bloomingdale Bros., 996 Third avenue; John Daniell & Sons, 761 Broadway; E. J. Denning & Co., successor to A. T. Stewart & Co., Broadway and Tenth street (have also general house furnishings); Ehrich Bros., 365 Sixth avenue; J. A. Hearn & Son, 26 to 30 West Fourteenth street; H. C. F. Koch & Co., 319 Sixth avenue; Leboutillier Bros., 845 Broadway and 48 East Fourteenth street; Leboutillier Bros., 50 West Twenty-third street; J. Lichtenstein & Sons, 281 Grand street; Lord & Taylor, 895 Broadway and 257 Grand street; James McCreery & Co., 801 Broadway; J. McCutcheon & Co. (linens), 64 West Twenty-third street; R. H. Macy & Co., Fourteenth street and Sixth avenue (have also general house furnishings); E. A. Morrison, Broadway near Eighteenth street; H. O'Neill & Co., 321 Sixth avenue; Edward Ridley & Sons, 301 Grand street; Simpson, Crawford & Simpson, 309 Sixth avenue; Stern Bros., 32 West Twenty-third street; A. A. Vantine & Co. (Oriental), 879 Broadway.

Florists.—Bebus, 1,153 Broadway; Hanft Brothers,

224 Fifth avenue; Hodgson, 545 Fifth avenue; Klunder Co., 1144 Broadway; McConnell, 546 Fifth avenue; Stumpp, 615 Madison avenue.

FURRIERS.—C. G. Gunther's Sons, 184 Fifth avenue; Jaeckel, 11 East Nineteenth street; Shayne, 103 Prince and 124 West Forty-second streets.

FURNITURE DEALERS.—Cottier & Co., 144 Fifth avenue; Herter Brothers, 154 Fifth avenue; Herts Brothers, 894 Broadway; Marcotte & Co., 298 Fifth avenue; Pottier, Stymus & Co., 375 Lexington avenue; Roux & Co., 133 Fifth avenue.

GLOVERS.—Harris Brothers, 865 Broadway. See also *Dry Goods.*

HABERDASHERS.—See *Men's Furnishing Goods.*

HARNESS.—Demarest & Co., 51 Warren street; Wood Gibson, 222 Fifth avenue; J. Newton Van Ness & Co., 50 Warren and 120 Chambers streets.

HATS.—Dunlap & Co., 181 Broadway and 180 Fifth avenue; Knox, 212 Broadway and 194 Fifth avenue; Youmans, 180, 719 and 1107 Broadway.

JEWELERS.—Black, Star & Frost, 251 Fifth avenue; Benedict Brothers, 171 Broadway; Jaques & Marcus, 857 Broadway (Union square); Theodore B. Starr, 206 Fifth avenue; Schumann & Sons, 860 Broadway; Tiffany & Co., Fifteenth street and Union square.

MEN'S FURNISHING GOODS.—Samuel Budd, 1101 Broadway; John Forsythe, 201 Broadway; Ingersoll & Glenney, 1129 Broadway; Kaskel & Kaskel, 20 West Twenty-third street; Michaelis & Rohman, 14 West Twenty-third street; F. Miller & Sons, 1151 Broadway; Ward, 395 Broadway. See also *Dry Goods.*

MILLINERS.—Halsey, 253 Fifth avenue; Jacquin & Co., 68 West Twenty-third street; Snedden, 183 Fifth avenue; Tierce, 381 Fifth avenue. See also *Dry Goods.*

MUSIC STORES.—G. Schirmer, 35 Union square; E. Schuberth & Co., 23 Union square; Novello, Ewer & Co., 21 East Seventeenth street; C. H. Ditson & Co., 867 Broadway: W. A. Pond & Co., 25 Union square.

NEWSPAPERS AND PERIODICALS.—There are news-stands in the principal hotels and at railroad and L R.R. stations. Brentano's, 5 Union square, deals largely in domestic and foreign newspapers and periodicals.

OPTICIANS.—Levy, Dreyfus & Co., 11 Maiden Lane;

Mayer, 2 Astor House; Waldstein, 41 Union square; Pike, 12 East Twenty-third street; Cross & Co., 18 West Twenty-third street.

PHOTOGRAPHERS.—Falk, 947 Broadway; Fredericks, 770 Broadway; Hargrave and Gubelman, 38 West Twenty-third street; Kurtz, 6 East Twenty-third street; Sarony, 37 Union square.

PHOTOGRAPHIC APPARATUS.—E. & H. T. Anthony & Co., 591 Broadway; Loeber Brothers, 111 Nassau street; Newcome & Owen, 69 West Thirty-sixth street; Scoville & Adams Co., 423 Broome.

SILVERSMITHS.—Black, Star & Frost, 251 Fifth avenue; Gorham Manufacturing Co., 889 Broadway; Tiffany & Co., 15 Union square; Theodore B. Starr, 206 Fifth avenue; Whiting Manufacturing Co., 31 Union square.

SPORTING GOODS.—Haas Brothers, 60 West Twenty-sixth street; Horsman, 341 Broadway; Peck & Snyder, 126 Nassau; Spalding Brothers, 241 Broadway; Squires, 178 Broadway.

STATIONERS.—Brentano's, 5 Union square; Dempsey & Carroll, 36 East Fourteenth street; Tiffany & Co., Fifteenth street and Union square.

TAILORS.—J. W. Bell & Son, 172 Fifth avenue; Cooper & Jarvis, 54 Broadway; Everall Brothers, 236 Fifth avenue; John Patterson & Co., 25 West Twenty-sixth street; Brooks Brothers, 938 Broadway; Redfern, 210 Fifth avenue.

TOYS.—Scharles Brothers, 24 West Twenty-third street; Schwarz, 42 East Fourteenth street.

TRUNKS AND TRAVELING BAGS.—Cattnach, 736 Broadway; Crouch & Fitzgerald, 556 Broadway, 123 Sixth avenue; Bazar du Voyage, 1 Wall and 1 Cortlandt streets; Roemer, 82 Fifth avenue; Prichard, 74 West Twenty-third street.

UMBRELLAS.—See *Dry Goods* and *Men's Furnishing Goods*.

WATCHMAKERS.—See *Jewelers*.

LAW COURTS.

UNITED STATES COURTS.

United States Circuit Court.—Federal Building, Broadway & Park row. Jurisdiction in appeals from

United States District Court, and original jurisdictions in civil law and equity suits between citizens of different States; also in suits arising under the revenue, copyright and patent laws.

United States District Court.—Federal Building, Broadway and Park row. Jurisdiction in admiralty and maritime cases; in cases where an alien sues on tort in violation of a treaty or the laws of nations; suits instituted by the United States, suits by and against foreign consuls.

The Supreme Court of the United States sits in Washington.

STATE COURTS.

Supreme Court.—County Court House, City Hall Park. The general law and equity court of the State of New York. The appellate branch known as the General Term passes on appeals from the trial judges of this court, the final appeal being from the General Term to the Court of Appeals which sits at Albany.

Oyer and Terminer.—County Court House, City Hall. The criminal branch of the Supreme Court.

CITY COURTS.

Court of Common Pleas.—County Court House. Concurrent jurisdiction with the Supreme Court within the county limits (actions involving real estate *within the city*, etc.).

Superior Court of the City of New York.—County Court House. Jurisdiction similar to that of the Court of Common Pleas. Both these courts hold General Terms, the final appeal being to the Court of Appeals.

City Court.—City Hall. Jurisdiction in smaller civil cases and a limited maritime jurisdiction. Also a General Term, final appeal being to the Court of Common Pleas.

District Courts.—Inferior civil courts; appeals being to the Court of Common Pleas.

Surrogate's Court.—County Court House. Jurisdiction in matters relating to wills and administration of the estate of a decedent.

Court of General Sessions of the Peace.—32 Chambers street. Criminal jurisdiction concurrent with the Court of Oyer and Terminer within the limits of the county.

Held by the Recorder, City Judge and Judge of the Court of General Sessions. Appeals to General Term of Supreme Court and finally to Court of Appeals.

Court of Special Sessions of the Peace.—Tombs, Centre street, between Leonard and Franklin streets. Jurisdiction over all misdemeanors.

A building for the City Criminal Courts is being erected on Centre street, one block above the Tombs.

Police Courts.—Inferior criminal tribunals.

CHARITY.

HOSPITALS.—The most important hospitals besides charity hospitals are: *New York Hospital*, 7 West Fifteenth street. *Mt. Sinai Hospital*, Lexington avenue and Sixty-sixth street, a general hospital for patients of all creeds and classes, with a capacity of two hundred beds. It treated last year 2,563 cases. Visiting days: Saturdays and Sundays, 2 to 4 P. M; Wednesdays, 2 to 3 P. M.; to the children's ward, Saturdays only, 2 to 4 P. M. Those able to pay board are charged $7 per week. *Presbyterian Hospital*, occupying, with its dispensary, the entire block between Madison and Fourth avenues, Seventy and Seventy-first streets. Visiting days: Tuesdays and Fridays, from 2 to 4 P. M., known also as the Lenox Hospital, having been founded by the late James Lenox. *German Hospital*, Fourth avenue and Seventy-seventh street, notwithstanding its name, open free to the sick poor of every nationality, color or creed. Private patients, $15 to $35 per week. Visiting days, Wednesdays and Thursdays from 2 to 4 P. M. *Hahnemann Hospital*, Park avenue between Sixty-seventh and Sixty-eighth streets, as the name signifies, a homœopathic hospital, but designed for the better class of poor who can pay a small sum per week. Private patients $10 to $40 per week. *Roosevelt Hospital*, Fifty-ninth street and Ninth avenue, endowed by the late James H. Roosevelt, a member of one of the oldest and best known families in the city, is one of the greatest institutions of its kind in the city. Free to all who cannot afford to pay. It is built on the pavilion plan and has a capacity of one hundred and seventy beds. According to its last report it treated, in one year, 2,754 cases in wards, and 3,226 in the accident-room.

Visiting days: Sundays, Wednesdays and Fridays from 1 to 3 P. M. *St. Luke's Hospital*, Fifty-fourth street and Fifth avenue, a hospital connected with the Protestant Episcopal Church, but affording medical and surgical aid and nursing without distinction of age or creed, in acute, curable and non-contagious diseases. Friends of patients admitted on Tuesdays, Thursdays and Saturdays from 10 to 12 M. Chapel service on Sundays at 3:30 P. M., which relatives of patients who cannot call on visiting days may attend with the privilege of remaining in the wards after worship until 5 P. M. Capacity two hundred and twenty beds. Treated 2,051 patients last year. *Sisters of the Poor of St. Francis*, 603 to 617 Fifth street, running through to Sixth street, a Roman Catholic institution, but non-sectarian in its reception of patients. Capacity, two hundred and forty beds. Treated 2,766 patients last year. Visiting days, Sundays and Thursdays from 3 to 5 P. M. Maintains also *St. Joseph's Hospital* East One Hundred and Forty-third and One Hundred and Forty-fourth streets, between Brook and St. Anne avenues; capacity two hundred and fifty beds.

BENEVOLENT SOCIETIES.—*Colored Orphan Asylum*, West One Hundred and Forty-third street and Boulevard, receives colored orphans of both sexes between the ages of 2 and 10, and provides for them gratuitously except when they are intrusted to the institution by a parent or guardian, when 75 cents per week is charged. Full orphans are instructed in home industries, and indentured into families or trades at the age of 12. Three hundred and sixty-seven inmates last year. Visiting days: Mondays and Fridays from 1 to 4 P. M. *Institution for the Improved Instruction of Deaf Mutes*, 904 to 922 Lexington avenue, corner of Sixty-seventh street. Pupils able to pay are charged $400 per annum. Imbeciles not received. Here deaf mute children from 6 to 14 years of age are taught by the most improved methods to use articulate sounds. *Catholic Protectory*, Westchester, Westchester county, cares for destitute Catholic children as follows: Children under 14 years of age intrusted for protection or reformation; between 7 and 14, committed by a police magistrate as truant, idle, vicious or homeless; between like ages, transferred by the Department of Public Charities and Correction. Boys, who are in charge of the Brothers of the Christian Schools, receive a common school education and are taught trades. The girls, who are in charge of the Sisters of Charity, receive a common school education and are taught industrial employments. Cared for 3,320 last year. *Children's Aid Society*, 24 St. Mark's place, seeks to elevate poor children by gathering those who attend no schools into its industrial schools, caring and providing for homeless children in its lodging-houses, and procuring homes for them in the rural districts in the West. Under proper conditions the Society will assist families with children to the South and West. It had charge last year of 38,853 children. Its most interesting lodging-house and school is the Newsboys' Lodging House (page 142). *Five Points House of Industry*, 155 Worth street (page 147). *Five Points Mission*, 61 Park street (page 145). *Hebrew Benevolent and Orphan Asylum*, Amsterdam avenue and One Hundred and Thirty-sixth street. *Institution for the Deaf and Dumb*, Eleventh avenue and One Hundred and Sixty-third street, for the free education of the deaf and dumb without regard to the circumstances of the parents, except that they must reside in the State of New York. The children are taught various trades by which they may support themselves on leaving the institution. *Isabella Home*, Amsterdam avenue and One Hundred and Ninetieth street, founded by Oswald Ottendorfer in memory of his wife. A home for the care and maintenance of aged indigent persons over 60 years of age, without distinction as to age, creed, color or nationality, and a hospital and dispensary for chronic invalids and convalescents. *Juvenile Asylum*, One Hundred and Seventy-sixth street and Amsterdam avenue, a reformatory for vicious children of both sexes between the ages of 7 and 14 years. Visiting days at the asylum: Last Thursday of each month. *St. John's Guild*, 21 University place, organizes water excursions for sick children in summer and maintains a seaside nursery at Cedar Grove, New Dorp, Staten Island. *Sheltering Arms*, Amsterdam avenue and One Hundred and Twenty-ninth street. For the care of homeless and destitute children from 5 to 12 years of age, for whom no other institution provides, such as those who are at once blind, deaf and dumb, and also children who are deserted or temporarily homeless. Children are trained in household and other work. *United Hebrew Charities*, 58 St. Mark's place, is a union of some of the most important Hebrew benevolent societies in the city. *Charity Organization Society*, 21 University place, directs persons in search of relief to the institution covering their special cases, and is therefore one of the most important adjuncts to the public and private charitable ministrations of the city. In the "New York Charities Directory" ($1), published by this Society, detailed information regarding all these institutions may be found.

COLLEGES.

Columbia College, Forty-ninth street and Madison avenue; University of the City of New York, Washington Square and Waverly Place; College of the City of New York, 17 Lexington avenue; College of Physicians and Surgeons, Fifty-ninth street, near Ninth avenue; University Medical College, foot of East Twenty-sixth street; Carnegie Medical College, Twenty-sixth street and First avenue; College of Pharmacy, 209 East Twenty-third street; New York College of Dentistry, 245 East Twenty-third street; General Theological Seminary of the Protestant Episcopal Church, Twentieth street, between Ninth and Tenth avenues; Union Theological Seminary, 1200 Fourth avenue (near Seventieth street.

CLUBS.

Aldine Club, chiefly a publishers' club, 20 Lafayette place. *Arion Society*, a vocal society, with a fine club-house at Fifty-ninth street and Park avenue. *Authors Club*, 19 West Twenty-fourth street. *Calumet Club*, Twenty-sixth street and Fifth avenue. *Century Association*, composed chiefly of litterateurs, artists and connoisseurs of literature and art, Forty-third street, between Fifth and Sixth avenues. *German Club*, Fifty-ninth street, near Sixth avenue. *Harmonie Club*, 45 West Forty-second street, and *Progress Club*, Sixty-third street and Fifth avenue, wealthy and influential Hebrew clubs. *Knickerbocker Club*, Thirty-second street and Fifth avenue, the most exclusive club in the city. *Lawyers' Club*, 120 Broadway. *Lotos Club*, north-east corner Twenty-first street and Fifth avenue, numbering many actors, artists and other professional men among its members. *Manhattan Club*, Thirty-fourth street and Fifth avenue, the principal Democratic club in the city. *New York Club*, Thirty-fifth street and Fifth avenue. *New York Press Club*, 120 Nassau street. *The Players*, of which Edwin Booth, the tragedian, is president, 16 Gramercy park. *Union Club*, north-west corner Twenty-first street and Fifth avenue, the most widely known social club in the city. *Union League Club*, Thirty-ninth street and Fifth avenue, the most influential Republican club in the United States. *University Club*, Twenty-sixth street and Madison avenue; membership restricted to graduates of colleges or similar institutions or to those who have attended such at least three years.

ATHLETICS AND SPORT.

Athletics.—The leading athletic club in New York is the New York Athletic Club, with a fine club-house at Fifty-fifth street and Sixth avenue, with all conveniences for athletic and gymnastic exercises and social enjoyment. The club also owns Traver's Island, near New Rochelle, where it has a club-house, boat-house, baseball and tennis grounds and an athletic track. The Manhattan Athletic Club has a handsome and well-appointed building, with a roof, summer garden and other attractive features, at Madison avenue and Forty-fourth street, and owns Berrian's Island in the East river, off Astoria. The Racquet and Tennis Club, 27 West Forty-third street, has racquet courts and complete gymnastic and athletic equipment. The Young Men's Christian Association has a gymnasium at Fourth avenue and Twenty-third street, and grounds and a boat-house at Mott Haven on the Harlem river. The Staten Island Athletic Club, with grounds and boat-house at West Brighton, S. I.; the New Jersey Athletic Club, at Bergen Point, N. J., and the Orange Athletic Club, at East Orange, N. J., are the most important suburban athletic clubs. Athletic games are held in the fall and spring. The Berkeley Ladies' Athletic Association has a well-appointed building in Forty-fourth street between Fifth and Sixth avenues, next to the Berkeley Lyceum.

Driving.—The most fashionable drive in New York is through Central Park, the main drive entering at Fifth avenue and Fifty-ninth street, leading around the park and back again to this entrance. Another beautiful drive is that along Riverside avenue (see Riverside Park). St. Nicholas avenue, a fine road, begins at Sixth avenue and One Hundred and Tenth street, at the upper end of Central Park, and runs to Fort Washington, joining there the Kingsbridge road and its continuation (Broadway) to Yonkers. The Boulevard, another broad thoroughfare, begins at Eighth avenue and Fifty-ninth street, and, crossing St. Nicholas avenue, finally joins the Kingsbridge road. Central avenue (or Jerome avenue), begins at McComb's Dam (or Central Bridge) and continues to Yonkers, crossing Moshola Parkway, which will connect Bronx and Van Cortlandt Park. This is where the owners of fast trotters speed their horses. Gabe Case's, "Judge" Smith's and Florence's are well-known road houses on this avenue, which is best reached by Seventh avenue, above Central Park. The Southern Boulevard starts from the bridge across the Harlem river at Third avenue, gradually swinging westward, and finally joining Jerome avenue at Jerome Park.

Riding.—There are fine bridle Paths in Central Park and a bridle path in Riverside Park. Riding in the ring may be practiced at the following well-equipped riding-schools: Dickel's (the oldest in the city), 124 West Fifty-sixth street; Durland's, at the Grand Circle, Eighth avenue and Fifty-ninth street, opposite the entrance to Central Park; Central Park Riding Academy, Fifty-eighth street and Seventh avenue; Antony's, Ninetieth street and Fifth avenue; West End, 139 West One Hundred and Twenty-fifth street; Belmont, One Hundred and Twenty-fourth street and St. Nicholas avenue; Boulevard, Sixtieth street and the Boulevard. An hour's ride in the ring costs about $1.50, and on the road from $2.50 to $3.00.

Base-ball.—The base-ball season lasts from May to

November. The location at which the games take place being subject to change, the reader is referred to the advertisements in the daily papers and the placards on the L railroad stations. One of the best known amateur clubs in the vicinity of New York is the Staten Island Cricket and Base-ball Club, with grounds at Livingston, S. I.

Cricket.—Cricket has never been able to supplant or to seriously encroach upon the prerogatives of base-ball as the "national game" of the United States. There are several cricket clubs in New York and vicinity, among them the St. George, with grounds at Hoboken, and the Staten Island, with grounds at Livingston.

Bicycling.—The roads of Central Park, Prospect Park (Brooklyn), and those around Orange, N. J., on the Morris and Essex Branch of the Delaware, Lackawanna and Western Railroad are well adapted to bicycling. Bicycles may be purchased at any of the sporting goods stores. The principal clubs are: The New York, 146 West End avenue, and Ixion, 4 East Fifty-ninth street.

Tennis.—A number of tennis clubs have headquarters in a tennis court building on the south side of Forty-first street, near Seventh avenue; and there are tennis courts on the grounds of the various athletic clubs, and in the buildings of the larger of these clubs.

Aquatics.—The most accessible rowing course is on the Harlem river. Boats may be hired in the vicinity of the bridge crossing the Harlem at Third avenue, at One Hundred and Fifty-fifth street (terminus of the Sixth and Ninth avenue L railroads), and at High Bridge. The Columbia College Boat Club, Gramercy and Nassau, and the Young Men's Christian Association, have boat houses on the Harlem; the New York and Manhattan Athletic Clubs respectively, at Travers' and Berrian's Island; the Alcyone, foot of Court street, Brooklyn; the Staten Island Athletic Club, at West Brighton, S. I.; the Argonauta and New Jersey Athletic Clubs, at Bergen Point, N. J. There is also a fine rowing course at Newark, on the Passaic river. The usual rate of boat hire is fifty cents for the first hour, the rate for time after the first hour being considerably less.

Canoeing.—The principal clubs are the New York, with a house at Tompkinsville, Staten Island, and the Knickerbocker, at the foot of West One Hundred and Fifty-second street.

Yachting.—The foremost yacht club of New York and vicinity is the New York Yacht Club, which boasts a fleet of some 265 vessels, among them some fifty steam yachts. Its trophies include the famous "America Cup." Club-house, 67 Madison avenue. Other clubs are the Atlantic, at Bay Ridge; the Seawanhaka, at Tompkinsville, S. I.; the Harlem, at 519 East One Hundred and Twenty-first street; the Larchmont, at Larchmont, on the Sound; and the American, at Rye, Westchester Co. For regattas and steamers going over the course, see advertisements in the daily papers. At 45 Beaver street, yachts may be chartered for a cruise or season.

Skating.—This sport may be enjoyed free of charge on the lakes in Central Park, Prospect Park (Brooklyn), and Van Cortlandt Park (reached by New York and Northern Railroad). At Central and Prospect Parks commodious structures with restaurants and other conveniences are erected, and skates can be hired for 25 cents an hour.

Turf.—The New York Jockey Club has superbly appointed tracks and buildings (in the Pompeian villa style), at Morris Park, Westchester, New York. The Coney Island Jockey Club has its tracks at Sheepshead Bay near Coney Island. The Monmouth Park Racing Association has beautiful grounds and buildings at Monmouth Park, near Long Branch, N. J., its first meeting opening July 4th. Other race tracks worthy of a visit are at Linden and Elizabeth, N. J. The meetings, the routes to the various tracks and railroad and admission charges are duly advertised in the daily newspapers.

Fox Hunting Clubs.—The Rockaway Hunting Club, at Far Rockaway; The Meadow Brook, Hempstead, near Garden City, L. I.; The Essex County, a branch of the Essex County Country Club, Orange, N. J. Mounts cannot be hired as readily as they can in England. The hunts are drag hunts, a fox being sometimes turned loose at the end of the drag.

MONEY.

The money ordinarily in use in the United States consists of the following coins: 1 cent (copper), 5 cents (nickel), 10 cents, 25 cents (quarter of a dollar), 50 cents (half a dollar), and 100 cents or $1.00, the last three being of silver. There are also $2.50, $5.00, $10.00 and $20.00 gold pieces, and $1.00, $2.00, $5.00, $10.00 and $20.00 bills, and so on up to $10,000. An English pound sterling is worth $4.86, subject to variations in exchange rate.

DIRECTORIES AND RAILWAY GUIDES.

Trow's New York City Directory contains, besides a list of names, a great amount of miscellaneous information, such as the official register of the City Government, lists of churches, clubs, etc. Mackey's A B C Guide and Bullinger's Counting House Monitor, both issued weekly, give the latest local railroad and steamboat information, movements of ocean steamers, postage and telegraph rates, etc. These publications are found at all hotels and other semi-public places, and Trow's is also to be consulted at most drug stores. Railway guides for the whole country are: Official Railway Guide, 50 cents; Rand, McNally & Co.'s Official Guide, 25 cents; Knickerbocker Railway Guide, 25 cents; X Y Z Guide, 25 cents. The Pathfinder covers New England only, 25 cents.

CHAPTER I.

BEDLOE'S, ELLIS AND GOVERNOR'S ISLANDS.

STATUE OF LIBERTY.—Auguste Bartholdi's "Liberty Enlightening the World," the largest statue of both ancient and modern times, stands on Bedloe's Island, part of the State of New Jersey, a mile and three-quarters from the Battery, and about the same distance from the other shores of the harbor. It is reached by steamer from the Battery, hourly every day, from 9 A. M. to 5 P. M. Fare for the round trip, 25 cents.

Bedloe's Island derives its name from Isaac Bedloe, a Dutch settler, who purchased it of the Colonial Government. During the Revolution, Captain Kennedy, commander of the British naval station in New York, bought it for a summer residence, and it was called Kennedy Island. In 1800 the United States acquired it and erected a fort on it. The present double star-shaped fortification, Fort Wood, within which the pedestal for the statue stands, and which is a feature of great architectural value in the view of the colossal monument, was built in 1841.

The idea of executing a colossal statue, emblematic of Liberty, and commemorative of the traditional good-will between France and the United States, to be presented by the former to the latter, seems to have been conceived by Bartholdi soon after the establishment of the French Republic in 1872. In order that the work should be truly international, it was decided that, while the statue should be presented by the people of France, the pedestal should be erected by the people of the United States. The undertaking was launched at a banquet at the Hotel de Louvre, Paris, November 6, 1875. A committee was formed in the United States, and the necessary legislation securing Bedloe's Island as a site for the statue was procured from Congress. Richard M. Hunt and Gen. Charles P. Stone (Stone Pacha) acted respectively as architect of the pedestal and engineer-in-chief.

The right arm of the statue was exhibited at the Centennial in Philadelphia (1876) and afterwards in Madison Square, New York. The head was executed for the Paris Exposition of 1878. October 24, 1881, the anniversary of the battle of Yorktown, all the pieces of the base and frame-work were put in place; Levi P. Morton, then United States minister to France, riveting the first piece mounted, the left foot. Ground for the pedestal was broken in April, 1883, and the work was continued until December, 1884, when, owing to a lack of funds, it was suspended. Finally these were supplied by a popular subscription through the New York *World*, and the statue, having been brought over from France in the transport *Isère*, was unveiled with appropriate ceremonies, October 28, 1886.

The colossal proportions of the statue forbidding its being carved in stone or cast in metal, the sculptor determined upon sheets of copper (*repoussé*) laid upon a skeleton of stone, wood and iron, a method which had been employed on the immense statue of Carlo Borromeo, cardinal and saint, erected two centuries ago on the shore of Lago Maggiore. The statue is supported by an iron truss-work, the core of which is formed by four large stanchions, bound together by St. Andrew's crosses, from which outgoing braces support the surface of the statue. From the foot of the stanchions bolted braces run 26 feet into the masonry of the pedestal, where they are connected with an iron frame-work.

The pedestal is an admirable work of architecture, supporting without dwarfing the statue, whose noble proportions thus produce their full effect upon the beholder. The solid concrete foundation, ninety feet square at the base, sixty-five feet square at the top and sixty-five feet ten inches in height, is the largest single block of artificial stone in the world. The pedestal itself is eighty-nine feet high, so that the surface upon which the statue stands is one hundred and fifty-four feet and ten inches above the base of the foundation. The statue itself rises one hundred and fifty-one feet and one inch, so that the whole work is three hundred and five feet eleven inches in height. The statue weighs

450,000 pounds, or 225 tons; the bronze alone 200,000 pounds. In money, value of services which were given free, etc., the statue cost about $200,000; the pedestal about $300,000. Following are a number of interesting measurements:

	Feet.	Inches.
Height from base to torch	151	1
Foundation of pedestal to torch	305	11
Heel to top of head	111	6
Length of hand	16	5
Index finger	8	0
Circumference at second joint	7	6
Size of finger nail ...13x10 inches.		
Head from chin to cranium	17	3
Head, thickness from ear to ear	10	0
Distance across the eye	2	6
Length of nose	4	6
Right arm, length	42	0
Right arm, greatest thickness	12	0
Thickness of waist	35	0
Width of mouth	3	0
Tablet, length	23	7
Tablet, width	13	7
Tablet, thickness	2	0

Other famous statues of colossal size compare with the "Liberty Enlightening the World" as follows:

	Feet.
Jupiter Olympus	43
Memnon	62
Borromeo, at Lake Maggiore	66
Arminius, in Westphalia	92
Colossus, Rhodes	105
Nero (about)	118
Statue of Liberty	151

The statue may be described as a draped female figure, crowned with a diadem, a flaring torch in the uplifted right hand, and a tablet held close to the body by the left. Its artistic value has been seriously questioned, but the fact remains that it is, next to the East River Bridge, the most imposing feature in the view of New York harbor from the south, and unqualifiedly the most imposing in any view of which the bridge is not a part. On fair days the steamer plying between the Battery and Bedloe's Island is crowded every trip. Admission to the pedestal and statue is free, a special permit being, however, required for admission to the right arm and torch. These permits are issued by the Major General commanding the Department of the Atlantic on Governor's Island, and by the Engineer and Inspector of the Third Lighthouse District, Tompkinsville, Staten Island. One hundred and seventy-three steps lead to the balcony on the pedestal; one hundred and sixty-four from the balcony to the head, which will comfortably hold forty people; and fifty-six from the head up the arm to the balcony around the torch, which will hold twelve people. In all, therefore, the steps number three hundred and ninety-three. Before beginning the ascent visitors are obliged to check overcoats, wraps, canes, umbrellas, etc., with the guard, who also lets out lanterns for a small fee. As the passage up and down the spiral stairways within the statue itself is in places very dark, the use of lanterns is advisable. The ascent to the balcony is easy, and one which all visitors should make, as from this point a superb view of New York and of the East River Bridge is had. Governor's Island, with its green mounds and its fortifications mellowed by age; the superb sweep of the waters of the harbor around the Battery into the North and East rivers, the cluster of towers and spires and the noble span of the bridge, a model of strength and grace—these are the chief elements in a view in which the grand and the picturesque are wonderfully harmonized. The ascent through the statue itself is arduous, and should not be attempted by any one who is nervous or not in prime physical condition. There are windows in the diadem from which a magnificent view is to be had, and that from the torch balcony is still grander.

The statue forms part of the light-house system of the United States, there being nine duplex electric lights in the torch. This light is visible 24½ miles at sea, or more than ten miles beyond the outside light-ship. Beside this there are five single arc lamps on the salients of the fort within which the statue stands, so that the light will be thrown on the statue, thus making it even more striking by night than by day. This beacon is not included in the system of lights for New York harbor. As many as 1,500 birds have killed themselves in a single night, flying against the lighted torch.

ELLIS ISLAND.—The facilities of the Barge Office, (p. 76), having proved entirely inadequate to dispose quickly of the immigration passing through it, there has just been completed on Ellis Island, which lies between Bedloe's Island and the New Jersey shore, a new landing depot for immigrants.

Ellis Island, area two-and-a-half acres, was formerly the site of Fort Gibson, dismantled in 1861, when the island was occupied as a naval magazine. It at one time belonged to the Ellis estate, and every child born on it has been christened Ellis. Nearly fifty years ago, three pirates, among them the noted Gibbs, were executed there. The superstitious Battery boatmen tell a romantic story about a young girl, who assisted her soldier lover to escape from confinement on the Island in a boat, but the boat was capsized and both were drowned, and the boatmen are fully convinced that the spirits of these two lovers are seen strolling along the beach of the island, arm in arm, on the night of the anniversary of their death.

Ellis Island is reached by ferry from the Battery. In an indentation on the south side is a fine basin 800 feet long by 200 feet wide. The dirt dredged from this basin was used to add to the area of the island. The island is protected on the northeast side by a crib-work breakwater, 356 feet long and 40 feet wide, which runs past the opening of the basin so as to keep it clear from all obstructions. A short distance back from the basin, facing it and the Narrows, is the building for the reception and registration of immigrants. The main structure is 250 feet long by 200 feet wide, with two wings, one story in height, 120 feet long and 80 feet wide, so that the entire frontage is 490 feet. Four towers, each four stories high, rise at each corner, and in the front center is a pediment with three story towers on each side. On the first floor are the general, local and railroad baggage offices and offices for baggage checkers. On the east end of the second story are rooms for the officials. The offices of the physicians and the receiving hospital are in a separate building. Immigrants enter double door-ways on either side of the main entrance, and pass upstairs into three compartments, after which they pass through narrow aisles before the registry clerks. North of these rooms are two large waiting-rooms. West of the registry department, on the second floor, are the telegraph offices, money exchange, and the railroad and ticket offices. Drinking water is furnished from artesian wells. Immigrants, having been registered, and having purchased railroad tickets or met their friends, proceed downstairs to the baggage-room and pick out their baggage. As immigrants from all parts of the world come to New York, it is necessary that the registry clerks speak from six to eight languages. There are, besides the official attendants, a number of missionaries who distribute Bibles, and are also ready to give advice to immigrants. The physicians in charge of the dispensary give treatment on the spot, or in serious cases transfer the patient to some hospital. About five hundred people a month are treated, immigrants being entitled to free treatment for a year after the date of arrival.

The number of immigrants of all nationalities—and it is most interesting to watch the strange faces and costumes of those who pour into the country out of this office—in 1890 was 356,310. In 1888 the number was 383,595, and in 1882, 455,000.

Governor's Island.—On Governor's Island, 65 acres in area, and a mile and a quarter in circumference, situated about 1,000 yards off the Battery, and separated from the Brooklyn shore by what is known as Buttermilk channel, formerly so shallow that there was at low tide land connection between Governor's and Long Islands, are the headquarters of the Military Department of the Atlantic. It is reached by government steamboat from foot of Whitehall street.

The Island is well shaded and swarded, having been in the earlier days of the Dutch settlement one of the richest pastures in the province. Its most striking feature from the water is Castle Williams on the northwest point, a stone work completed in 1811, with three tiers of casemates from which cannon protrude. On the seawall in front of it is the sunset gun, which is discharged at sunset as a signal to vessels to display their lights. On the northern shore of the Island is the New York arsenal of the United States Ordnance Department, the ground being covered by pyramids of cannon-balls and by large guns. A little beyond this is a building in which the United States Military Service Institution maintains a military museum, among the objects of interest being the well-mounted stuffed skin of Rienzi, the charger who bore General Sheridan on his famous dash of twenty miles from Winchester to Five Forks, where his timely arrival turned a rout into a victory for the Union arms. Fort Columbus, a stone work containing several commodious buildings used chiefly as administrative offices, is situated at about the center of the Island. The parade ground is a beautiful stretch of smooth lawn. The South Battery is a small triangular work on the southern point. Although every provision is made for adding to the strength of the fortifications by throwing up earthworks, Governor's Island is not a very formidable means of defense, but it is preserved as a military post largely because of the ease from which troops could be landed from there should it be necessary to suppress a riot in New York. The cattle from the first two ships dispatched by the West India Company in 1625 for Manhattan Island were landed on Governor's Island; but want of water necessitated their speedy transfer to Manhattan. In 1637 Governor Van Twiller bought the Island, then called Nutten, and since his purchase it has been known by its present name.

CHAPTER II.

BATTERY TO WALL STREET.

THE BATTERY.—The Battery, the southernmost point of the Island of Manhattan, is upon made ground, the island having extended originally only to about Pearl street. In 1693, there being rumors of a French expedition against New York, the "The Whitehall Battery" was erected on a heavy platform laid upon Schreyer's Hook, a ledge extending from the southern end of the island, and ending in "The Capske," a number of jutting rocks. According to a description of the city in 1756, this battery was built of stone, and the merlons of cedar joists filled in with earth, and mounted ninety-two cannon. From this point the British evacuated New York, November 25, 1783.

The water-front was originally at what is now Pearl street, and Water, Front and South streets were subsequently formed by filling in. Similarly much of the Battery was made. It is now largely occupied as a public park with thirty-one acres richly laid out, well shaded and open to all the sea breezes. It was in colonial days the most fashionable part of the city, lined with residences of wealthy citizens. These were long since converted into office buildings, mission houses or warehouses. Here are the South, Hamilton, Thirty-ninth Street (Brooklyn), Bay Ridge and Staten Island Ferries and the boats for Ellis, Liberty and Governor's Island. All the elevated roads have their southern terminus at this point.

Barge Office.—The first building of any note on the water front west of the ferries, is the Barge Office. Here are a branch office of the Surveyor of the Port and the headquarters of the Customs Inspectors, and here during the interval between the abandonment of Castle Garden and the occupancy of Ellis Island, was the depot for the landing of immigrants.

U. S. Marine Hospital.—Adjoining the Barge Office on the east side is the United States Marine Hospital. Here there is a dispensary, the hospital being at Stapleton, Staten Island. Sailors of the American merchant marine are entitled to free treatment at this dispensary and hospital. Here men for the revenue marine and for the life-saving service are examined, and pilots undergo a special examination for color-blindness. The office registers about six hundred visits a month.

Next to the Barge Office on the west side is the landing for the boat to Bedloe's Island (p. 69). Adjoining this is an L-shaped basin where the Battery boatmen keep row-boats, holding from twelve to fourteen persons, the charge being $1.00 an hour. Between here and Castle Garden is a fine sea-wall, from which one has a superb view over the water, and can watch the lively panorama of ferry-boats, tow-boats, steamers, tugs and sailing-craft.

Castle Garden.—Castle Garden, which stands upon this sea-wall, was until the spring of 1890 the landing place for immigrants, the control of immigrants being then taken from the State authorities by the United States Government. It was erected during the war of 1812 as a fortification, and was reached by a bridge, but afterwards the space between it and the shore was filled in. Being comparatively useless as a fort, it was converted into a summer garden. Here, August 16, 1824, Lafayette landed upon a carpeted stairway under an arch decorated with flags and wreathed with laurels. In the evening an immense balloon, representing a knight mounted upon the famous racer Eclipse, was sent up from the Garden. In 1832 President Jackson, and in 1843 President Tyler held receptions here, and September 7, 1850, Jenny Lind made her American debut under the management of P. T. Barnum. It was opened as a landing depot for immigrants in August, 1855. The first immigrants who passed through it came on the German bark *Europa*, and walked ashore from the vessel's gangplank. It will soon be converted into an aquarium.

Pier A.—Beyond Castle Garden is Pier A. where the police boat *Patrol* has its landing. At the pier are the headquarters of two police precincts, the Twenty-fourth and the Twenty-eighth, and the Department of Docks. The *Patrol* is the station of the Twenty-fourth Precinct, which is thus always afloat. Besides the steamboat this precinct has seven row-boats, four of which are continually on patrol along the wharves, looking out for smugglers, river thieves, and for lost articles and suicides, or cases of accidental drowning. The jurisdiction of the precinct extends as far south as Robins Reef, and up the Hudson and East river to the ends of the city boundaries. On the *Patrol* are fine fire pumps, which have often been brought into successful requisition quelling conflagrations along shore. The precinct has also done capital service in suppressing mutinies on vessels anchored in the harbor, and in restoring order upon excursion boats, where free fights have been in progress. The Twenty-eighth Precinct does important duty in patroling the docks and bulk-heads on the west side up to Fourteenth street, and on the east side to Pier 25 at Gouverneur's Slip.

Adjoining Pier A is the Iron Steamboat Company's Pier, and next to this, on West street, is *Pier* 1, occupied by the Pennsylvania Railroad Company as a freight depot. This corner gives the stranger an excellent idea of the enormous amount of business transacted along the water front. Bales, cases, and barrels are heaped up on this pier, and dozens of carts and drays are engaged in loading and unloading freight. All is seemingly bustle and confusion, and yet everything is conducted according to a system.

The elevated railroad runs in an undulating line through the Battery into Greenwich street. Near the sea-wall between the Barge Office and Castle Garden is a band stand where concerts are given in summer, and on such occasions there is an immense outpouring of humanity from the lower wards of the city. The Battery is bounded on the north by State street, which sweeps around to West street. To the east of South Ferry, South street begins and Whitehall street leads directly up from the ferry to Bowling Green.

Battery to Bowling Green.—Between the ferry and Bowling Green are several of the oldest city streets, but before beginning a tour in this direction, it may be well for the visitor to take a glance down *South street*, where a perfect forest of masts will give him an excellent idea of the vast amount of shipping carried on from this port. At the foot of Moore street, and also at Coenties Slip, both of them but a short distance from South Ferry, innumerable canal-boats and barges are moored, for it is here that most of the large tows are made up or dispersed.

Moore street is particularly interesting because the first wharf of the city was built on its line. This wharf is mentioned as early as 1644, and extended from the present Pearl street, whose north side then touched the river, only far enough out to make possible the landing of goods by scows and small boats. In 1659 it was extended fifty feet, and near it on Pearl street, between Whitehall and Broad streets, some of the Dutch merchants had their principal warehouses. Whitehall street derived its name from a large dwelling supposed to have been erected by Petrus Stuyvesant (p. 19) at the corner of Whitehall and State streets. Water street is interesting because it marks the first attempt of the city to win territory from the harbor. The city sold water lots between the present Whitehall street and Old Slip, on condition that the purchasers should fill in the street and protect it by a line of bulkheads in front of their lots. Front and South streets were subsequently added. Bridge street derived its name because on its line a bridge crossed the ditch which anciently ran through the middle of Broad street. Stone street was so named because it was the first street to be paved with stone under an ordinance of 1667. On Whitehall street is the United States Army building, which occupies the east side of the block between Water and Pearl streets. It has a fortress-like base of granite extending two stories in height, the rest of it being in brick. Its entrance resembles a sallyport, and over it the seal of the War Department is hewn in granite. This building is a branch of the War Department, and is under its orders only. It is a depot for quartermaster's supplies and the like.

Fraunces' Tavern.—A short detour from Whitehall street through Pearl street to Broad leads to one of the most famous historic sites and buildings in the city, the old Fraunces' Tavern, which is still a public-house.

It was originally built by Etienne Delancey, a Huguenot, who arrived in New York in 1686. He was a merchant of considerable wealth, to which he added greatly by his commercial successes here. When, in 1700, he married into the Van Courtlandt family, his father-in-law conveyed this property to him. When Delancey, in 1762, built a new residence at what is now the Boreel Building, 115 Broadway, Samuel Fraunces opened the Pearl street house, under the sign "Queen Charlotte," as a tavern. It owes its historical fame to the fact that in its great room, which is still preserved, in the second story, Washington delivered his farewell address to his officers in 1783. Here, also, in 1768, the New York Chamber of Commerce began to hold its meetings. The old room is now somewhat gaudily papered. On the south wall hangs a cheap portrait of Washington, a cheap print of Washington bidding farewell to his officers, and a pair of horns which, when alterations were being made in the building, were dug out from near the foundations. On the west wall are copies of minutes of the Chamber of Commerce, showing that it was instituted here April 5, 1768, the tavern then being kept by Bolton & Siegel, and copies of another minute dated Tuesday, the 6th December, 1768, which reads:

"Resolved, a proper room for the meeting of the members of the Chamber of Commerce is to be provided and the Treasurer is to have, Bread, and Cheese, Beer, Punch, Pipes and Tobaco, provided at the expence of the members present, so that it doth not exceed one shilling each man, which each person is to pay to the Treasurer at their respective meeting."

On the same wall hangs a fac-simile of a hand-bill, which Fraunces issued September 10, 1770, when he again became proprietor of the tavern. This hand-bill reads:

"On Thursday the 20th instant, will be opened the Queen's-Head Tavern near the Exchange, for many years kept by the subscriber, (late by Bolton & Siegel), is now fitting up in the most genteel and convenient manner for the Reception and Entertainment of those gentlemen, Ladies and others, who may please to favor him with their company. As the best clubs and the greatest entertainments in this city were at the above tavern, in the time of the subscriber, he flatters himself the public are so well satisfied of his ability to serve them as to render the swelling of an advertisement useless other than to assure his former friends, and the public in general, that every endeavor will be used to give them the highest satisfaction, and the utmost respect on all occasions shown by their already much obliged and very

Obedient servant,
SAMUEL FRAUNCES.

N. B.—Dinners and suppers dressed to send out for lodgers and others who live at a convenient distance. Also cakes, tarts, jellies, whip-sillybubs, blaumage, sweetmeats, etc., in any quantity. cold meat in small quantities, beefsteaks, etc., at any hour, pickled oysters for the West Indies or elsewhere."

In this famous room where the beaux and belles of old New York feasted, during the intervals between dancing, on tarts and sillybubs, the guest can now sit down to a meal of Frankfurter sausages and sauerkraut.

PRODUCE EXCHANGE.—On the east side of Whitehall street the block between Stone and Beaver streets is occupied by the superb fire-proof granite, brick, terra cotta and iron building of the New York Produce Exchange, finished May 1, 1884. The building is 300x150 feet, and opens on the northeast side upon a broad terrace. From the street to the roof of the main structure the height is 116 feet, to the coping of the tower 225 feet, and to the top of flag-staff 306 feet. The tower clock measures 12 feet in diameter, each number on its face is a foot in length, and the flag 50 feet by 20 feet is said to be the largest ever made. The ground floor is occupied by the Produce Exchange Bank, a branch of the United States Post-office, the Western Union Telegraph Company, the chief New York branch of the Pennsylvania Railroad Company and the Maritime Exchange. On the second floor is the enormous hall of the exchange, 220 feet by 144 feet, and 60 feet high to the skylight. It is said that 7,000 men could transact business comfortably on this floor. The long tables provided with drawers and compartments contain samples of various articles dealt in on the exchange, and are leased to men bers. Wheat is dealt in around a circular series of steps sunk into the floor of the exchange and called the pit. Scattered over this room are telegraph and telephone booths, tables for reporters and boards on which the prices are listed, Back of the pit is what is known as the call-room, in which 500 seats arranged like those of an amphitheatre ascend from the floor. Here grain and and provisions are dealt in. On the third floor there is a visitors' gallery, from which the bustling life of the exchange may be watched. Of course, the business is transacted in a much quieter manner than that of the Stock Exchange (p. 98). There is a steady hum, and at times perhaps a roar, but there is a certain continuity of sound here, very different from the screeches and yells so characteristic of the Stock Exchange. On the third floor are rooms for various officers and committees, and in the reception-room is a large picture of the laying of the corner stone in which numerous portraits are introduced. Above this are four stories of offices. In the basement are vaults for deposit and storage, and Turkish and Russian baths.

A feature of the Produce Exchange that is appreciated by about 300 visitors daily, is the tower, built in the style of a campanile and reached by one of the elevators on the Stone street side which ascends 14 stories; a flight of stairs leading one story higher to the roof. From here is had a superb view of the city and its environs. Everything lies spread out to beholders like a map. To the south is Battery Park, the Barge Office and the undulating line of the elevated road as it curves around towards Greenwich street. Governor's Island, Bedloe's Island lie like restful spots of green in the shimmering expanse of harbor. Beyond are the Narrows. The view to the east embraces Brooklyn Heights, the East River Bridge and the East river as far as the bend which it makes towards the east. Nearer by is the Cotton Exchange, a yellow brick building on Hanover square. Straight north is a view of Broad street and Wall street, and above the roofs on Broadway is Trinity spire. The Hudson river can be followed north to the beginning of the Palisades. To the west are the Orange Mountains, and nearer by Castle Garden and the Washington Building at No. 1 Broadway.

The Produce Exchange represents a total expenditure of about $3,200,000. The following statistics in regard to the material employed will be of interest as showing the grand scale on which buildings in New York are erected: It consumed 12,000,000 brick, 15 miles of iron girder, 1¾ miles of columns, 2,061 tons of terra cotta, 7½ miles of sash cords and chains, and 29 miles of steam pipes. The elevators carry about 23,000 people a day.

The first meeting of an Exchange in New York was on a bridge which, at Exchange Place, crossed the ditch once running through Broad street. This was March 24, 1670. The first Exchange building was erected in 1690, at the foot of Broad street. In 1754 the Royal Exchange was built upon arches over a canal at the foot of Broad street. From this the Exchange went to the Merchants' Exchange, now the United States Custom House in Wall street. The New York Produce Exchange assumed its name and succeeded to the rights of various bodies in 1868. It was then located at the corner of Whitehall and Pearl streets, the building having been erected in 1860. The present site was purchased in 1880. The membership of the Exchange is limited to 2,000. It is controlled by a President, Vice-President, Treasurer and twelve Managers, who together constitute the Board of Managers. Besides arbitration committees for each trade appointed by the President, there is a general final arbitration committee of five members not managers, elected by ballot of the Board. Attendance of witnesses is compulsory, and no appeal is admissible unless fraud or corruption is alleged. A complaint committee takes cognizance of accusations against members, and seeks to restore harmony or to induce arbitration; if the committee fails in these points, the dispute is referred to the Board of Managers, whose action is final. The rooms of the Exchange are open for business from 9 A. M. to 4 P. M., excepting Saturdays, when the Exchange takes a half-holiday. The Exchange is believed to do the largest business of any similar institution in the world.

A few statistics will give an idea of the amount of business transacted on the Exchange: In 1889 2,947,005 barrels of flour were dealt in; 1,123,148,600 bushels of wheat; 253,135,800 bushels of corn; 90,108,000 bushels of oats; 823,050 bushels of rye; 1,317,150 bushels of barley; 73,080 barrels of pork; 1,029,855 tierces of lard, and 21,569,000 pounds of tallow.

The Maritime Exchange, to the left of the Beaver street entrance, is open from 8 A. M. to 5 P. M. Its large membership is composed chiefly of persons interested directly or indirectly in maritime commerce. It reports maritime and commercial news, and more especially furnishes a record of the movements of vessels in advance of the daily papers. It has an excellent maritime library, and the Hydrographic Office of the Navy Department, which publishes the valuable *Monthly Pilot Chart*, has its quarters in the Exchange. For a fee of $1 the Exchange will send to any point in the city notice of the arrival of a vessel in time for the person notified to reach the wharf before the vessel

Bowling Green.—The site now inclosed by Bowling Green, Whitehall, Bridge and State streets is perhaps the most interesting historical portion of the city. This was the original lower end of Manhattan Island, and within its limits, early in the spring of 1615, a small log fort was erected. In 1626 this small fort was replaced by a red cedar palisade surrounding a storehouse, the whole being erected by an engineer brought over for that special purpose by Minuit. It could not have been a very formidable fortification, for there is a tradition that a goat which once assumed the offensive was able to fight its way through the palisades. Near by it the erection of the first church on Manhattan Island (Reformed Dutch) was begun in 1633 (p. 124).

The fort was demolished in 1787, and a Government

house was built, it being then supposed that the United States Government would be permanently located in New York. It was a stately red brick structure, with Ionic columns. After the seat of government was removed to Philadelphia it served as a residence for the State Governors, among them George Clinton and Jay, but became, soon after the beginning of the present century, the United States custom-house. It was taken down in 1815, and the present block of houses now occupied by steamship offices and foreign consulates was put up for purposes of residence.

Bowling Green is the old drill-ground in front of the sallyport of the ancient fort. Two roads ran from it, one along the present line of Broadway as far as City Hall Park, the other to the Long Island Ferry at what is now Peck Slip. In 1659, and for thirty years thereafter, Bowling Green was the scene of an annual cattle fair which drew great crowds to town, many inducements being held out to visitors, among them exemption from liability to arrest for debt. In 1732, the space in front of the fort was leased to several residents on Broadway, and was converted into a bowling green. In the fall of 1770, about the time the angry feelings which finally led to the Revolution had been temporarily subdued by concessions on the part of Great Britain, a leaden equestrian statue of George III arrived and was erected on Bowling Green, the space being inclosed by an iron railing built by the city at a cost of £800. The statue stood there until the evening of July 9, 1776, when the Declaration of Independence having been read from the City Hall in Wall street, it was demolished by the excited soldiers and populace. The pieces into which it was hewn were sent to Oliver Wolcott, at Litchfield, Connecticut, whose wife and daughters manufactured 42,000 bullets from the lead. The crowns which ornamented the railing were hacked off at the same time. This railing is one of the city's most interesting Revolutionary relics.

Broadway runs out of Bowling Green on the line of the old road which extended straight up to City Hall Park.

No. 1 Broadway.—No. 1 Broadway, which occupies the west corner at the beginning of this great thoroughfare, is not only a handsome and important office-building, but it also stands upon a site of considerable historic interest. Here stood the Kennedy mansion, built in 1745 by Archibald Kennedy, the eleventh earl of Cassilis. It would be considered a fine dwelling even to-day. It was entered through a handsomely carved doorway, the halls were wide, the staircases broad and the rooms spacious. The parlor measured about fifty feet in length, and opened through an arch upon a porch which could accommodate a cotillon. No. 3 Broadway was the Watts mansion, and the two houses were connected by a bridge, so that when large entertainments were given they could be thrown into one. The gardens extended to the North River and were overlooked by broad piazzas. General Putnam had his headquarters at this house, and here, July 20, 1776, Washington received Colonel Patterson, Lord Howe's Adjutant-General, who came charged with what the British considered conciliatory overtures. Lord Howe had sought previously to communicate with Washington, in a letter addressed "George Washington, Esq." This the American Commander-in-chief had declined to receive. At the meeting at the Kennedy house Colonel Patterson produced a letter addressed "George Washington, Esq., etc., etc., etc.," explaining that the three etceteras were intended to cover Washington's official title. Washington declined to receive any communication not addressed to him by his full official title, saying that the etceteras might mean anything. Colonel Patterson then communicated verbally the substance of the letter, namely, that Lord and General Howe were empowered to pardon the rebellious colonists. The American Commander-in-chief replied that the colonists had committed no wrong which required pardon. The interview was without result other than to induce the Howes to address Washington by his official title in future. Washington entertained Colonel Patterson at a collation at which he met the American General's officers. In taking leave he asked Washington, "Has your Excellency no command to my Lord or General Howe?" "None, sir," was the reply, "but my particular compliments to both of them."

In 1780, after Benedict Arnold's treason had been discovered and he had escaped into the English lines, he had quarters at the Kennedy house. About 33 years ago this was converted into the Washington Hotel, which in turn gave way to the present building.

To stand at the head of Bowling Green and look up Broadway, gives one a continuous sense of motion as the crowds pour like a steady stream up and down the street. Horse cars and other vehicles of all description are also in line, moving up or down town. Broadway is gradually being transformed into a lane between huge office buildings. The smaller structures are giving way and their giant successors are rearing their heads aloft. From the head of Bowling Green the most conspicuous is the fine granite building which runs through an L from Broadway to Beaver street, and is known as the Wells building, 18 Broadway. Adjoining it is the Standard Oil Building, a granite pile as massive as the wealth which built it. Running from 41 to 45 Broadway is Aldrich Court. This and the site occupied by No. 39 Broadway, a small brown-stone office building, comprise the ground where the first habitation of white men on Manhattan Island was located. An early American explorer, Captain Adrian Block, whose vessel, the *Tiger*, had been destroyed by fire, erected four houses or huts here for himself and his men in November, 1613. This same Captain Block (after whom Block Island is named) built a new vessel called the *Unrest*, of 38 feet keel, 44½ feet on deck, and 11½ feet beam, which, except the canoes of the aborigines, was the first vessel launched in the waters of New York. Aldrich Court is an effective piece of architecture of brick upon a granite base. The Tower building at 50 Broadway, with its 11 stories, is a remarkable example of a clever utilization of a narrow plot of ground.

At the north-east corner of Broadway and Exchange place is the handsome building of the *Consolidated*

Stock and Petroleum Exchange, a rival of the Stock Exchange. In 1837, while the New York Stock Exchange held its meetings in a room of the Merchants' Exchange, now the Custom House, an open board of brokers in opposition to it was organized in the Rotunda. Unable to force itself into the regular Stock Exchange room, its members cut away portions of the beams and dug out bricks at points in the flooring and walls of the board room, and obtained quotations by listening at the holes so made. This open board, however, proved a failure. A second one was organized in 1863 in a William street basement, sarcastically called "The Coal-hole." It gained members enough and did sufficient business to force the regular Exchange into a consolidation. The Stock Exchange has, however, never had so great a rival as the Consolidated Stock and Petroleum Exchange, which originated in 1875 as the New York Mining Stock Exchange, and has by consolidation with various other Exchanges acquired its present name and influence. It moved into its handsome new building in April, 1888. This fronts 91 feet on Broadway, 132 on Exchange place, and 87 on New street. The board-room contains nearly 10,000 square feet of space, and the ventilating and lighting appliances are of the best.

At 80 Broadway is the huge yet graceful granite structure of the Union Trust Co., built by George B. Post. It is one of the handsomest buildings in the city, and a fine example of Romanesque, now being widely introduced. It fronts 72 feet on Broadway and is 196 feet high.

Trinity Church.—On the west side of Broadway, at the head of Wall street, is the most famous church edifice in the United States, Trinity Church, which, with its ancient graveyard, forms a wonderfully restful spot at the junction of the two greatest business arteries of New York, and, indeed, of the New World. No greater contrast can possibly be imagined than the sense of peace which overcomes one when entering Trinity Church after leaving the turmoil of Broadway and Wall street.

TRINITY CHURCH.

History.—Trinity parish is of great historic interest, being the parent of the Episcopal Church, not only in New York, but of the United States. The first home of the Church of England in America was in a little chapel near the Battery, which had been vacated for larger quarters by the Dutch church. In 1697, under William and Mary, a grant was made under the title of the Parish of Trinity Church of a parcel of land described as "In or near to a street without the north gate of the city, commonly called Broadway." A further grant was made in 1705 of Queen Anne's farm, which lay along the North river, between what are now Vesey and Christopher streets. The present Trinity Church is the third building of that name on the same site. The first structure was 148 feet long and 72 feet broad, with a steeple 175 feet high, and history says that it was ornamented beyond any other place of worship in the city. The first and second rectors were Mr. Vesey and the Rev. Henry Barclay, after whom respectively Vesey and Barclay streets are named. During Mr. Barclay's ministry the church became too small to accommodate the congregation, and St. George's Chapel, which is now a distinct parish, was erected (p.167). By 1763 a third church was needed, and St. Paul's was erected.

When the Revolution broke out Trinity was strongly loyal. Dr. Auchmuty, the rector, having retired from the city, Mr. Inglis, who officiated in his stead, persisted in praying for the king, and this even in the face of a band of 150 armed men, who, one Sunday morning, marched into the church with loaded muskets, bayonets fixed, and drums and fifes playing. The congregation was affrighted, but Mr. Inglis, notwithstanding the fact that he invoked the blessings of God upon "our most gracious sovereign, King George," was not molested. It was thought wise, however, to close the church, and it remained so until the British army entered New York. A few days afterwards it burned down, with the rectory and the parish school. It was rebuilt in 1778, but the structure then erected being in 1839 adjudged unsafe, the erection of the present building was determined upon. This was completed in 1846.

Trinity Parish is commonly supposed to be an enormously wealthy institution, applications for charity falling upon it as if it had unlimited pocket-money. As a matter of fact, however, it cannot be said to have more than enough for its own support and the support of other churches and charities, many in number, dependent upon it. These about absorb its annual income, which reaches something like half a million dollars. Had the parish been able to foresee the wonderful rise in value of New York real estate and held on to all the land granted it, the wealth now at its disposal would be fabulous, but until it was confronted with the actual necessity of retrenching it was almost recklessly generous. Struggling sister churches and charities, educational institutions, and even persons without the slightest claim to its bounty, received from it donations of land and money for the asking.

The parish now contains seven churches. These are the historic St. Paul's (p. 125), St. John's, in Varick street; St. Augustine's, on East Houston street near the Bowery (p. 151); Trinity Chapel, Twenty-fifth street near Broadway; St. Chrysostom's, Seventh avenue and Twenty-ninth street; St. Agnes' (just completed), Ninth avenue and Ninety-first street; and St. Cornelius's, on Governor's Island. Pews are free, with the exception of those in Trinity Chapel, and others in the older churches held by inheritance.

For many years Trinity Church at the head of Wall street has been an object of veneration to the citizens of New York. A writer (W. H. Rideing, in the *Century* magazine) has well expressed these feelings in the following words: "There are few persons, believers or infidels, who do not possess an affectionate interest in 'Old Trinity.' Its history is, in a measure, the history of the city. For over two hundred years its worshippers have included the most honored citizens, many of whom have gone from their seats in the naves to graves in the burial ground outside. It has survived many changes, many vicissitudes, and in meditative retrospect we see many pictures in the vista of its past. The first building was outside the upper gate of the city, and now the site is near the lower extremity. Under the King and under the Republic, it has existed for one purpose, and that is expressed when, above the noise of the traffic that plies around it, the chimes in its high steeple ring out their melodious proclamations. In this vicinity Broadway is crowded to excess. From early morning until late at night busy or careworn business men hasten past the church or pause to talk in its shadow; and the fine gothic pile of brown sandstone commemorating the generations associated with it can hardly fail to awaken a thought of more enduring things than the commerce which impels these eager merchants, bankers and brokers."

Exterior and Interior.—Trinity Church building is considered one of the finest specimens of Gothic architecture in the city, and in spite of the many enormous structures devoted to secular purposes which have sprung up in its neighhorhood, it still remains the most interesting and most conspicuous building in the lower part of the city. It is open daily, and visitors are constantly entering and going out of the gate. Many of these visitors are strangers in the city, attracted simply by curiosity, but others leave their places of business or interrupt their walk for the purpose of spending a few moments in devotion in this venerable structure. Perhaps the contrast between the world outside and this sanctuary is all the greater for the fact that the turmoil of Broadway and Wall street is not entirely shut out, but is heard like the constant roar of a distant cataract. The groined roof is supported by rows of carved Gothic columns; daylight is warmed and toned by the richly stained windows by which it enters the interior, and the beautiful altar and reredos effectively end off the vista.

The altar and reredos, memorials of the late William B. Astor, were erected by his sons. The altar is of pure white marble with shafts of red upon which are capitals carved in foliated designs. These shafts divide the front and sides into panels. The design of the central panel includes passion flowers, a Maltese cross in mosaic set with cameos, a Christ head, and symbols of the Evangelists. It is flanked by two kneeling angels.

Ears of wheat, also in mosaic, form the carvings of the other panels. The cornice is designed in grape vines inlaid with five crosses of red marble, and supports a white marble slab. The super altar is red Lisbon marble, and on its face are the words "Holy! Holy! Holy!" in mosaic. On each side there is an extension forming a shelf along the whole length of the reredos, and designed for the reception of flowers at festivals. The reredos is of Caen stone carved in foliated designs, the whole being in perpendicular Gothic style. In the base are three square panels filled with colored mosaic conventional designs. Above the super altar seven panels of white marble sculptured in alto relievo show scenes in the life of Christ immediately preceding and subsequent to the Last Supper. Buttresses divide this reredos into three bays ; conspicuous on either are statuettes of the twelve apostles. The center piece represents the crucifixion, and at the points of the buttresses stand seraphims playing tambourines, lutes and timbrals. Behind the reredos is a large stained glass window with pictures of Christ and the apostles,

The steeple and spire of Trinity Church are 284 feet high. The ascent of this steeple was formerly one of the usual incidents of a visit to New York, but strangers are no longer admitted unless they obtain a permit from the rector, whose office is in the building behind St. Paul's Church, corner of Vesey street, where he may be seen from 1 to 3 P. M. It may be said, however, that permits are granted only in special cases, and that, as a rule, applications for them would only be a waste of time. The view from this steeple is one of the finest to be had in the city. To the north one looks straight up Broadway to Grace Church. The crowds below are so small that they look like swarms of bugs rather than human beings, and horse cars and vehicles seem moving in opposite directions with a regularity almost resembling files of soldiers. Broadway is about the only street that can be distinguished in this direction. The city looks like a desert of house-tops, the monotonous line of which is broken only here and there by chimneys, wreaths of white smoke and spires. Looking toward the North river one looks right down upon the decks of sailing vessels and schooners, and across the river, beyond the heights behind Jersey City and Hoboken are the Orange Mountains and the Jersey Highlands. To the south is the glistening harbor with its emerald islands, the gateway of the Narrows, and in the extreme distance Sandy Hook and the ocean. Eastward Wall street runs like a mere lane to the river, Brooklyn Heights rounding off the view.

Mr. William Waldorf Astor is planning to erect as a memorial to his father, the second John Jacob Astor, a massive bronze gateway to the old church. The plan includes a massive pair of bronze doors to the front entrance and swinging inward. These doors are to bear designs from sacred history and allegory, and to include the finest features of the famous Baptistry gates of Florence.

The Graveyard.—As interesting as the church itself, and possibly more interesting to strangers is the graveyard in which it stands. Several headstones in this date back to the time of the first Trinity Church building. Around the walls of the church are sepulchures and vaults. The most conspicuous monument near the entrance is that of Captain James Lawrence, U. S. N., which is near the south gate.

This monument stands in a square plot of grass, surrounded by chains suspended from eight trophy cannon. It is in the form of a sarcophagus in brown stone, and is fittingly massive and effective. In the east end of the bier are carved an anchor and laurel wreath, and on the west end part of a sloop of war. On the north face of the pedestal is a laudatory, but unexaggerated inscription, which tells also the leading events in the hero's career.

"In memory of Captain James Lawrence of the United States Navy, who fell on the 1st day of June, 1813, in the 32d year of his age, in the action between the frigates Chesapeake and Shannon. He was distinguished on various occasions, but especially when commanding the sloop of war Hornet, he capture and sunk his Brittanick Majesty's sloop of war Peacock, after a desperate action of 14 minutes. His bravery in action was equalled only by his modesty in triumph, and his magnanimity to the vanquished. In private life he was a gentleman of the most generous and endearing qualities. The whole nation mourned his loss, and the enemy contended with his countrymen who should most honor his remains."

The east face bears the following inscription, referring to his last words, which have become almost a motto with the American navy:

"The heroic commander of the frigate Chesapeake whose remains are here deposited, expressed with his expiring breath his devotion to his country. Neither the fury of battle, the anguish of a mortal wound, nor the horrors of approaching death could subdue his gallant spirit. His dying words were, 'Don't give up the ship.'"

Captain Lawrence's widow and Lieut. Augustus C. Ludlow, who was his executive officer and fell with him, are buried with him beneath this memorial.

On the south side of the cemetery, about half-way between Broadway and New Church street, is the monument erected by the corporation of Trinity Church to the memory of Alexander Hamilton, a small obelisk on a broad pedestal and bearing the inscription:

"The patriot of incorruptable integrity, the soldier of approved valor, the stateman of consummate wisdom, whose talents and virtues will be admired by a grateful posterity long after this marble shall have molded into dust."

At the foot of this memorial his wife is buried. Near the southwest end of the church is the grave of Albert Gallatin, who was Secretary of the Treasury in 1801–1813, and near by is the grave of Phil. Kearney, who fell in 1862, at Chantilly. Kearney, born in New York, June 2, 1815, was a famous fighter. After graduating at the United States Military Academy, he went to France and took part as a cavalry officer in the Algerian war in 1839–1840. In the Mexican war, after the battle of Churubusco, he pursued the fleeing enemy at the head of a company of dragoons into the city of Mexico itself. In cutting his way out again he was shot in the left arm, which had to be amputated. After this he rode into battle with his bridle between his teeth, his sabre in his right. In 1859, he again went to France, and served in the French army in the war with Italy, leading several decisive charges. He was on a reconnoitering expedition when killed at Chantilly.

At the head of the first path on the northern side of the church, is the grave of William Bradford, the printer of the first newspaper in New York, who died here on the 23d of May, 1752. The stone having become marred by age, it was restored with the original inscription by the vestry of Trinity Church in May, 1863. This inscription is worth quoting for its quaintness, in which particular it resembles many of the other old head-stones in the graveyard :

> " Reader, reflect how soon you'll quit this stage ;
> You find but few attain to such an age.
> Life is full of pain : Lo ! Here's a Place of Rest,
> Prepare to meet your God, then you are blest."

William Bradford was born in Leicester, England. He came to this country with William Penn in 1682. In 1685 he set up at Philadelphia the first press south of New England, and the third in the colonies. In 1693, on account of political differences, he came to New York and set up here the first press in the province. On the 16th day of October, 1725, he began the issue of the *New York Gazette*, which was the first paper printed in the city.

Diagonally across the path from Bradford's grave a plain slab sunk in the sod marks the last resting-place of the ill-fated Charlotte Temple, a beautiful girl, who before the Revolution, eloped from England to this country with a British officer, and was here betrayed and deserted by him, dying insane and in bitter poverty. This is a place of pilgrimage for many people, and the grave is rarely without flowers, some cut, some growing in pots, placed there by loving hands.

In the northeast corner of the burying-ground is the large Gothic memorial to "Those brave and good men who died while imprisoned in this city for their devotion to the cause of American independence." This is directly opposite the head of Pine street. It was erected at the time when it was feared that the city would continue the street through the graveyard, and its erection was regarded as a clever ruse on the part of the church corporation to prevent the extension of the street. The oldest headstone in the graveyard is a small brown stone in memory of Richard Churcher, bearing date 1681, and standing directly opposite Charlotte Temple's grave.

Charities.—The wealth of Trinity Church is estimated at about $5,000,000, and, as has been stated, the income derived from this goes not only to the support of the parish and its missionary work, but also to that of some twenty sister churches. Large sums are annually paid to the Episcopal funds of the diocese and to the diocesan fund, and the expenses of the convention fall in a large measure on the vestry of Trinity Church. Numerous charitable societies are connected with the parish. A large school building stands back of the church on New Church street. Here there are both day and night classes. There is also an industrial school for the exclusive purpose of teaching young girls to sew. Trinity Church Association was formed in 1879 and incorporated in 1887 to carry on charitable work down-town. This association supervises and supports a mission house at 209 and 211 Fulton street, in charge of the Sisters of St. Mary. This is the headquarters for work among the poor. Here are a dispensary, a kindergarten, a training school in household service for young girls, a relief bureau, a kitchen garden, and here also are given entertainments and lectures. The Association also maintains a seaside home for children at Great River, near Islip, L.I. The separate chapels of the parish have also numerous charitable societies. The parish as a whole also maintains a hospital where, during the year, an average of 250 patients are treated.

CHAPTER III.

WALL STREET.

Wall street runs along the line of outer fortifications, which in 1644 were erected as a defense against the Indians, the Governor ordering at the time that a good solid fence be built across the island. For nine years this fence formed the northern boundary of a sheep pasture, a part of which was then granted to a number of influential citizens, who seem to have held the land for speculative purposes. In 1653 the wall was strengthened, and a gate known as the "Land Gate" was built at the present junction of Wall street and Broadway, right in front of the site on which Trinity Church now stands. The first building of any note on the street was erected in 1656 on the spot now occupied by the Custom House. Lots ranged in price from $50 to $100. North of the street was an orchard, and there is an account of a bear hunt in it about this time. It is not improbable that an occasional bull may have strayed into the sheep pasture at the south, so that in those days already Wall street had its bears, bulls, and lambs. In 1699 the wall was finally demolished, and in 1700 the City Hall, the predecessor of the famous Federal Hall, was erected where the Sub-Treasury, facing Broad street, now stands. Opposite it, on the upper part of Broad street, were a cage, pillory, whipping-post and stocks, but not the kind of stocks that are now dealt in in this vicinity. In 1766 William Pitt was honored for having espoused the cause of the colonists by a marble statue at Wall and William streets. But during the British occupancy of the city in the Revolution, the statue was beheaded and otherwise disfigured, and in 1789 it was removed, and is now in the building of the New York Historical Society.

On the north corner of Wall street and Broadway, is the *United Bank Building*, occupied by the First National Bank, known among financial circles as Fort Sherman, from the favor with which Senator Sherman, when Secretary of the Treasury, is said to have regarded it, the Bank of the Republic and numerous offices. Between this building and Nassau street, on the north side of Wall, are the Schermerhorn and Astor buildings. On the opposite side of the street is the handsome Mortimer building, on the east corner of Wall and New streets. This is a structure of dark, buff brick, with an entrance in the form of a deep arch, through which a stone stairway curves up to the first floor, an unusual architectural effect in the business quarters of the city.

New York Stock Exchange.—Next to this is the narrow Wall street entrance to the Stock Exchange, the main fronts being on Broad and New streets; but of course it would have been absurd for the institution which rules and sometimes almost ruins the country financially, not to have an entrance on Wall street. Strangers gain admission to the visitors' gallery by this entrance.

The first New York Stock Exchange was formed by seventy-four brokers, who in 1792 met under a button-wood tree in front of the present No. 60 Wall street. Until 1817 its business was chiefly transacted at the Tontine Coffee-house, at the corner of Wall and Water streets. From that time until 1865, when it moved into the present edifice, it had various meeting-places, among them a private office and an upper room in the Merchants' Exchange (on the site of the present Custom House).

The present building was designed by James Renwick. Its greatest front is on New street, where it occupies 152 feet. It also has a frontage of 70 feet on Broad street, where the main entrance is. The part on Wall street is really only an L, yet the Stock Exchange is always associated with Wall street. The best view of the building is obtained on Broad street. It is a substantial five-story white marble structure, with the columns and upper stories of colored granite built in the French Renaissance style, costing about $2,000,000, the title being vested in the New York Stock Exchange Building Company. The annual expenses for wear and salaries are about $200,000.

Board Room.—That portion of the building which the stranger will want to see first is the Board Room, the financial nerve center of the country. The turmoil of this room must be heard to be appreciated—to describe it is impossible. It surpasses even the proverbial bear garden. Perhaps it is more like a tribe of Indians executing a war dance than anything else. The transactions which take place in it are telegraphed all over the civilized world, and it is not exaggeration to say that the business interests of the whole country throb in unison with it. A panic in Wall street means financial disaster throughout the United States. This Board Room is on the New street side of the ground floor, and is 260x98 feet. At 10 A. M. a gong strikes for the opening of business, at 2:15 P. M. for deliveries, at 3 P. M. for closing. Strangers are not admitted to the ground floor except as a matter of courtesy through a member, but an excellent view is had from the galleries on the second floor, which are reached from the Wall street entrance. Besides the Board Room, there are on the ground floor the Long Room for telegraph apparatus for subscribers at $100 a year, and the Reading Room. The click of the famous "tickers" running out their paper ribbons of quotations makes music joyous or sad, according to the information which the ribbon conveys to the speculator who consults it.

In the Board Room every stock has its special location, which is designated on a row of sign pillars running along the middle of the room from end to end. For purpose of communion with the outside world each broker is numbered and if he is wanted a knob bearing his number is pulled, and instantly this number appears conspicuously in a space in front of the visitors' gallery. The room is electrically lighted from three chandeliers and is admirably ventilated, Clocks announce both Washington and New York time.

Since 1879 the limit of membership of the Exchange has been eleven hundred. Its government is vested in a Governing Committee of forty, in four classes, one of which retires every year, and in its President and Treasurer. The President serves gratuitously. The initiation fee is $20,000, or if membership is acquired by purchase of a seat, $1,000. The latter is the usual method. As high as $36,000 has been paid for a seat. No initiation fee was demanded under the button-wood tree in 1792. In 1823 it was $25; in 1827, $100; in 1833, $150; in 1842, $350; in 1862, $3,000, and in 1866, $10,000. The present rate was established in 1879.

Brokers are of three classes—the first do a regular commission busines and never speculate; the second are the "scalpers," who buy with the intention of selling to other brokers at a rise; the third are the "traders," who confine their operations for a long period to a certain line of stocks or even to one particular stock. A division of "scalpers" are known as "guerrillas." These deal in inactive stocks. Certain parts of the floor have, through guerrilla transactions, become known as "Hell's Kitchen" and "Robber's Roost." Members of the Exchange in dealing with non-members are required to charge a commission of at least ⅛ of 1 per cent. Even offering to do business for less is punishable by expulsion and the sale of the offending member's seat.

Exchange Slang.—The slang of the Exchange is a fit subject for a linguistic study, There are many terms besides those of "scalper," "guerrilla" and "trader," which have a special meaning on the floor of this institution, "bull" and "bear" being the most familiar. A "bull" is an operator who is "long of stock," *i. e.*, who has "loaded" himself with a large number of stocks, bought perhaps in a large quantity at a time, and who expects to "unload" on a rising market. Naturally his tendency is to "bull the market," send up the prices of stocks. Sometimes he has to resort to fictitious measures such as "ballooning"—circulating rose-colored reports anent its value, making fictitious sales, etc., and may even be forced to "fly kites"—expand his credit injudiciously. If he operates so skillfully that he raises or depresses the stock at will he "milks the street." "Bears" are those who agree to deliver stock at a future date at a certain price, lower, of course, than its price at the time the contract is made. The bear's policy is to so depress the stock between the date of the contract and the date of the delivery that he can buy it at a lower price than that at which he is to deliver it, thus making the balance. Hence, the "bear" is usually found "gunning a stock," for he is obliged to depress or "break" the market in order to "cover his shorts," *i. e.*, buy in the stock he has to deliver at a figure low enough to yield him a profit or at least save him on the transaction. Sometimes he is "cornered" by a "pool" or a combination of operators who are bulling the stock. The conflict between bull and bear is irrepressible, and at any particular time it is simply a question as to whether the bull can toss the bear or the bear can get his arms around the bull's neck and squeeze him.

U. S. Sub-Treasury.—The most interesting building on Wall street is undoubtedly the Sub-Treasury, and this not only because of the vast sums of money deposited there—at times $200,000,000—but also because it occupies the site of the old Federal Hall, on the balcony of which Washington took the oath as the first President of the United States. It stands on the east corner of Wall and Nassau streets.

History.—When in 1699 the old fortifications on Wall street were torn down, the stones from the bastions were appropriated to the building of the City Hall on this site. This became, of course, the center of political life in the city. It was not only a City Hall, but a Municipal and Colonial Court House, a jail and the Capitol of the province. Here the freedom of the American Press was established in 1735 at the trial of John Zenger; here in 1765 the people of New York protested against the Stamp Act; here, July 18, 1776, the Declaration of Independence was read to the excited populace, and here for a time sat the Continental Congress and the old Congress after the Revolution. When Congress had selected New York City as the Capital of the Nation, the citizens of New York determined to transform their City Hall into the more imposing Federal Hall. An archway through the basement formed a promenade. Four heavy Tuscan columns supported the grand balcony, and four high Doric pillars a pediment on which were carved a great American eagle having thirteen arrows, the arms of the United States and other ornamental figures. The furniture used by this Congress, and Washington's desk and table may be seen at the Governor's Room in the City Hall (p. 134).

Washington Inauguration.—Washington traveled to New York by way of Baltimore, Wilmington, Philadelphia, Trenton, New Brunswick and Elizabeth. From Elizabeth he was rowed, April 23, 1789, to New York in a superb barge by thirteen masters of vessels in white uniform with black caps ornamented with fringes. As the barge drew up to Murray's wharf, near the foot of Wall street, cannon were fired and the bells of the city were rung. Washington was escorted by a procession composed of troops, the officers of the State and city, the clergy, the French and Spanish embassadors and citizens to the Franklin House, which stood at the intersection of Franklin square and Cherry street, then a lovely retreat, a strikingly pretty feature of which was a fine cherry orchard from which Cherry street derived its name. The 30th of April, the day on which he took the oath as the first President of the United States, was ushered in by a discharge of cannon at sunrise at old Fort George near Bowling Green. At half-past nine services were held at all the churches in the city. At noon the military paraded in front of the house on Cherry street, and at half-past twelve marched to Federal Hall, where they were drawn up on either side of the street, Washington passing through the lines and proceeding to the Senate Chamber. He was almost immediately conducted to the grand balcony in front of the Senate Chamber which looked out on Broad street. Near him stood Vice-President John Adams, Governor George Clinton, Chancellor Livingston, Roger Sherman, Richard Henry Lee, Generals Henry Knox and Arthur St. Clair, Baron Steuben and Samuel Otis, the Secretary of the S nate. In the center of the balcony was a table, the covering of which was red velvet. On this lay a crimson

WASHINGTON STATUE.
(U. S. SUB-TREASURY.)

velvet cushion and on this a large Bible. This Bible had been borrowed at the last moment of St. John's Lodge, No. 1, F. and A. M., it having been discovered just before the oath was to be administered that there was no Bible in Federal Hall. Washington, with due solemnity, advanced to the front of the balcony, laid his hand on his heart, bowed several times, and retired to an arm chair near the table. When the universal shout of joy and welcome had subsided, and profound silence reigned all about him, Washington arose and came forward. Chancellor Livingston read the oath, and Washington, resting his hand upon the table as he stood, repeated it. Mr. Otis then took the Bible and raised it. Washington stooped and kissed it. As he did so, a flag was raised upon the cupola of the Hall, and, as it was unfurled to the breeze, there was a discharge of artillery at the Battery, the bells of the city rang out, and the multitude sent up a great shout. Washington bowed to the people and then retired into the Hall. In the Senate Chamber he then delivered his inaugural address, and afterwards, accompanied by the Vice-President, the Speaker, the two houses of Congress, and those who had been invited to the inauguration ceremony, proceeded to St. Paul's Church (p. 125) where a service of thanksgiving was conducted. The Washington Inauguration Centennial celebration is too recent to require a detailed account. It lasted three days, beginning April 29, 1889, the principal ceremony taking place on the steps of the Sub-Treasury.

The *Statue of Washington* which stands upon these steps was unveiled November 26, 1883. It is a bronze figure of colossal size by J. Q. A. Ward, and represents Washington taking the oath. It was erected by voluntary subscription under the auspices of the Chamber of Commerce of the State of New York. Sunk in the pedestal in front of the figure is a large brown stone slab bearing the following inscription: "Standing on this stone in the balcony of Federal Hall, April 30th, 1779, George Washington took the oath as the first President of the United States of America."

Present Building.—After the seat of government of the United States was removed to Philadelphia, Federal

Hall was occupied by the State Assembly and the Courts. In 1813 it was taken down and the buildings erected on its site gave way in 1842 to the old Custom House, which is now the Sub-Treasury. This is a large, light granite building, in Doric style, extending from Wall to Pine street. On the Wall street front eighteen granite steps extending the entire breadth of the building lead to a dignified portico supported by eight marble columns. Within is a rotunda of sixty feet diameter, sixteen Corinthian columns, fifteen of which are monoliths, supporting the dome, a gallery running around the rotunda. On the floor are ranged the desks of the various departments of the Sub-Treasury. This branch of the Treasury department has been here since 1862, when the Custom House was removed to the building on the south side further down the street which it now occupies.

Transactions.—This institution received during the last fiscal year $1,157,931,582.23, and paid out $1,130,-598,102.68. Its receipts come from the Custom House, the Post Offices of this district, and from the Treasury Department, for disbursing officers, such as army and navy paymasters, and for pensions. Its disbursements were made up largely of Treasury drafts, money paid out to disbursing officers, the redemption of United States bonds, the payment of coupons and interest on bonds, and the redemption of mutilated currency. It will redeem any piece of paper money which is not mutilated more than two-fifths. If mutilated to a greater extent, the request for redemption has to be accompanied by an affidavit explaining the manner in which the mutilation occurred. The extent to which mutilated money is redeemed through this agency is shown by the following statistics for one year: Gold certificates, $49,141,000; silver certificates, $15,983,000; United States notes, $20,345,000; National Bank notes, $2,812,000; fractional notes, relics of war days still in circulation, $1,500. It may be said of this institution in a general way that it transacts two-thirds of the financial affairs of the United States Government. Some 375,000 pension checks are cashed in this office each quarter, making about 70 per cent. of the entire pension list of the United States. The largest single check ever drawn in the office was one for $30,000,000, and it is offset by the smallest single transaction, which was for one cent.

Gold Vaults.—The vaults in which the gold and gold certificates are stored are on the floor of the rotunda on the north side, respectively to the left and right of the passage-way, and are well lighted, and cheerfully carpeted; quite different from the vaulted and gloomy recesses which one would naturally expect to enter. But, however cheerful they are, they are as secure as if they were the darkest of dungeons, being separated from the rotunda by four huge, heavy doors with the most modern lock appliances. The vault in which gold exclusively is kept is to the left of the passage-way. It is fitted up with one hundred and thirty closets, each holding one hundred bags, each bag containing $5,000 in gold coin, so that each closet contains half a million dollars. There has been as much as $64,000,000 stored in this vault at one time. The other vault is used not only for the storage of gold coin, but also for the storage of gold certificates. These are done up in packages of one hundred notes, and ten of these packages go into a bundle, so that each bundle contains one thousand notes. At the time when the author visited this vault he was allowed to hold in his hand a package containing $10,000,000 in gold certificates. It was made up of one thousand $10,000 certificates, and the package represented the smallest space into which that amount of money could be compressed. It was the length of an ordinary bill, and about four inches in thickness. It was almost as light as a feather, but represented a weight in coin of 18½ tons. There are, besides these two large vaults on either side of the passage, a small vault for the reception of nickels and pennies.

Coin Division.—Passing out of the rotunda toward Pine street, there is on the right-hand side of the building the coin division. Here business houses and corporations requiring large sums of money in small change receive this in exchange for coins and bills of larger denominations. Retail firms during the Christmas season will draw at one time $10,000 in pennies. The Manhattan Elevated Railroad, on the other hand, which receives large quantities of small coin, exchanges this three times a week for large bills. At the time of deposit a certificate is given, then the coin deposit is carefully examined, and whatever is light-weight, mutilated or counterfeit is thrown out and charged against the depositor. Counterfeits are, before they are returned, so effectually marred that they cannot be passed upon unsuspecting persons. It is learned from the experience of this department that counterfeiting is carried on to an extraordinary extent. A favorite method is to dig out the metal from between the two faces of the coin, and then fill it up with metal of about the same weight. Even one cent pieces are counterfeited, and there is a counterfeit penny in circulation upon which is stamped "Not one cent." Of course the experts who receive the coin at the Sub-Treasury can determine at the first touch, in nearly every instance, that a coin is a counterfeit, and there are also expert counterfeit detectives among the men who handle paper money.

In the upper story is an armory, where various weapons are kept in readiness for defense in case of riot. The shutters are of steel and the building is fortified in various ingenious ways, not only on all sides, but on the roof, to ward off an attack from the adjoining buildings which are higher than the Sub-Treasury. The system of defense is naturally kept secret.

The silver vault is in the basement in the northwest corner of the building. Here the silver is stacked up in bags like bags of salt. The bulk is in dollars. The smallest silver coin now in circulation is the dime. A few half-dimes and three-cent pieces are occasionally presented, but these are retired as rapidly as they are received, as are also the two-cent copper pieces. A thousand dollars' worth of coin is packed in each bag. There has been about $38,000,000 worth of silver in this vault at a time. The silver is shipped in large quantities to the South, when the cotton crop is being picked, as the negroes prefer the bright coin dollars to the paper dollar. The general public is not admitted to a detailed inspection of the Sub-Treasury, but applications made to the Sub-Treasurer will receive consideration.

U. S. Assay Office.—Adjoining the Sub-Treasury is the United States Assay Office, a marble building in classic style, erected 1823, for a branch of the United States Bank. It is the oldest structure on Wall street. It is a branch of the United States Mint, and everything is done here which is done at the Mint, except coining. Domestic bullion, domestic coin which is uncurrent on account of mutilation or light weight, foreign bullion, foreign coin, jewelers' bars, watch-cases, old plate, the latter class of articles often from "fences" (receivers of stolen goods), are brought here to be melted up and cast into bricks.

Operations.—the operations of the Assay Office during the last fiscal year are represented by the following statistics: There was deposited, in gold, bullion to the value of $16,365,923.27, partings $1,443,136.61; in uncurrent coins of the United States, $417,000; in foreign coins, $1,117,659.06; in silver, bullion to the amount of $4,166,044.17, partings $92,941.62; in coins, $3,001.05. The work of the assay department of this institution comprised the testing of some 10,000 melts of gold and silver, besides many other melts of the fine metals, and the testing of some four hundred barrels of sweeps, and many hundreds of special assays. Sweeps are obtained from the retorts, cloths, strainers, brushes, brooms, dusters, and other articles which are apt to catch silver or gold dust, or to become in any way impregnated with the precious metals used in the Assay Office. These are ground up, placed in barrels, and assays from each barrel made so as to determine its general value. The barrels are then put up at auction and sold to the highest bidder, a report of the assays being first made to the bidders.

In the melting and refining department there were refined last year by acid 2,232,101 gross ounces. There were prepared and delivered to the superintendent 18,234 bars of gold and 25,993 bars of silver, a total of 44,227 bars; and 1,104,255 pounds of sulphuric acid were used in the parting operations, and 1,592,545 pounds of spent acid and 129,913 pounds of blue vitriol were sold during the year, realizing $9,015.03. Sixty-one thousand ounces of silver from the acid refinery were used over in parting gold deposits.

The melter and refiner operated during the year on 970,792 standard ounces of gold and returned a surplus of 416,394 standard ounces. The same officer operated on 4,294,094 standard ounces of silver and returned an excess of 5,021.30 standard ounces. The bars of precious metal refined here are sold largely to manufacturing jewelers, are sent to the mints for coinage, and are also used as exchange when the rate of exchange reaches what is known in financial circles as the shipping point.

Vaults.—In the vaults of the Assay Office millions of dollars' worth of gold and silver is piled up in bricks of various sizes ranging in value from $100 to $8,000. The gold vault, on the ground floor of the building on the Wall street side, is a little room, and yet it will hold $70,000,000 worth of gold.

Refining.—The most interesting operation to the visitor is undoubtedly the refining department on the Pine street side of the building. The bullion being received on the ground floor, is here granulated by being melted in crucibles and then thrown into water. Having been granulated, it is sent up to the acid-room on the top floor, where it is boiled seven times in sulphuric acid. This eliminates the silver from the gold, leaving the gold in a dirt colored powder in a filter-box, but a box of this dirt is worth about $100,000. The powder having been thoroughly washed, is placed into a press, and, under a pressure of two hundred tons, the moisture is squeezed out of it, and the powder assumes the form of a round cake. It is then ready to be refined. Silver undergoes a more complicated treatment. Having been boiled in sulphuric acid and eliminated from the gold, it runs down in a liquid form as sulphate of silver through pipes to the story below, where it is received into vats lined with copper plates. These copper plates separate the silver in the form of a gray powder, leaving sulphate of copper in the vats which flows down into the floor below where it is crystalized on copper plates. The silver powder is treated like the gold in the press, and is then ready to be melted. The crystalized sulphate of copper is sold. The melting furnaces are on the same floor on which the granulation takes place. The cakes are thrown into large black lead crucibles, which are placed in furnaces. When the metal is sizzling and bubbling in the crucible, a thick covering of bone ash is spread over it, and through a little hole made in this bone ash nitre is poured on the molten metal. The nitre draws up the copper impurities which form a slag with the bone ash. This is removed from time to time, and the process repeated for about three hours. When the metal is refined, it is dipped out in ladles, and poured into forms from which it is lifted as red-hot bricks of gold and silver and placed upon tables to cool. The glow of a red-hot gold brick is something which possesses a glory all its own, being like the gorgeous golden hue of a sunset sky.

Assaying.—The process of assaying is somewhat more complicated, and is not as readily understood as the simpler process of refining. All bullion, whether it is simply for assay, or for refining purposes, is received in a room on the ground floor on the Wall street side of the building. Here it is weighed and receipted for. It is then run into bars, "pig" gold and "pig" silver one might call them, from which delicate slips are taken. These slips are sent up to the assay department, which occupies the upper stories on the Wall street front of the building, and here delicate portions are weighed out on scales which will weigh the $\frac{4}{1000}$ part of a drachm. They are wrapped up in a thin strip of pure lead shaped somewhat like a cornucopia and technically called cornets, and put in little calcined bone cupels. These are then deposited in gas cupel furnaces and as the lead melts the base metals are carried with it into the bone of the cupel or are oxidized, leaving a button of pure gold and silver in the bottom. This is then weighed, and the loss shows the amount of base metal contained in the original. The button is then rolled out into a thin strip which is boiled in nitric acid, the acid eating out the silver and leaving the pure gold. The best time to visit the Assay Office is about 10.30 A. M., when the refining is most apt to be in progress.

The Sub-Treasury stands opposite *Broad street*, one of the main arteries of business running into Wall street. Originally the ground here was marshy, and a brook ran from the marsh through the middle of Broad street to the river. In 1657 the sides of this brook were lined with plank so that it might better serve its purpose as an open drain. The marsh ended at Exchange Place, which is one block below Wall street, and the ground between the end of the swamp and Wall street itself was a sheep pasture, so that sheep were sheared in this part of New York long before the Stock Exchange was established here. In 1676 the marsh and the ditch were filled up, and the street made level. The corners of Wall and Broad streets are considered among the most valuable parcels of real estate in the City of New York. The west corner is occupied by the Wilks Building, sufficiently imposing to make it worthy of its costly site. Next to it stands the Broad street front of the Stock Exchange, and beyond this a branch of Delmonico's. The eastern corner is occupied by the Drexel Building, a white marble six-story building in the Renaissance style, and built for the banking firm of Drexel, Morgan & Co. The superb brick structure adjoining it on Broad street, occupying a frontage of 175 feet and ten stories high, is the Mills Building. This has an L opening on Wall street, where the building occupies a frontage of 25 feet. On busy days the elevators in this building have carried as many as 17,000 passengers. The view down Broad street from the corner of Nassau is gracefully ended off by the distant campanile of the Produce Exchange.

Exchange Place, which runs from Broadway to Hanover street, crossing Broad street, is interesting, because in the old days a bridge crossed the ditch at Broad street at this point, and on this bridge the first Merchants' Exchange was organized, March 24, 1670; its members meeting on the bridge every Friday morning at 11 o'clock. The small boys of the vicinity having been accustomed to coast in winter down the hill from the country road which is now Broadway, to the sheep pasture, which is now Broad street, they were ordered by the Mayor to suspend their sport on Fridays, between 11 and 12, so as not to disturb the deliberations of the Exchange. The Long Island Ferry once started from this bridge at Exchange place, the skiff proceeding down the ditch through Broad street into the river, the ferry house standing at the present corner of New street and Exchange Place. Nassau street is a narrow thoroughfare leading from Wall street to City Hall Park. It follows the line of an old lane, which, when a petition for the opening of the street was presented in the early days of the city, was quaintly described as a "cart lane running by the pie woman's to the Commons," City Hall Park then being the common pasture of the town. This is now the great thoroughfare for lawyers on their way from this part of the city to the Court House in City Hall Park, and here are the stores of law-book publishers and secondhand book dealers, and it is also occupied by numerous handsome office buildings.

Proceeding down Wall street, from Nassau, the next building to attract attention is that of the Mechanics Bank at Nos. 31 and 33, built of granite and Indiana limestone and presenting an imposing front of nine stories. Conspicuous on this front is a bronze casting of a mechanic's brawny arm and hand wielding a hammer. The bank acquired this property in the last century and the deeds to it are said to run back to the days of Queen Anne. Another conspicuous building housing one of the historic banks of the country, the Bank of the Manhattan Company is the nine story granite structure built conjointly by the bank just named, and the Merchants' Bank at Nos. 40 and 42 Wall street. One of its finest features is the grand entrance arch. The *Manhattan Company's Bank* was organized by Aaron Burr in opposition to the Bank of New York, one of whose founders was his bitter political rival, Alexander Hamilton. Its banking privilege was secured by clever ruse. Just after the yellow fever scourge in New York, when it was thought that the epidemic might have been caused by the brackish water in the wells which then furnished the only water supply to the city, Burr obtained a charter for a water company with $2,000,000 of capital, but in this charter there was a clause permitting the company to use its surplus capital in any way not inconsistent with the laws and constitution of the United States or of the State of New York. This clause was utilized in a manner which the Legislature granting the charter little dreamed of, for it led to the incorporation of the Manhattan Company's Bank in 1799. The Manhattan Company did, as a matter of fact, construct water-works and for some time supplied the city with water, and it still, in order to retain its charter, maintains in a building on Centre street a huge tank. Opposite the building of the Manhattan Company is the nine story building of the United States Trust Company, Nos. 45 and 47 Wall street. It is built of granite varied with brownstone, the carving on which is as delicate as lace-work. On the northwest corner of Wall and William streets is the handsome building of the Bank of America, while the *Bank of New York*, the oldest bank in the State and the second bank organized in the United States, occupies a fine building on the northeast corner. This is the bank founded by Alexander Hamilton, which Burr sought to antagonize when he incorporated the Manhattan Company's Bank. The Bank of New York commenced business on the 9th of June, 1784, being then located in the Walton mansion on Franklin square, at 156 Pearl street, about opposite the structure now occupied by Harper Bros. (p. 141). In 1787 the bank removed to No. 11 Hanover square, and in 1798 to the site it now occupies. The Walton house remained standing until 1881, having fallen, however, upon sorry times, being last occupied as a lodging house for immigrants. The Bank of New York was formally incorporated in 1791, re-organized under the Free Banking Act in 1852, and in July, 1879, became a national bank.

Proceeding down William street to the south, the visitor will reach, near the corner of Beaver street on the east side, the handsome building of the Farmers' Loan and Trust Company, and near it, on the corner of William street and Hanover square, the yellow brick structure of the *Cotton Exchange*. This Exchange was organized August 15, 1870, and occupied, until May 4, 1872, premises at 142 Pearl street, from that time to April 29, 1885, premises in Hanover square, and moved into the present building April 30, 1885. It is calculated that the cotton crop of the United States is nearly 6,940,000 bales or nearly 3,440,410,000 pounds. For the year ending May 1, 1890, the sales of spot cotton on the Exchange aggregated 315,443 bales, and for future delivery 21,084,100 bales. Diagonally across the street is the new Delmonico building, occupying the site of the first restaurant established by this famous house. Returning to Wall street, the next object of interest is the United States Custom House.

United States Custom House.—This occupies the entire block bounded by Wall, William, Hanover streets and Exchange Place, and is connected by a bridge with another building on the southern side of Exchange Place, where the Naval Officer has his headquarters. The Custom House building is of Quincy granite, in Ionic style, with a portico of granite columns, each 38 feet high and 4½ feet in diameter. Its main entrance is on Wall street, and leads into a fine rotunda with a dome supported by 8 pilasters of marble. The building was originally constructed for a Merchants' Exchange, but when the Sub-Treasury was established in 1862, it was purchased by the National Government for customs purposes. It may be said without exaggeration that every man, woman and child in the United States is affected by the business transactions of this, the principal Custom House of the country, for there duties are collected on wearing apparel, articles of ornament, house furnishings, food and drink, all of which cost more because the United States Government levies duty upon them.

The New York Custom House has less proportion of expense to the amount of duties collected than any other in the land, and is an enormously profitable institution to the Government. Its receipts in 1889 were $154,831,162.38; its expenses only $2,800,000. Altogether there were 275,000 entries for merchandise, and the record of vessels entered was as follows: From foreign ports, 5,557, and from domestic ports, 2,477; while there cleared for foreign ports, 4,948, and for domestic ports, 2,773. The mode of passing goods through the Custom House is very complicated, and requires for its proper supervision the division of the customs service into several branches, at the head of which is the Collector of the

Port. All the work done in the Collector's office is then verified by the Naval office. The employees number about 1,700 people, including several female inspectors, whose business it is to prevent women from smuggling articles through the customs in their wearing apparel. The inspectors have their headquarters at the Barge Office, which has already been described (p. 78). The routine through which a passenger's baggage must pass before a passenger can take it or have it removed from the port has already been explained (p. 29).

The unloading and delivery of goods from the vessels at the wharf involves more circumstance. The captain proceeds to the Custom House and delivers the manifest of his cargo and other papers to the Collector, this being technically described as an "entry" of the vessel. Until this and other incidental acts are performed by him, the cargo of the vessel can not be touched. When all preliminary steps have been taken and bulk is broken, the goods are passed from the vessel to the dock under the supervision of two inspectors, who see to it that samples of the goods are sent for appraisement to the Public Stores, and also that the regulations of the customs are otherwise complied with. When the goods at the Public Stores have been examined and appraised, the consignee is notified of the amount of duty payable. He will already have paid duties on the face of the invoice, but the result of the appraisement may be to either lower or increase these, in which case part of his payment is refunded, or he is obliged to make an additional payment. The process is, of course, much more complicated than this, so complicated in fact that merchants usually employ Custom House brokers to transact this branch of their business, but the above is about the simplest way of describing the method.

Opposite the Custom House, on Hanover and Wall streets, is the old banking firm of Brown Bros. & Co. There is nothing of especial interest beyond here to the foot of the street, where along South street another busy, bustling shipping scene greets the eye. The Elevated Railroad crosses Wall street at Pearl street. Pearl street, it will be remembered by those who have followed the itinerary of this guide, begins at State street, and therefore has swept around in a semi-circle to this point, and from here on it makes another sweep joining Broadway above Duane street, running a semicircular course. Its peculiar line is due to the fact that it was built up along an old cow-path which ran from the old fort along the outlying settlements to the common pasture which is now City Hall Park. At the foot of Wall street is a ferry to Brooklyn, having its Brooklyn landing at the foot of Montague street.

CHAPTER IV.

WALL STREET TO CITY HALL PARK.

Broadway above Wall street to City Hall Park is still a succession of large buildings. At No. 111 Broadway, opposite Pine street, is the Trinity Building, whose southern windows look out on the old churchyard. The block above this on the same side is occupied by the *Boreel Building*, 115 Broadway, the site of the old De Lancey mansion, where the Washington Inauguration Ball took place, and which was subsequently occupied by the City Hotel, a famous hostelry in its day. Pine street, which runs into Broadway at the head of Trinity cemetery, is a narrow thoroughfare lined on either side with office buildings.

EQUITABLE BUILDING. — Between Pine and Cedar streets, on the east side of Broadway, stands the building of the Equitable Life Assurance Society, which houses 3,500 tenants, and through which pass more than 30,000 people a day. Almost every kind of business capable of being transacted in offices is represented in this building. It is a granite structure in classic style, a certain large effect being introduced by an architectural device in giving two stories the external appearance of one very high story. The present structure was built in 1885, the company at that time acquiring the whole block on Broadway, and a large portion of the block on Nassau street. The entrance is a massive coffered granite Roman arch, leading into a double vestibule with pilasters of yellow marble with capitals of Mexican onyx and lintels of Knoxville marble, ceiled with polished marble and bronze friezes. The arcade beyond is 30 feet broad by over 100 feet long, with a great arched skylight of stained glass and polished marble, the walls being lined like the vestibule. In the tympanum of the arch at the end of the main corridor is a mosaic by F. Lathrop, representing the tutelary significance of life insurance. In the corner of the building at Broadway and Pine street is the Café Savarin, and back of this across the hall, the restaurant of the same name. The Mercantile Trust Company, several banks, and the well-known banking firms of Winslow, Lanier & Co., August Belmont & Co., and Kountze Bros. & Co., have offices here. A large portion of the fifth and sixth floors is reserved for the Lawyers' Club and a fine law library, the building being a great headquarters for lawyers.

A portion of the tower is used by the *U. S. Signal Service*, and it is from this point that New Yorkers ascertain why they are either freezing or sweltering. Here the famous humidity statistics originate. This tower, however, is used chiefly for the office of the Signal Service, the various instruments for measuring the barometric and atmospheric pressure, for determining the temperature, the direction of the wind, the velocity of the wind, and the amount of rain-fall being exposed on an iron tower built up from the roof and considerably higher than the Broadway tower, to the office in which, however, the records are automatically transmitted. In this office is a small printing outfit for printing signal office charts, made up from reports and observations received from all over the country at 8 A. M. and 8 P. M. On a flagstaff attached to the Broadway tower weather signals are raised, warning mariners against cold waves and storms—flags by day and lanterns by night. The highest temperature reported from this office was 100 degrees on June 6, 1881; the lowest, 6 degrees below zero Jan. 10, 1875. The wind attained its greatest velocity, 72 miles, on Dec. 31, 1880. The tower roof is no longer accessible to the public, but it is interesting to stroll around the roof of the main building and observe the number of superstructures upon it, which form a little village all by themselves. The view, however, is much cut off by tall buildings.

Passing out of the Equitable Building, on the Nassau street side, and proceeding to the corner of Cedar street, the fine building of the *Mutual Life Insurance Company* (C. Clinton, architect), occupying the block between Cedar and Liberty streets, and one of the finest specimens of Italian Renaissance in the city, is seen. Its most impressive feature is a portico two stories high, the capitals of the polished granite columns on the second story being carved heads emblematic of America, Europe, Asia, and Africa. This building stands upon an historic site, that of the old Middle Dutch Church (p. 123), which, during the Revolution, was occupied as a riding-school by the British calvary, and also as a prison. Subsequently it passed into the possession of the United States, and was occupied as a post-office until the present Federal building on Broadway and Park row was erected. The *Chamber of Commerce* of the State of New York occupies quarters in this building. It collects and publishes annually valuable statistics relating to the commerce of the State and city. Being composed of leading men in commercial and financial circles it exerts considerable influence upon legislation. The walls of its spacious headquarters are hung with the portraits of many of its distinguished members. Four of the portraits were painted for or purchased by the Chamber. These are of Cadwallader Colden, Lieutenant-Governor of the Colony, painted 1772, by Matthew Pratt; Alexander Hamilton and De Witt Clinton, by Trumbull; and of John Sherman, by Huntington—the last in honor of the resumption of specie payments effected by Sherman while Secretary of the Treasury. The Chamber was instituted April 5, 1768, at Fraunces' Tavern, and has an unbroken record of the minutes of every meeting from that date down.

Passing up Nassau street to Liberty street and through Liberty street to Broadway, there stands on the north side of Liberty street, No. 57, the *Real Estate Exchange*, the object of which is to facilitate the sale and transfer of real estate, primarily in the City of New York, but furthermore, also, throughout the United States. Formerly the public sales of real estate were effected in the basement of Trinity Building at 111 Broadway. The present Exchange was opened on the 14th of April, 1885. All sales of land in New York City under decrees, orders or judgments have to be made in the rooms of this Exchange. The Building Material Exchange occupies quarters in the rear part of the auction room. The Exchange keeps books in which it registers, for a fee of five dollars, property within the city limits, and even considerable property without the city boundaries offered for sale. It has, also, valuable records, and offers its members other privileges. The first private deed on record in New York City is a conveyance of a lot 30 x 110 feet on Bridge street, between Whitehall and Broad streets, for twenty-four guilders, which is about $9.50 in our money. Auction sales of real estate on the Exchange last year amounted to $44,083,763.

Leaving the Exchange and proceeding to and up Broadway, the next street is *Maiden Lane.* This was once a country lane crossing the island along a stream with marshy shores, and it was called the Maiden's Path, T'Maagde Paatje in the original Dutch, because washwomen plied their occupation along the banks of the stream. Here, also, the tanners once had their pits. The street entering Broadway opposite is Cortlandt street, named after the old Van Cortlandt farm, part of which was appropriated for opening the street. On the southeast corner of Cortlandt and New Church streets stands the large building of the Coal and Iron Exchange, and on the north side of the street, not far from Broadway, is the Telephone Building.

WESTERN UNION BUILDING —The next street entering into Broadway on its west side is Dey street. Here stands one of the most conspicuous buildings in the city, housing one of the greatest corporations in the United States, the *Western Union Telegraph Company.* When this company began operations in 1856, it had 37,318 miles of poles and cables, 75,686 miles of wire, and 2,250 offices. The statistics for messages, receipts, expenses and profits do not exist for this year, but in the following year the company handled 5,879,282 messages, its receipts were $6,558,925.36, and its profits $2,624,-919.73. The average toll for a message was a little over $1.04. The marvelous increase in the company's business, and the manner in which it, itself, has grown with its growth of business, is clearly shown by the statistics for 1890. It had 678,997 miles of wire. Its offices numbered 19,382. It handled 55,878,762 messages. Its receipts were $22,387,027.91. Its profits were $7,312-725.10, and the average cost for a message had fallen from a little over $1.04 to a little over 32 cents. In this building is the nerve-center of the network of wire which stretches all over this country, and runs along the bottom of the sea to nearly all civilized countries of the globe; and one can sit in this building and by simply touching a knob communicate with every place in the world where there is a telegraph station. In July, 1890, the upper stories of the Western Union Building were destroyed by fire. The building, remodeled by J. H. Hardenbergh, occupies a frontage of 75 feet on Broadway, and including an adjoining building, runs 200 feet on Dey street. The Broadway building is nine stories high, and is built of brick with terra cotta trimmings. The principal feature of the Broadway front are three wide arches on piers which extend through two stories, and are crowned with capitals. There are seven arches on the Dey street front, and the top story is formed by an arcade of arched openings, the whole being surrounded by a heavy cornice of terra cotta. The adjoining building on Dey street is of the same general character and design, but the structure is ten stories high. The seventh and eighth stories, communicating with those of the Broadway building, form immense operating rooms 75 x 100 feet, fitted up with the most improved apparatus.

There are employed in all departments in these buildings about 1,200 people; over 2,000 wires center in the operating room; 100,000 messages are handled, on the average, in the operating room every day. There are 175 branch offices in the city. From this building telegraphic communication can be had with any part of the world. The company's own submarine cables, which land at Whitesand Bay, Devon, England, and at Coney Island, N. Y., with land wires in England, and underground and aerial cables across Long Island and the Brooklyn Bridge at this end, give a direct connection with London. Thence messages are transmitted, either by the various government systems or submarine cable companies, or by both, to all parts of Europe, Asia, Africa and South America. The company has also direct connection, through its own submarine cables, which lie between Florida and Havana, with Cuba, all the West India Islands and the northern parts of South America; and by means of the cables of the Mexican and Central and South American Telegraph companies, which start from Galveston, Texas, it reaches all the important places in Central America and on the west coast of South America, and has an alternate route, via the land lines from Valparaiso across the Andes, to the Argentine Republic, Brazil, etc.

In the basement of the building are immense boilers and engines which furnish power for the dynamo machines and for the operation of the pneumatic tubes, which extend to down-town offices in the neighborhood of the exchanges, and to the principal up-town sub-offices, nine in all, and terminate at the up-town central office at Twenty-third street and Fifth avenue. Through this pneumatic system, which comprises about 16 miles of brass tubes, an endless procession of leather boxes, in which are messages of every conceivable import, is kept moving either by the compression or exhaustion of air.

John Street M. E. Church.—Opposite Dey street John street runs into Broadway. On the south side of John street, between Nassau and William, is the oldest Methodist Episcopal Church in the United States. It is preserved chiefly for memorial purposes, but also for a business men's prayer meeting, which is held from 12:15 to 1 P. M. during the week, although the worshipers sometimes become so excited that they prolong the meeting, their shouts of praise and joy, and their wailings of contrition being heard on the street above the noise of the traffic. The history of this edifice is interesting. In 1766 a few Methodists held services at a private house, and afterwards in a room in the barracks near Chambers street and Broadway, where the New York Hospital afterwards stood. A Captain Thomas Webb, who was a Methodist minister as well as a soldier, spent the winter of 1766–67 in New York. As he preached in his regimentals, and was also a man of eloquence, he attracted such great crowds that the room in the barracks became too small and the services were transferred to a rigging loft in William street. Here the society prospered, and in 1768 a little rough stone church was erected on the site of the present edifice. As dissenters were not allowed to worship in churches, a fireplace and mantel were built in order to give the place a resemblance to a private house. Philip Embury, the famous carpenter preacher, built the pulpit with his own hands, and preached the dedicatory sermon the 30th of October, 1768. The gallery was reached by a ladder. In 1817 the structure was taken down and a larger one built on the site. By 1841, however, the up-town movement had drawn most of the congregation away from its vicinity, and the ground upon which it stood being valuable, the church was torn down, and a smaller one built, the rest of the land being utilized for business structures.

Back of what is now 17 John street, though the site is also given as No. 15 and No. 21, stood the famous old *John Street Theatre.* This was not absolutely the first place of amusement in New York, for there is a vague record of a theatre as far back as 1740, and in 1750 a company acted in a building on the east side of Nassau street, between Maiden Lane and John street. The John Street Theatre was opened in 1767. The performances began at 6 o'clock, and ladies who desired good places were requested to send their servants by 5 o'clock to secure them. The theatre stood 60 feet back of the street, and its patrons were compelled to walk through a badly lighted wooden passage. The interior accommodations were a pit, two rows of rough boxes, and a gallery. The theatre was lighted by candles. During the Revolution it was called the Theatre Royal, and amateur theatricals, some of the plays being written by Major André, were acted by British officers. Washington patronized it during the time that he resided in the city as President of the United States. Above John and Dey streets, Broadway is crossed by *Fulton street,* one of the most crowded thoroughfares of the city. This street runs from river to river, and has on its western end Washington, and on its eastern end Fulton Market. At the latter point is also the Fulton Ferry to Brooklyn. The southeast corner of Fulton street and Broadway is occupied by the *Evening Post Building.* From here to Fulton Ferry (East River) the street is largely given over to retail business establishments.

Fulton Market, Fulton street and East river is one of the best known establishments of its kind in New York. Including restaurants there are 218 stands, and everything in the way of meats, poultry, vegetables, fruits and fish are supposed to be had here. On April 1st, when the trout season opens, there is an especially brilliant display of fish at the market. Opposite, on the east side of South street, next to the river, is a wooden structure, three stories high, which is utilized for a wholesale fish market. Here the fishing-smacks discharge their cargoes, and early in the morning the place is made hideous with the shouts of licensed venders and retail dealers laying in their stock for the day. *Washington Market*, at the western end of Fulton street, is a somewhat similar structure. It is surrounded by the great produce district of New York, virtually the distributing center of the country. Saturday evenings, the booths which abound in Vesey and Barclay streets, and from which fruit and produce, hardware, stationery, toys and in fact almost every variety of cheap merchandise is sold, are illuminated by oil torches, which throw a weird, reddish light, veiled by clouds of thick smoke, over the scene, the spectacular effect being heightened by the hoarse shouts of venders and the more subdued, but also more steady, roar of the surging crowd.

Oldest House in New York.—Between Fulton and John streets is No. 122 William street, which is considered by good authority the oldest house in New York. When William street was opened in 1692 from Wall street to Fulton, lots were granted on condition that stone houses at least two stories high should be built within two years. No. 122 was built at that time, and therefore must have been erected between the years 1692 and 1694. The house is two stories high with dormer windows in the roof, and is built of narrow Holland bricks. There were large open fire-places in the house, one of which, in the second story, still remains. They were decorated with white and blue tiles representing Biblical subjects, and several of these have been preserved. The house is now occupied as a restaurant. Right back of this house was Golden Hill, where the first blood of the Revolution was shed (p. 131), and in the house which once stood opposite, Washington Irving was born.

Fulton Street Prayer Meeting.—At 113 Fulton street are the offices of the oldest church organization in the United States, the Collegiate Reformed Protestant Dutch Church, of which the Fulton Street Prayer Meeting is a chapel, known as the North Church Chapel.

The Fulton Street Prayer Meeting being decidedly the most interesting adjunct of this ancient organization to the public, and also the only adjunct of it accessible to the public on week-days, this is the proper place in which to give a history of this venerable body.

The Collegiate Dutch Church was organized in 1628. In 1623 the first church services on Manhattan Island were held by Dutch and Walloon immigrants in the loft of the first horse-mill built on the island, and in this loft the church was organized in 1628. In the spring of 1633, when the Rev. Everardus Bogardus came out from Holland, the erection of a building exclusively for purposes of worship was begun on the north side of Pearl street, about midway between Whitehall and Broad streets. During the Indian War of 1642, a stone church was erected inside the fort. The old Middle Church, which occupied the site between Cedar and Liberty streets, where the Mutual Life Insurance Building now stands (p. 118), was built in 1729, and was kept in use until 1844, when it was leased to the government of the United States, and was used as a post-office until 1875. The Collegiate Church maintains three churches and three chapels; the churches being at 14 Lafayette place, which is the old Middle Church, Fifth avenue and Twenty-ninth street, and Fifth avenue and Forty-eighth street.

The *Fulton Street Prayer Meeting* is held on the second story of 113 Fulton street. It is capable of seating over 500 persons. Signs on the wall tell the visitor that "No person is allowed to consume over five minutes in prayer or testimony," "No controverted religious subjects allowed to be introduced." On other cards are scripture exhortations. Every day a different leader conducts the meeting, so that the style and experience may be varied. As soon as the clock strikes 12, the leader gives out a hymn, generally a familiar one, in which the whole congregation can join heartily. Then there is reading and an introductory prayer. After more singing, the leader reads extracts from the letters which have been received since the meeting of the day before. These number from 50 to 100, and are requests for prayers either for the writer or for some relative or friend, for the reform of a drinking father or neglectful husband, for the forgiveness of some sin that weighs heavily upon the conscience, for children who have been led into sin, for the conversion of infidels. These letters come from all parts of the United States, and even from foreign countries, showing how wide-spread is the fame of the Fulton Street Prayer Meeting. The leader calls on some brother to pray as requested in the letters, and, after singing, the meeting is thrown open to all, and prayer follows prayer, the supplications telling of many experiences similar to those which were related in the letters. After this experience meeting the proceedings are brought to a close with the Doxology.

St. Paul's Chapel.—On Broadway, between Fulton and Vesey streets, stands St. Paul's, a chapel of Trinity Parish and the only colonial relic among the churches of New York. It was the third Episcopal church built in the city. Its corner-stone was laid in 1754 and it was finished in 1756. It seems curious to the beholder to-day that its rear should be towards Broadway, but when the church was built the space between it and the North river was clear of buildings, and the frontage in that direction was considered far more attractive. It is a venerable classic structure, the air of antiquity being enhanced by the graveyard which surrounds it. The rear on Broadway is a portico supporting a pediment, in which is a niche occupied by a statue of St. Paul.

Within this portico, and set in the rear wall of the church, is a monument to General Richard Montgomery, the Revolutionary soldier, bearing the following inscriptions:

The State of New York caused the remains of Major-General Richard Montgomery to be conveyed from Quebec and deposited beneath this monument the 8th day of July, 1818.

This monument was erected by the order of Congress the twenty-fifth of January, 1776, to transmit to posterity a grateful remembrance of the patriotism, conduct, enterprise and perseverance of Major-General Richard Montgomery, who, after a series of successes amidst the most discouraging difficulties, fell in the attack on Quebec, 31st December, 1775, aged 37 years.

A rough-hewn design of military accoutrements is a feature of the memorial. Richard Montgomery, whom this memorial honors, was born near Raphoe, Ireland, December 2, 1736. He was commissioned an officer in the British army when he was only eighteen years old. He was conspicuous at the siege of Louisburg, and in the expeditions against Martinique and Havana. In 1772 he came to New York and married a daughter of Robert R. Livingston. After a series of successes which made him master of the greater part of Canada, he effected a junction with Arnold, and at 2 A. M., December 31, 1775, attempted to capture Quebec by a *coup de main.* The first barrier was carried, but as he was pressing on to the second at the head of his troops, he fell with two of his aides, killed at the first and only discharge of the British artillery, and his army retreated.

In view of Montgomery's Irish birth, it is interesting to know that on either side of him lie the remains of two Irish patriots. To the north of the rear of the chapel is a tall monument erected to the memory of Dr. McNevin, and to the south is an obelisk in memory of *Thomas Addis Emmet.* In the east face of this obelisk not far below the pyrimidian is a bust of Emmet in relief, and below this about 6 feet above the pedestal an oval in which is a relief design of clasped hands, the shamrock being on the wrist of one, and stars on the other. Another interesting monument in this cemetery is that to *George Frederick Cooke*, the English actor. It stands in the central part of the graveyard, and was erected by Edmund Kean. Cooke, born at Westminster, April 17, 1756, died from the effects of intemperance at New York, September 26, 1812. His first appearance in the United States was October 21, 1810, at the Park Theatre, New York, on the site of 23 Park row, not so very far from where he lies buried. The inscription on his monument:

> "Three kingdoms claim his birth;
> Both hemispheres pronounce his worth,"

was written by Halleck. Upon the monument is also engraved "Erected to the memory of George Frederick Cooke, of the Theatre Royal Drury Lane, 1821." Kean's son, Charles Kean, finding, when here in 1846, that his father's monument to Cooke had fallen into decay, had it repaired, and added to the inscription

"Repaired by Charles Kean, 1846." It was, as further inscriptions upon it tell us, again repaired in 1874 by E. A. Sothern, and in 1890 by Edwin Booth, a graceful tribute from the greatest American tragedian to a great English predecessor.

After Washington had been inaugurated on the balcony of Federal Hall (p. 101), he proceeded to St. Paul's Church, where services where held, and the same religious formality was observed at the Washington Inauguration Centennial, when Bishop Potter preached the sermon, President Harrison occupying the pew which Washington had used, which is on the left side of the church and is marked by a bronze memorial tablet donated by the Aisle Committee at the Centennial service. On the opposite side of the church is the pew occupied by Governor George Clinton.

On the block above St. Paul's is the Astor House, one of the best-known hotels of the city. In the rotunda, reached through the Broadway entrance, from 2,000 to 2,500 take their luncheon every day of the year, except Sundays.

Post-Office.—At the point where Park Row runs into Broadway, forming a triangle bounded by Park Row, Broadway and Chambers streets, was, until the erection of the Federal or Post-Office Building, the beginning of the old common pasture now City Hall Park. Broadway originally ran in a straight line only as far as the point where Park Row now diverges from it. The road then continued on the present line of Park Row to Chatham Square, where there was a hill, the Square being formed by the necessity of laying out the road in a circuitous line so as to make the ascent of the hill as easy as possible; and it was not until Broadway was continued in a straight line from the point where the old Commons began that the triangle, at whose lower end the Post-Office stands, was formed.

It is worth while to stand at the point of this triangle to watch the mighty tide of travel that surges and roars in its course up and down Broadway. Great buildings catch the eye in either direction, but hold it only for a moment, for the panorama of humanity, of men, women and children, of millionaire and beggar, of vehicles of every description, allows of no diversion.

The Building.—The Post-Office Building is used not only for a post-office, but also for the United States Courts, the United States District-Attorney's office and other Federal purposes. Its architecture is Doric, with a suggestion of Renaissance, and has been severely criticised. The fact remains, however, that, possibly only by reason of its massiveness or its superior position, it has the effect of a dignified and imposing structure. It is a granite building fronting 340 feet on Broadway and the same distance on Park Row, and 290 feet on Mail street, which runs along its northern end. An effective feature of the building is an entrance looking down Broadway, from which the two great fronts on Broadway and Park Row spread out. A large dome, modeled after that of the Louvre, rises above the sky-line on the middle of the Broadway side.

Business.—The New York Post-Office, like the New York Custom House, is a source of profit to the Government, yielding some $3,500,000 above expenses. From the last official statement of transactions of the New York Post-Office, prepared for the annual report of the Chamber of Commerce, it appears that during the year 1889, 542,096,905 pieces of mail matter were handled, in 3,236,820 bags, weighing 233,637,960 pounds. The sales of postage stamps, stamped paper and postal cards amounted to $5,192,903.61 ; the sales of newspaper and periodical stamps to $380,213.61 ; the box rents to $50,953.33 ; and the total business of the money-order department embraced 3,183,620 items, amounting to $91,004,253.55. In the registry department 7,471,083 packages of letters were handled. Several statistics relating to the inquiry and dead letter department are also interesting; 46,923 letters and packages were refused by persons to whom they were addressed, for postage due ; 8,432 letters were sent to fictitious addresses ; 42,292 letters remaining unclaimed at hotels were returned to the Post-Office ; 553,080 letters were either misdirected or insufficiently addressed, and of these 480,067 were corrected and forwarded. Among those insufficiently addressed was one from Germany, directed "To my dear son John, New York." This letter was sent to the dead letter office along with 1,162,902 others. In the foreign department 26,058,734 letters were forwarded and 21,601,619 letters were received.

The average daily business of the New York Post-Office involves the handling of over 600,000 letters and about 9,000 bags of newspaper mail. The most interesting operation of the Post-Office, the receiving and distribution of letters, can be watched from a gallery which runs along the Park Row side of the mezzanine floor. It is most easily reached from the entrance at the point of the triangle looking down Broadway, from which a flight of stairs leads to the floor upon which it is located. Guards are in attendance, whose duty it is to direct visitors to this or any other part of the building. The gallery looks down upon the ground floor. On the southern end of the Park Row side is the city department, and on the Broadway side the outgoing domestic. In these departments are shelves with pigeon holes arranged according to mail routes in the outgoing domestic department, and according to carriers' boxes and branches in the city department. On both sides are long tables where the stamping is done. As fast as the letters are received through the various drops in the corridors on the ground floor, they fall upon a table, and as they do so they are faced up and passed on to a long table where they are stamped. From the stamper they pass to the separator, and from him to the mail-maker, who verifies the separation, ties the letters according to routes into bundles, putting on each bundle a printed label marked with its direction. The mail-maker's work is in turn verified by the route agent in the postal car, who marks any errors he may discover upon the labels, which are returned to the New York Post-Office, where a strict account is kept. On the Mail street side are large pouch racks, in which pouches with open maws, receive the letters that are showered into them. The foreign department is on the extreme northeast end. Everything in the Post-Office is done on schedule, and a person can ascertain by inquiry of the proper official at what hour a letter posted at some lamp-post up-town should reach its destination in the city, or for that matter, in any part of the United States. It may be said, in fact, that the Post-Office grinds out letters like a machine, for if the visitor will watch the carriers' table in the center of the floor, he will see that the carrier has hardly taken the mail for his route out of the box before the assorter is throwing mail into the box for the next delivery.

CHAPTER V.

CITY HALL PARK AND VICINITY.

City Hall Park, which, before 1875 and before the Post-Office was erected, occupied the entire triangle bounded by Broadway, Park Row and Chambers street, is one of the old historic sites of the city. It was the old Commons, used for a pasturage and for public celebrations. Five times each year during one period of the city's history, a public bonfire was lighted, and wine and victuals distributed at the town's expense. Not far from where the Register's office now is, stood the gallows; afterwards a powder-house was built on the site, it being considered sufficiently remote from the city for the storage of so dangerous an article.

In the years preceding the Revolution, when public sentiment here was in a constant state of ebulition, this part of the city witnessed many exciting scenes. A contest between the noted Liberty Boys and the British garrison resulted in the first shedding of blood on behalf of American liberties, two months before the Boston massacre, to which event that honor has generally been assigned. January 4, 1770, when the news of the repeal of the odious Stamp Act reached New York, the Liberty Boys erected a large liberty pole on the Commons, opposite the barracks. Several times it was destroyed by the soldiers, and as often re-erected by the people. January 18th, two days after the soldiers had destroyed the pole, several Sons of Liberty caught three soldiers in the act of posting insolent hand-bills, apprehended them, and marched them toward the Mayor's office. A crowd gathered, and when a band of some twenty soldiers attempted to rescue their comrades with cutlasses and clubs, the citizens drove them back upon Golden Hill, the highest point of which was just in the rear of what is now 122 William street, the oldest house in New York (p. 123). Several citizens were wounded, and one of them killed in the affray. The Sons of Liberty then purchased a plot of land on the Commons, directly opposite what is now 252 Broadway, and there erected another pole, upon which "Liberty and Property" was inscribed.

The Park is now an exceedingly attractive spot and resting-place. At the junction of Park Row and Nassau street is the triangular point upon which the handsome granite Romanesque structure of the *Times* building stands, one of the happiest architectural creations in the city. This and the Pulitzer Building (see below) are by George B. Post. Here is "Printing House Square," entirely occupied by newspaper offices. The statue of Benjamin Franklin, the tutelary divinity of printing in this country, was erected in 1872, after a design by Plassman, at the expense of Captain De Groot. Diagonally opposite the *Times* building on the corner of Nassau street, is the structure occupied by the *Tribune* building, conspicuous by reason of its tall tower, and a good example of the Neo-Grec style of architecture. In front of the *Tribune* publication office is a fine statue of *Horace Greeley*, founder of the *Tribune*, by J. Q. A. Ward, which represents the great journalist seated and apparently pausing a moment to think before putting his pen to paper. Adjoining the *Tribune* is the *Sun* building. On the opposite corner of Frankfort street is the large new building of the New York *World*, the Pulitzer Building, with its great dome, affording from its elevation of 309 feet a superb view of the city and its environs.

The municipal buildings in City Hall Park are the City Hall itself, the new Court House and the Register's office, or Hall of Records, and two other structures in the north-east corner.

City Hall.—The City Hall, although it was built early in this century, is still considered one of the finest, if not the finest, public building, from an architectural point of view, in the United States. The first City Hall in the history of Manhattan Island was a tavern built in 1642 on the north-west corner of Pearl street and Coenties alley, then close to the shore, and ceded after the organization of a city magistracy in 1653 to the city as a *Stadt Huys*, as which it was used until 1700, when the City Hall on Wall street, at the head of Broad, was built. In 1788 this was enlarged and converted into Federal Hall. In 1803 the corner-stone of the present City Hall was laid by Mayor Edward Livingston. It was finished in 1812 at a cost of more than half a million dollars. Its architect was John McComb, whose work, though characteristic enough to be justly praised as original, shows the influence of the Adams Bros. and of Sir William Chambers. The City Hall, when cross-sectioned north and south, resembles the Register Office in Edinburgh, built by the Adams Bros. in 1774, and the main stairway is somewhat like that built by the same architects in the Glasgow Assembly Rooms. The architecture is classic. The building consists of a central structure of two stories and an attic, surmounted by a cupola, and two wings of two stories each, the whole resting on a basement of brown freestone. The front and sides are of white marble, the rear of freestone. There is a tradition that freestone was used for the rear, because the building then stood so far out of town that it was thought the rear would not be noticed sufficiently to make it worth while to build it of marble. A broad flight of steps leads from the south to an Ionic colonnade, and thence to a large vestibule opening into a corridor communicating with the staircases, halls and rooms. A large circular stone staircase faces the entrance from the center of the structure, and on the second floor a circular gallery runs around ten marble Corinthian columns. The cupola is surmounted by a statue of Justice and a flagstaff. A person looking at the building from a position in front of it, is apt to be struck by the want of something to lessen the effect of tallness produced by the cupola, and also the monotony of the straight roof line, The architect had, in fact, designed a pedimental foil for the base of the cupola, showing the city arms and statuary, so that from this point of view, at least, the building is unfinished. In August, 1856, a spark from the fireworks set off from the roof of the City Hall, at the celebration of the laying of the first Atlantic cable, ignited some materials stored near the base of the cupola, and the latter was entirely destroyed.

The building contains the offices of several city officials, among them the office of the Mayor, which is in the western wing on the ground floor. This office is connected with the Council Chamber, in which hangs a large painting of Washington by Trumbull, ordered of him by the City of New York in 1790. This is a full length portrait, and is highly interesting not only for its subject and the fact that it commemorates an event of the greatest historical importance, the evacuation of the city by the British, but also because it is an example of a noted early American painter's work. Washington stands beside a white charger, which is pawing the ground, its head lowered. The Commander-in-chief's right hand holding the reins rests upon the horse's croup; his left arm is akimbo, the hand upon his sword-hilt, holding at the same time his chapeau. He is watching the evacuation of the city by the British in the distance.

Governor's Room.—The most interesting room to strangers in the City Hall is the suite of large apartments on the second floor front, known as the Governor's Room. In this is the furniture used by the first Congress of the United States in the old Federal Hall. Directly opposite the entrance is the large desk used by Washington while President; and between the doors leading to the East Room of the suite stands another desk also used by Washington. The furniture is all of mahogany, and calculated to excite the envy of people who can appreciate its beauty and its value as relics.

In this room are numerous portraits of State Governors and Mayors. These paintings are not catalogued, and are somewhat difficult of identification, but they are nevertheless a valuable portrait gallery of State and local interest. There are three Trumbulls in the Governor's room, chief among them being the fine portrait of Governor George Clinton, who was Governor of the State at the time Washington was inaugurated President. He was a distinguished soldier as well as a statesman of force and influence, and it is as a soldier that Trumbull has painted him. He stands in uniform with drawn sword, his strong face wearing a look of determination. A battle scene in the background adds to the spirited effect of this picture, which hangs in the east wing of the Governor's Room. Among the other portraits in this wing are those of Alexander Hamilton by Weimar; and of Van Buren by Inman, the latter hanging over the desk used by Thomas Jefferson, which stands in the space between the two doors leading into the main room. On the Jefferson desk is a bust of DeWitt Clinton. Under the desk is a huge punch bowl, which was used in this city at the banquet and celebration of the opening of the Erie Canal. It was presented to the city by General Jacob Morton. Inside is the bibular exhortation: "Drink deep! You will preserve the city and encourage canals." Many, doubtless, would be willing to preserve numerous cities and encourage any number of canals upon similar terms. In the south doorway between the east wing and the main room is a portrait of Washington woven in silk in Lyons, France, at a cost of $10,000. In the main room, there is above the small Washington desk, between the doors leading to the east wing, a copy of Gilbert Stuart's full-length portrait of Washington. On the north wall is a life size portrait of John Jay, by Weimar. Jay, a typical statesman of the wig and knee-breeches school, is standing, his right arm resting on the back of a high chair, his left on a book upon a table. Between the doors leading into the West Room is a full-length portrait of Lafayette, by Morse. Lafayette stands upon a tiled terrace. He wears a black coat, roomy buff trousers, and a brown cloak lined with red is draped about him. In the background are busts of Washington and Franklin. In the west wing are two Trumbulls, the most important of them being a portrait of Governor Morgan Lewis on the extreme right of the west wall. Governor Lewis was a great fighter, not only in the Revolution, but in the war of 1812, and Trumbull has painted him as a soldier. A small portrait of Gen. Williams, who was killed in the second war with England at Lake Champlain, is the other Trumbull. It hangs on the south wall, beside a large iron statue of Jefferson, which was presented to the city by Commodore Uriah Levy. Other portraits in this room are a full-length likeness of William H. Seward, by Inman, and Hamilton Fish, by Hicks, and small portraits of De Witt Clinton and Baron Steuben. Seward is shown as a sandy-haired young man in evening dress, standing by a rustic chair amid rural surroundings.

On the same floor with the Governor's Room, in the northwest corner of the building, is the Aldermen's Chamber. In this room are six full-length portraits, one of Jefferson at a table, quill in hand, looking up from his writing as if wrapped in thought. Monroe, by Vanderlyn, whose most familiar work, by the way, is the Landing of Columbus, an engraving of which on our five dollar notes makes parting with these less sad than would otherwise be the case, is shown standing in graceful pose in black coat, buff vest and knee breeches. The portrait of General and President Taylor, and that of Andrew Jackson, who is shown with uncovered head and drawn sword, his eyes flashing with the fire of battle, are also by Vanderlyn. A strong portrait of Clay is by Jarvis.

While on the subject of the paintings belonging to the city, it may be stated that in the office of the Commissioner of Public Works, No. 31 Chambers street, about opposite the new Court House, are Jarvis' portrait of Bolivar, Morse's of Monckton, and Jarvis' painting of Commodore Perry, a picture of some spirit, but open to the criticism that the small boat in which Perry stands would inevitably have upset had he in reality struck the attitude in which he is.

Back of the City Hall stands the white marble building of the *New Court House*, a structure of Corinthian architecture, three stories high, 250 feet long by 150 wide. Its most imposing feature is the portico and steps with columns on the Chambers street front. The State Courts and several of the city departments are located in this building.

Register's Office.—To the east of the City Hall stands the old Hall of Records or Register's Office, which is one of the most noted historic buildings in the city, being a relic of the Revolution, and in fact the only public building directly connecting us with Revolutionary times. Beginning with the occupation of New York by the British until Evacuation Day in 1783, it was crowded with American prisoners of war and others who had incurred the enmity of the British authorities, and was ruled over by the infamously brutal Provost-Marshal Cunningham.

In 1757, when the city was below Wall street, and City Hall Park was in the suburbs, the additional room needed in the City Hall, which then stood on the site of the present Sub-Treasury in Wall street, made it necessary to build a new jail. Thus originated the present Hall of Records, which, when it was finished, stood far in the fields adjoining the high road to Boston, surrounded by the pillory, the whipping-post, the stocks and the gallows. In the stormy days which preceded the Revolution, obnoxious patriots were imprisoned therein. Its interest as a Revolutionary prison begins with the occupation of New York by the British. There is a tradition that Hale, the martyr spy, spent his last night here, in charge of Cunningham, his executioner. The American prisoners were half-starved, and otherwise most cruelly treated, and to add to the horrors of this dungeon, they were obliged to mingle with the worst classes of criminals who were also incarcerated here. The well, the sick, the dying, the new-comers, and the prisoners emaciated by long confinement were here huddled together. An account written by a prisoner says: "So closely were we packed that when our bones ached at night from laying on the hard plank and we wished to turn, it could only be done by word of command, being so wedged and compact as to form almost a solid mass of human bodies. The allowance to each man was 2 pounds of hard biscuit, and 2 pounds of raw pork per week, but no fuel with which to dress it was allowed." It is also charged that American generals and soldiers were here slowly starved to death, or poisoned by having arsenic mixed with their rations, and here these staunch patriots suffered the tortures of the damned rather than gain their freedom by entering the British service. Ethan Allen, who was confined here, also gives a description of the suffering which the prisoners endured. It is said that on evacuation day, Cunningham refused to release his prisoners, and, when the approach of Washington rendered longer stay dangerous, he threw away the key. It is believed to be the only Revolutionary prison remaining in the country.

East River Bridge.—Next to the Pulitzer building, is the New York terminus of the East River Bridge, to a stranger, perhaps, the most imposing public work in the United States, and probably the most interesting sight in New York. It is the largest suspension bridge in the world, so grand and yet so graceful that it is impossible to convey a sense of its beauty in words. To be fully appreciated it should be seen from the river, which is best accomplished by crossing over to Brooklyn and back by the Fulton Ferry, or if one desires a more distant view, by the Wall street ferry. It should then be crossed from the Brooklyn side on foot. As early as 1865, plans for a bridge to Brooklyn from this point were prepared, and in 1867 a company was formed. In 1875 the enterprise was made a State work. Its construction was begun after the plans and under the supervision of John A. Roebling, the originator of wire suspension bridges. Work was delayed by tardiness of appropriations and other vexatious incidents. The piers were built with the aid of caissons of a size hitherto unknown, that on the New York side weighing 7,000 tons, with a concrete filling of 8,000 tons. The Brooklyn tower was finished May 18, 1875, it having been built up from a clay bottom 44½ feet below low-water mark. The tower on the New York side was completed in July, 1876, being built up from bed rock 78½ feet below low-water mark. The first wire was run across in June, 1877, and the four huge cables were completed by October 7, 1878. The bridge was opened May 24, 1883. In the course of construction there were twenty fatal and numerous disabling accidents. In the first accident John A. Roebling was injured and he died of lockjaw, July 22, 1879. His son, Washington Roebling, succeeded him. In 1870 he was stricken with caisson disease, the result of a fire in the Brooklyn caisson, but he was able, through his wife, to

EAST RIVER BRIDGE.

superintend the construction, and later was moved to a residence in Brooklyn in view of the bridge, from which point he could direct the work.

The towers are pierced by two archways, 31½ feet wide and 118 feet above high water. The arches are 120½ feet high. The floor of the bridge runs through these. This is supported by four cables 16 inches in diameter. The bridge is divided into five parts. On the outside on either side are the roadways for vehicles. On the inside of these roadways are the roadbeds for the trains, which are run on the cable system, and between these roadbeds, that is, in the middle of the floor, is the walk for foot passengers. This is upon a higher level than either of the other divisions. Fares: foot passengers 1 cent; cars 3 cents (10 tickets 25 cents); vehicles 5 cents.

The following statistics give an idea of the immensity of the work:

Size of New York caisson, 172x102 feet; size of Brooklyn caisson, 168x102 feet; timber and iron in caisson, 5,253 cubic yards; concrete in well-holes, chambers, etc., 5,669 cubic feet; weight of New York caisson, about 7,000 tons; weight of concrete filling, 8,000 tons; New York tower contains 46,945 cubic yards masonry; Brooklyn tower contains 38,214 cubic yards masonry; length of river span, 1,595 feet 6 inches; length of each land span, 930 feet; length of Brooklyn approach, 971 feet; length of New York approach, 1.562 feet 6 inches; total length of bridge, 5,989 feet; width of bridge, 85 feet; number of cables, four; diameter of each cable, 15¾ inches; first wire was run out May 29, 1877; cable-making commenced, June 11, 1877; length of each single wire in cables. 3,579 feet; length of wire in four cables, 14,361 miles; weight of four cables, inclusive of wrapping wire, 3,588½ tons; ultimate strength of each cable, 12,200 tons; weight of wire (nearly) 11 feet per lb.; each cable contains 5,296 parallel galvanized steel, oil coated wires, closely wrapped to a solid cylinder 15¾ inches in diameter; depth of tower foundation below high water, Brooklyn, 45 feet; depth of tower foundation below high water, New York, 78 feet; size of towers at high water line, 140x59 feet; size of towers at roof course, 136x53 feet; total height of towers above high water, 272 feet; clear height of bridge in center of river span above high water, at 90 deg. F., 135 feet; height of floor at towers above high water, 119 feet 3 inches; grade of roadway, 3¼ feet in 100 feet; height of towers above roadway, 159 feet; size of anchorages at base, 129x119 feet; size of anchorages at top, 117x104 feet; height of anchorages, 89 feet front, 85 feet rear; weight of each anchor plate, 23 tons. Attached to the four large cables are 2,172 hanging cables.

The view up and down the river on a clear day is

superb. One can see beyond Governor's and Bedloe's Islands; down the harbor to Staten Island and the Narrows; up the East river to the bend at Corlears Hook, getting a glimpse of the Navy Yard. New York is a plain of roof tops pierced by innumerable spires and chimneys. Brooklyn, being situated on higher ground, shows perhaps to greater advantage. The river streets of both cities are lined with shipping of all kinds, and the river itself is alive with every variety of craft.

Traffic.—The report of the President of the trustees of the East River Bridge for the year ending December 1st, 1890, gives an excellent idea of the vast importance of this structure. The receipts from tolls were $1,127,094.50, divided as follows: Promenade, $18,614.68; carriageways, $76,465.59; railroad, $1,032,014.23. The number of passengers carried in the twelve months upon the railroad was 37,676,411. The whole number of foot passengers for the year was 3,222,073. The aggregate number of foot and railway passengers for the year was 40,898,484. The receipts from all sources were $1,239,493.90. The traffic reached its maximum on Nov. 24, when 154,550 passengers were carried in the cars. This has been exceeded only once in the history of the bridge, and that was on April 30, 1889, Washington Inauguration Centennial, when 159,259 passengers were carried. From the opening of the bridge until December 1 last, the number of passengers transported was 180,721,240.

CHAPTER VI.

DETOURS FROM CITY HALL PARK.

From City Hall Park several interesting detours can be made. On Frankfort street the huge arches upon which the New York approach to the Brooklyn Bridge is built can be seen. These have been utilized for business purposes. Between Frankfort and Fulton streets lies the headquarters of the leather trade, the "Swamp," so called from the swampy ground of the old Beekman farm, situated here; a pungent odor fills the air in this district. Frankfort street leads into Franklin Square (part of Pearl street), where the famous historic publishing house of Harper & Bros. is situated.

HARPER & BROTHERS.—This is an iron structure on the west side of the square, a few doors below Frankfort street. The firm was founded in 1817, by James and John Harper, and was at first a printing house only. The first book printed by the old firm of J. & J. Harper was "Seneca's Morals," and it is a curious coincidence that the firm of Harper & Bros. issued a new edition of this work on the day of the death of Fletcher Harper, who, with his brother, Joseph Wesley Harper, joined the original firm soon after its establishment. The first book published by the Harpers on their own account was "Locke on the Human Understanding." This was in 1818. About 1833 the firm was changed to Harper & Bros. December 10, 1853, the firm's buildings on Cliff and Pearl street were destroyed by fire, involving a loss of $1,000,000, only one-quarter of which was insured. Nevertheless, the business was continued without interruption in temporary quarters, and the present iron, fire-proof structure of seven stories, and occupying half an acre, partly on Franklin Square, and partly on Cliff street, was erected. It is still considered a model structure of its kind. A noteworthy feature is the absence of a staircase in the buildings themselves, a spiral stairway leading up from an open court, the buildings being reached by bridges from this staircase. *Harpers' Magazine* was established in 1850, *Harpers' Weekly* in 1857, *Harpers' Bazar* in 1867, and *Harpers' Young People* in 1879. These periodicals, and the long list of books published by Harper & Bros., are printed on the spot, the establishment being considered the most complete publishing house in the world; everything pertaining to the printing of books, including the illustrations and wood-cutting, being done under one roof. For this reason it is an interesting establishment to visit. Permits may be obtained on the premises.

Leading from Franklin Square in a northeasterly direction is *Cherry Street*, once a fashionable thoroughfare, Washington having had his first residence as President on the corner of Cherry street and Franklin Square. Now it is in the very slums, and is appropriately enough approached through the obscure shadows cast by the elevated railroad station. Here is the domain of some of the worst tenements in New York. Many of these are the old fashionable residences crowded with poverty-stricken occupants, but there are others of more recent building which are, if anything, worse. Filth, noisome odors, and a general appearance of dilapidation mark this street and its vicinity. Here are the famous double-decker tenements, as they are called, consisting of a huge tenement divided by a narrow alley, which usually reeks with filth, the building on either side of it being probably occupied by a population larger than that of many a country village or town. The visitor will hardly care to linger long in this street, and will probably be glad to retrace his steps up Frankfort street to City Hall Park again.

Opposite the New York entrace of the East River Bridge is Tryon Row, where the fine building of the *Staats Zeitung* stands. Park Row continues on toward the Bowery, and Centre street branches off to the left. Park Row is here a street of cheap hotels, pawnbrokers, clothing stores, jewelers and saloons. It is not a very attractive thoroughfare, but it leads to some rather picturesque portions of the city.

NEWSBOYS' LODGING HOUSE.—New Chambers street,

which runs out of Park Row on the right leads to the Newsboys' Lodging House, one of the buildings of the Children's Aid Society (p. 62), which also conducts an industrial school here. The Society strives to help children by encouraging them to be self-supporting. The boys pay six cents for lodging, and six cents for each meal, but will not be turned away if they cannot pay. The institution has sheltered since its foundation 37 years ago 239,560 boys, and the total expense of carrying on the work has been $433,256.76, of which the lads themselves have contributed $172,776.38. There is a good gymnasium, library and reading-room in the house, and a day and night industrial school. Last year 7,177 boys were registered, 59,522 lodgings and 82,081 meals were provided, and homes and employment were found for 337 boys, all this fine work being accomplished at a net cost of only $6,511.82.

Returning to Park Row, and continuing toward the Bowery, *Baxter street*, which enters the Row on the left-hand side, is reached. This is the headquarters of the cheap or second-hand clothing stores, and it is impossible to walk through it without being button-holed by the runners-in, who occupy the side-walks in front of the stores where clothing of all kinds is hung out and flapping in the breeze. A tour of this street is not particularly agreeable, but it is nevertheless a somewhat interesting experience. In the street below Baxter, *Mulberry*, where the Italians are packed like sardines, are other side-lights on life in New York. Where Mulberry street crooks like an elbow, not far from Bayard street, is the famous "Bend," where the sanitary police, during the summer, scatter disinfectants all day long, and where policemen are constantly making tours of inspection to find out whether the rooms of the tenements are not overcrowded to stifling. Here are the so-called two-cent restaurants, where a meal and a night's rest in a chair are furnished at the small price mentioned. The two-cent restaurant is really only a higher-toned name for the stale beer dive, and is usually situated in a damp, mildewed cellar. The beer is obtained by the keeper of the dive from the barrels which saloon-keepers put out on the sidewalk, and after it has been simmering all day long in the hot summer sun it is retouched with chemicals. Some of the dives have expressive names, such as the "House of Blazes," "Bandit's Roost," and the "Black and Tan."

Entering into Park Row one block further down is Mott street, which from Park Row to Bayard street is known as *Chinatown.* Looking down upon the curious and vicious life that is led there by the Chinamen and their victims, are the church and school of the Transfiguration, with an image of the Saviour in a niche above the portico. No stranger contrast exists in the city than this evidence of Christianity in this heathen quarter of the city, with its Chinese signs and lanterns swaying from every balcony and window, and on wires that are stretched across the street. At 6 Mott street, within a stone's throw of the church, is a Chinese temple. Some of the small shops in this street are great Chinese importing houses, and their owners who live here are wealthy enough to occupy Fifth avenue houses if they cared to. The whole of Chinatown is squalid in appearance, its buildings are rickety, old and ill-preserved, and the street is badly kept, but nothing about the whole place is as revolting as the faces of the white wives of these Chinamen, who are nearly all of them victims of the opium habit, and in the last stages of that decadence which overcomes those who fall low enough to seek relief from the woes of life in "hitting the pipe." It may be said here that this neighborhood belongs to what is known in police parlance as the "bloody Sixth," the Sixth Ward of the city being considered about the worst, and requiring the most surveillance; and a visit here, or in fact to any of the slums of New York—an amusement technically known as "slumming"—is best made at night, under the guidance of a detective, application for whose services may be made at Police Headquarters, which see. At the foot of Park Row is Chatham Square, nearly the entire space being occupied by the structure of the elevated railroad, for from this point the City Hall branch leaves the main line, and the Second avenue branch comes into it.

The Bowery, which begins here, is no longer what it used to be, but is still, especially at night, when the cheap stores, lodging houses and dime museums which line it on either side are brilliantly illuminated, a pretty lively thoroughfare. But the Bowery boy and his glory have departed from it, the change being chiefly due to the fact that the large section of the city lying to the east of it has of late years been taken up by Polish Jews. Near Canal street, on the west side of the Bowery, is the Thalia Theatre, once the principal German theatre in the city, but now occupied by a Hebrew company. It was once famous as the Bowery Theatre.

As several detours made later on in the course of describing the city from City Hall Park to Union Square will bring the stranger again to the Bowery, it will hardly be necessary for him to at present pursue its course further than Canal street. To see it thoroughly, however, he should visit it at night, when the east side population and the sailors' boarding-houses south of it pour out their denizens upon it. A curious feature of New York trade is witnessed in *Division Street*, which leaves the Bowery from Chatham Square. The south side of this street running from Chatham Square to Market street is taken up by an almost unbroken line of Hebrew millinery stores, the sidewalks being occupied by runners-in as importuning as those of Baxter street, but differing from the latter in that they are girls instead of men.

Five Points Mission.—Returning up Park Row to City Hall Park, there is an interesting detour down Centre street. Proceeding to Worth street, and turning into it to the east, the famous, or rather infamous, Five Points is reached, at one time the vilest spot in New York. An immense amount of noble mission work has redeemed it from the old reign of vice and debauchery, leaving, however, plenty of work for the missionaries in the neighboring streets. Dickens speaks of it in his "American Notes," saying: "Debauchery has made the very houses prematurely old. Where dogs would howl to lie, women, men and boys slink off the street." He speaks of hideous tenements "which take their name from robbery and murder," and dwells upon the coarse, bloated faces at the doors. In 1848 the city converted the little triangle formed by the meeting of Worth, Park and Baxter streets, which come together here in such a way as to form five corners, whence the name of the locality, into a kind of park, to which, as if in howling sarcasm, the name of Paradise Park was given. In 1850 the Ladies' Home Missionary Society of the Methodist Church was formed to redeem this spot, which one of the ladies connected with the mission described as a more vivid representation of hell than she had ever imagined. A room in one of the miserable buildings was hired, and an attempt was made to establish a Sunday school in it. The boys who were attracted to it by curiosity rather than by any desire to improve their condition, threw somersaults, fought and cursed; but instead of being disheartened, those in charge of the mission redoubled their efforts, and matters soon improved to such an extent that a day school was added. Temperance meetings also became a feature of the work, and as one of the best means of improving the condition of those living in this hopeless locality, employment was found for such as were willing to earn an honest living. By 1854 the mission had made such progress that its quarters became too cramped, and an effort was made to enlarge them. With this purpose in view, the society purchased what was known as the "Old Brewery," which was the special den of vice in this headquarters of iniquity. It had been erected as a brewery in 1792, and changed into a tenement in 1837. It was known as the "Den of Thieves," and the narrow alley which ran around it as "Murderers' Alley." Mysterious deaths, no doubt due to violence, occurred here, and the "sudden death of the Old Brewery" was an expression current in police circles. It was upon this infamous spot, 53 Park street, that the Ladies' Home Missionary Society erected the Five Points Mission House, which has done such noble work in redeeming this section of the city. Not only is religious instruction given here, but there is a day school with an important industrial department, including a cooking class and a fresh-air home. Deserving poor are supplied with clothing, food and medicines. Lodgings can also be had in the mission house, a feature of these being several suites of rooms for destitute families. A few statistics will give some idea of the work done annually by this mission. Relief was last year afforded to 632 entire families; to 6,160 individuals 26,791 articles of clothing were distributed; 91,400 dinners were served to pupils at the day school; 320 children were sent to the country during the summer, and a great amount of food was distributed to poor applicants.

House of Industry.—Opposite the Five Points Mission House, at 155 Worth street, the Five Points House of Industry, another admirable institution, was incorporated in 1854. It was originally an industrial school for adults, but is now for children only. It is a roomy, brick building, divided into a chapel, class-rooms, and living apartments. The babies' sleeping-room with about 40 tiny cribs and the babies' nursery adjoining, are always peculiarly interesting to visitors, as there are some 30 little ones usually at play here. The most touching sight, however, is to see them all taking their noon-day nap in their little cribs, or at their evening prayers, when they kneel down in their snow-white night-gowns and repeat, "Now I lay me down to sleep." On the top floor is a play-room, 90x45 feet, where the children romp and make merry during the play hours. The dormitories are also roomy and airy, and the beds are as clean and neat-looking as any to be found in the best-conducted households. The chapel is on the lowest floor, and is used not only for the inmates of the House of Industry and others from outside who choose to join in the services, but is also loaned to the City Mission for an Italian church. At one end is a raised platform with rows of tiny arm-chairs where the little folk are seated during service. The rest of the space is for adults, and a gallery is reserved for vistors. The best time to visit the institution is at the even-song service on Sunday, at 3 o'clock, after which the children go to supper, where they may also be seen. The manner in which they conduct themselves, and the general loveliness of the scene, are the most charming evidence of the admirable work done by the Five Points House of Industry. Connected with the institution is a homœpathic dispensary and hospital. The day school, under the supervision of the Board of Education, is graded up from a kindergarten. At the age of thirteen, the children leave the House of Industry, but the Trustees place them in homes both here and outside of the city, and seek in every way to keep track of any former inmate. Various industrial occupations are taught in the house, the course for boys including type-setting and carpentry. The work for last year is summed up as follows: 445,191 meals were given, the average attendance at school was 296, and the services of 40 teachers and employees were called into requisition. The pupils of the day school since its organization aggregate 41,010. The system of bringing pupils from outside into the house has worked very well, as it has prevented the stagnation of mind sometimes seen in institutions in which children are wholly isolated from outside influences.

THE TOMBS.—[Permit from the Commissioners of Public Charities and Correction, 66 Third avenue]. On the west side of Centre street, between Franklin and Leonard, stands the Tombs, the most famous of New York's city prisons. The granite structure is a fine example of Egyptian architecture, and is fittingly dark, gloomy and forbidding looking. No part of New York's topography has been so changed by the growth of the city as the site upon which the Tombs stands. Here was the old Collect or fresh water pond, a lovely sheet of water, the resort of anglers in summer, and of skaters in winter. In places the pond was 60 feet deep, and it had the common reputation of being bottomless. On an island in it, stood the gibbet upon which twenty negroes were hung during the negro riots (p. 20). On the waters of the Collect John Fitch conducted, in the summer of 1790, the first trial of the first steamboat with a screw propeller. The pond's outlet was along the present line of Canal street, and when, in 1809, Canal street was laid out and other improvements were made in this vicinity, the Collect was filled in, and the pretty sheet of water, which had been for so many years the delight of pleasure-seekers, disappeared from the topography of the city. The Tombs has been an abode of woe for nearly fifty years. It is not only a jail, but in its various departments exhibits the machinery of the criminal law in full operation. A broad flight of steps leads from Centre street to a hall into which the Tombs Police Court and the Court of Special Sessions open. In the Tombs Police Court, which is to the right, justice is meted out to some 20,000 people a year. On the opposite side of the hall is the Court of Special Sessions, which is connected by a bridge known as the Bridge of Sighs, with the prison. Across it prisoners are led after conviction. The prison itself is entered from Franklin street. In addition to the old granite building, two prison buildings of yellow brick have been erected in the yards. These are known as the new prisons. The cells are in tiers. If a condemned murderer is awaiting execution, and the day of execution is so near that the "death watch" has been set upon him, the visitor will see the murderer's cage, which is put up in whichever of the corridors happens to be most convenient at the time. In it the condemned are kept ten days before execution. It is made of wire netting, and usually occupies half the length of the corridor. It also has a wire ceiling to prevent any one in the cells above throwing any weapon, rope or poison to the condemned, by which he might be able to commit suicide. The Tombs is saddest during visitors' hours (10 A. M. to 2 P. M.), when mothers, sisters, wives, sweethearts and others interested in the prisoners hold whispered conversations with them through the bars of their cells, many of the women breaking down when the hour for parting comes. In the keeper's apartments is a cabinet of murderers' weapons, each of the implements there having a history.

CHAPTER VII.

FROM CITY HALL PARK TO MADISON SQUARE.

Broadway and the streets running into it are, from City Hall Park to the vicinity of Bleecker street, given over to the wholesale dry goods district. While the crowd and turmoil, the blockades of vehicles, the shouts of drivers, and the struggle of pedestrians at the crossings are interesting, there is no feature of special importance to call for particular mention.

Canal street (p. 148) is one of the main arteries of commerce from the Bowery and Broadway to the North river water front.

GRAND STREET.—An interesting detour from Broadway may be made at Grand street, which runs from Corlears Hook on the East river to Canal street, crossing it and entering Desbrosses street, which continues on to the North river. At Grand and Elm streets the *Board of Education* has its offices. The whole number of public schools in New York last year was 302. Grammar schools for males, 46; for females, 48; for both sexes, 13. Primary departments of grammar schools, 80; primary schools, 38; evening schools, 28; nautical school, 1; corporate schools under supervision of the Board, 48; number of teachers employed, 4,206; number of pupils, 307,108; total expenditures, $5,600,655.34. The most interesting portion of Grand street lies east of the Bowery, for here Grand street becomes the great retail shopping district for a densely populated section of the city. The Polish Jews throng this part of the city, and on Friday afternoons hold an open air market in Hester street one block below Grand, the vendors being most numerous in the neighborhood of Ludlow street. This is a picturesque feature of life in New York. In Ludlow street, just north of Grand, is Ludlow Street Jail, and back of it, on Essex street, the Essex Market Police Court. In Ludlow Street Jail prisoners arrested in civil suits or on process of the Federal Courts are held. It is the Elba of "Napoleons of Finance," who are often finally transported from here to the St. Helena of Sing Sing. Ludlow Street Jail is a county jail and permission to visit it must be obtained at the Sheriff's office, New Court House, City Hall Park (p. 136). On a little open space, known as Oriental Park, stands the famous printing press manufacturing establishment of R. Hoe & Co.

St. Augustine Chapel.—Returning to Broadway, and continuing along its course, a detour through East Houston street brings the visitor to St. Augustine Chapel, on the south side of this street, a few steps east of the Bowery. The purpose of this, the only Protestant Episcopal church, and one of very few churches in this neighborhood, is to provide means of worship in a handsome and comfortable structure to poor people, and also to instruct children. The chapel and mission house form a fine Gothic structure. On Sundays, holy days, and on nights when services are held, the cross on the spire is illuminated, and its gleam has cheered many a poor wanderer through a stormy night. The church is as handsomely decorated as if it stood in one of the wealthiest sections of the city, and is most commodious and cheerful. This doubtless is an important factor in its success as a mission station. There is a vista of 214 feet from the gate at the main entrance through a long vestibule to the stained chancel windows, whose cheerful colors seem a standing invitation to enter and be comforted. The chapel bell was cast in 1700, and given to Trinity by the Bishop of London in 1704. Beneath the chapel are Sunday-school class-rooms, which, with the other class-rooms in the mission house, will accommodate 1,600 scholars. A day school, an industrial school for boys and girls from a kindergarten upward, is in session here during the week, and the building is always open to visitors during the day.

In the building on the northwest corner of Bond street and the Bowery the *Commissioners of Excise* have their office. According to the last annual report of the Excise Board the total number of licensed drinking places in the city, other than hotels, restaurants and steamboats, was 6,742. Receipts from liquor licenses amounted to $1,442,740; distributed, after the expenses of the Excise Board had been deducted, among various reformatory and benevolent institutions. At the southwest corner of Houston and Mulberry streets is the large building occupied by *Puck*, and at No. 300 Mulberry street between Houston and Bleecker is the building occupied by the Police Department, and by the Board of Health. It is commonly known as Police Headquarters or the Police Central Office.

Police Headquarters.—The police force of New York City numbers 3,421, including one Superintendent, four Inspectors, each of them in charge of a certain district, 36 captains, 158 sergeants, 40 detective-sergeants, 163 roundsmen, whose duty is to see that patrolmen are on their beat, and 2,922 patrolmen, distributed in thirty-five police precincts and detailed for duty in the Police Courts, the Sanitary Company and the Tenement House Squad. The Nineteenth precinct, in what is known as the "Tenderloin District," in the heart of the city, into which large hotels, restaurants, theatres, gambling-houses and varied resorts are crowded, has the largest force, a total of 131. There is one policeman to about each 550 of the population of the city, as compared with one policeman to every 343 in the Metropolitan district of London, and one to every 100 in the ancient city of London.

The total annual cost of maintaining the New York police force is about $4,425,000. The first public watchmen were appointed in 1693, the ordinance stating that each watchman should be clothed in a "coat of ye citty livery, with a badge of ye citty arms, shoes and stockings." The entire force is now under the supervision of a Board of Police Commissioners, consisting of four members, one of whom is the president of the Board. To facilitate operations, there is a system of telephone and telegraph communication between Police Headquarters and all stations; and at Headquarters and each station are patrol wagons for the quick transportation of large bodies of the force. The "Broadway Squad," a body of policemen of conspicuous stature and strength, is charged with preventing blockades, escorting passengers, especially nervous females, across the street, and maintaining order on the crowded portions of Broadway below Fourteenth street. According to the last annual report the number of arrests made during the year was 82,200, of which 19,926 were females; 2,968 lost children were taken care of by the Police Matron at Headquarters (one of the most interesting departments to visitors), and all but 23 restored to parents or guardians; property to the value of $947,145.26 passed through the Property Clerk's office or was delivered at various precincts. Within the past ten years 745,946 arrests have been made. A record of cheap lodging houses and dormitories is also kept. Of these "hot-beds of vice" there are in the city 270, with 13,648 rooms, which received during the past year 4,974,-025 lodgers. The Detective Bureau, the most famous branch of the New York police force, attained its present proficiency under Superintendent Thomas Byrnes.

An interesting feature of Police Headquarters is a museum of criminal implements and the Rogues' Gallery, a cabinet of photographs of noted criminals, many of whom are fine-looking men and women, and the last persons in the world one would suspect of any crime. The contents of the museum include burglars' outfits, murderous instruments, each with a history and a victim; and, most ghastly of all, the nooses with which certain murderers have been hung, the black caps which were drawn over their faces, and the cords with which their hands and feet were bound before they were swung off.

Board of Health.—The Board of Health consists of a President, a Commissioner of Health, the Health Officer of the Port, the President of the Board of Police. According to the last annual report 363,875 inspections, including 10,987 tenement houses, were made by the Sanitary Bureau. The corps inspecting food and chemicals destroyed 1,495,630 pounds of fruit and vegetables; 1,763,283 pounds of meat and fish. The disinfecting corps fumigated 26,245 rooms and disinfected 83,452. The summer corps of physicians visited 264,520 families.

The Board of Health's last annual vital statistics show 14,400 marriages, 40,476 births, and 39,583 deaths.

One block above Houston street, at the northeast corner of Bleecker and Broadway, is the large building of the Manhattan Savings Institution, and next to it is a small classic building occupied by the Bleecker Street Bank for Savings, the oldest savings bank in the city. With Bond street, which runs into Broadway from the west one block above Bleecker street, the publishers', and more especially the retail booksellers' district, may be said to begin (p. 111). On the south side of Bond street, near Broadway, is the publishing firm of D. Appleton & Co.; Charles Scribner's Sons, who are also publishers of *Scribner's Magazine*, are at 745 and 747 Broadway, opposite Astor Place; and on Lafayette Place, which runs parallel with Broadway to Astor Place, are a number of publishing firms and the Astor Library, probably the best and most utilized reference library in the city, while the Mercantile Library building is a large structure on Astor Place.

St. Joseph's Home.—On the northeast corner of Great Jones street and Lafayette Place is St. Joseph's Home, under the Mission of the Immaculate Virgin for the Protection of Homeless and Destitute Children, a great Roman Catholic charity. It started in small quarters in Warren street in 1876, but by 1880 had grown into an institution which required the present ten-story building for the prosecution of its work. The interior management of the Mission House is under the care of the Sisters of St. Francis. There are, among the children, two divisions, having distinct dining-rooms and dormitories. Those in the first division, destitute, homeless boys, who await the time when sufficiently strong and possessed of a good rudimentary and industrial education they may enter some trade, store or office in which the Mission secures them work, reside in the home. The second division is for working boys who pay whatever they can for the excellent accommodations afforded them, and are apt, thanks to this Mission, to become self-supporting, honest and industrious citizens. There are about 1,800 children in the Home. Connected with the institution is Mount Loretto, a fine stretch of fertile farm land with a number of buildings upon it, situated on the south shore of Staten Island.

At the northeast corner of Lafayette Place and Fourth street is the large building of the De Vinne Press, and a few doors above on the same side of the street, in a private house, the old Middle Dutch Reformed Church (p. 124). At No. 27 on the opposite side is the Episcopal Diocesan House.

Astor Library.—On the east side of Lafayette Place, not far from the corner of Astor Place, in a large building of brown stone and brick is the Astor Library. It was originally endowed by John Jacob Astor, who died in 1848, leaving $400,000 for the library. His son, William B. Astor, and his grandson, John Jacob Astor, added respectively $550,000 and $700,000 to this endowment. The library, incorporated January 1, 1849, opened at 32 Bond street, with 20,000 volumes. The board of trustees included Washington Irving, as president, and J. G. Cogswell, as librarian. In 1854, the central portion of the present structure was opened. A wing was added in 1859, and another in 1881. Open, except Sundays and legal holidays, 9 A. M. to 5 P. M., closing, however, at 4.30 P. M. and 4 P. M. in winter.

The Astor Library is intended to be, above all, a reference library for students. It is not a circulating library. The entrance leads into a vestibule decorated in Pompeiian style, and containing twenty-four classic busts of Greeks and Romans. A flight of stairs rises to the floor above, where the librarian's assistants receive applications for and hand out books. Near this are the tables with catalogues, and also a cabinet containing a card catalogue of accessions since 1880. On this floor are, besides the distributing desks, the North and South Reading Rooms, surrounded by 90 alcoves, four stories in height, for the shelving of books, their capacity being 315,000 volumes. On the floor below 350,000 additional volumes can be placed. At the east end of the middle hall is a bust of the library's founder, John Jacob Astor, and at the west end one of Dr. Cogswell. A bust of Washington Irving is conspicuous in the south hall. Those desiring to prosecute special studies are allowed, on bringing a letter of introduction from some responsible person known to the librarian, to have access to the alcoves where they can make their notes or write.

Statistics.—There are now in the library, including pamphlets, about 268,000 volumes, and the library's estate is estimated at about $2,000,000. The whole number of readers for the past year was 64,210, of whom 10,226 were alcove readers. In the department of Science and Art 72,790 volumes were in use, and in the department of History and Literature 97,757, making a total for both departments of 170,547. In the former department the branch most consulted was Chemistry and Physics, 8,339 volumes; and the least consulted Domestic Economy, only 249 volumes. This last figure is an apt commentary on certain aspects of American life. It may be noted that 1,635 volumes on Music were in use, the library being especially rich in this department, containing the full orchestral scores of Wagner's operas and music dramas. In the department of History and Literature the branch of American History was most largely in use, showing a total of 17,916 volumes. British Literature was next with 17,629, and then American Literature with 9,162 volumes. Dutch Literature was last with only 11 volumes. It may be noted that in the branch of Heraldry and Genealogy there were 3,653 volumes used, showing an active hunt for ancestors on the part of some New York families.

Rare Books and Manuscripts.—The library has an interesting collection of rare books and manuscripts, the earliest date (870 A.D.) being an illuminated manuscript on vellum entitled "Evangelistarium, sive Lectiones ex Evangelis." The finest is, however, a superb manuscript of the seventeenth century on vellum parchment, of great size and beauty, and bound in purple morocco with gilt mountings. It is an "Antiphonale," containing 228 pages of the Antiphonal music in use in the Roman Catholic church service, 272 small and 53 large miniatures in the highest style of French art, the larger paintings representing scenes from the Bible, some of the work being authoritatively attributed to Lebrun.

The superb binding is ornamented with a fleur-de-lis, and with the cipher of Charles X, at whose coronation it was designed to be used. Another fine work in the collection is entitled "Graduale de Tempore Omnius Anni," 1494. It is finely illuminated on vellum with huge Gothic letters and square musical notes, and miniatures of sacred subjects. To judge by the arms and portraits of nobles which fill the borders, it was probably executed by order of the princes assisting at the coronation of Maximillian as King of the Romans in 1486. In the collection are also one of six copies of the first letter of Columbus, describing his discovery of a new world; the first edition of the Bible printed with a date, "Biblia Sacra Latina, 1462," an original copy of the Papal Bull against Luther, and three folio editions of Shakespeare (first, second and fourth), which are enough in themselves to attract many visitors. Their dates are respectively 1623, 1632 and 1685. Among letters and autographs are specimens from Franklin, Jefferson, Hamilton, Frederick the Great, Humboldt, Beethoven, Liszt, Cuvier, and Talma. Most of these rare works and autographs are arranged in cabinets and glass show-cases around the stairway, and each bears a card containing a full title and additional descriptive matter; but the rarest objects in the collections are shown only on application. (See also Lenox Library.)

Cooper Union.—At the junction of Third and Fourth avenues, fronting on Astor Place, is the brown stone building of the famous Cooper Union, founded by Peter Cooper, the American philanthropist.

The corner-stone of the Union was laid in 1854, and in 1859 Cooper deeded the property to six trustees to carry out the purposes which he had in view. It has been estimated that since the Union was opened 30,000 pupils have attended the classes alone, not counting the lectures which have an average attendance of 200, nor the reading-room and library, which are used by from 1,400 to 1,500 readers a day, and on holidays, such as Thanksgiving, by some 2,300.

Schools.—In the free night school of Science and Art (7:25–9:30 P.M.) a regular collegiate mathematical course can be had. Women are admitted to the Scientific but not to the Art department, except the class in perspective drawing, there being a free art school for woman during the day.

The *Woman's Art School* (9 A. M. to 1 P. M.) embraces a full theoretical and practical course in art. Many pupils of this school have secured situations as drawing teachers. Patterns designed by members of the class in design are bought by leading manufacturers in this country and woven and printed in fabrics, so that the taste and skill of the pupils in this department are displayed in dry goods stores in New York and other cities. The amount earned by the pupils of the term of 1889-90, and by the previous year's graduates is estimated at $22,494.92. There are also free day schools in stenography and type-writing and in telegraphy for women. Saturday nights free lectures are delivered in the great hall of the building in the basement, and there are lectures supplemental to the various courses.

The *Free Reading-Room* of the Cooper Union, 125x80 feet, with deep alcoves at the sides, is one of the largest and best equipped in the country. The chief and most useful resources of the frequenters of this reading-room are in the magazines and newspapers. Last year 218,986 books were drawn, of which 72,508 were in fiction. The attendance at the various departments in 1890, including 560,429, at the Free Reading-Room, reached a total of 564,019—certainly a magnificent showing, especially as the large attendance at the various lectures has not been taken into consideration.

Bible House.—The large brick building occupying the entire block bounded by Third and Fourth avenues, Eighth and Ninth streets, and just north of the Cooper Union, is the Bible House, in which the American Bible Society has had since 1853 its offices, composing and printing establishment and bindery, employing 500 hands in the work of printing the Bible in English and many foreign languages.

Instituted in 1816, the Society has since then distributed 52,736,075 Bibles.

The Society carries on its work by auxiliary branches, and by colporteurs. Bibles and other publications are sold at cost price to auxiliary societies for distribution. The total cash receipts for general purposes during the year ending March 31, 1889, were $597,693.05. In addition to this the sum of $43,316.05 was received and permanently invested. The disbursements for general purposes amounted to $529,955.74. The Society publishes Bibles and portions of the Bible in many foreign languages, including, besides those of Europe, Hebrew, Arabic, Chinese, Japanese, Zulu, Ponga, various Indian tongues, Hawaiian and Syriac, and volumes in raised letters for the blind. Among large editions of the Scriptures that have been printed in other lands at the Society's expense may be specified 32,700 volumes in Constantinople, 1,275 in Beyroot, 33,519 in Japan, and 223,100 in China. From its organization, the chief reliance of the American Bible Society, both for the circulation of Bibles and the subscription of funds, has been its numerous auxiliary societies throughout the United States. Recently the work of a fourth general re-supply of the United States has been undertaken. Over 6,300,000 families were visited; 8,146,828 copies of the Bible in 27 different languages being distributed. Some of the more important in foreign languages were as follows: German, 472,920; Swedish, 220,277; Norwegian and Danish, 153,707; Italian, 57,883; Welsh, 29,287; Finnish, 2,314; Polish, 2,317; Hungarian, 2,543; Bohemian, 9,924; Chinese, 7,243. One of the Society's important auxilliaries, The New York Bible Society, office at the Bible House, makes a specialty of distributing Bibles among immigrants and seamen. It keeps an agent at the immigrant landing office, where some 58,000 volumes are annually distributed, and has an agent working constantly along the water front of the city who, during the year last reported, visited 1,842 vessels, distributing 6,020 volumes.

In the Manager's room is the main part of the Society's valuable and unique collection of ancient and modern versions of the Holy Scriptures, including the two editions of 1611, the Oxford reprint of 1833, the the Cambridge Paragraph Bible, the Caxton Memorial Bible, the first English Bible printed in the United States, the Psalterium Americanum of 1718, the "Vinegar Bible" (Vinegar for Vineyard in headline of Luke xx), the "Breeches Bible" ("breeches" used in Gen. iii, 7), and the earlier editions of the Rheimish Testament and the Douay Bible. It is especially rich in works relating to the history of the English Bible and the efforts which have been made during two centuries to amend and improve it, and among its treasures are the archives of the American revisers and the collection of books made for their use. Among the few manuscripts owned by the Society is a Hebrew roll containing a portion of the Pentateuch, brought from China, where it is supposed to have been in use for several centuries.

On Stuyvesant Place, which runs into Astor Place and Third avenue, stands *St. Mark's Protestant Episcopal Church*, erected as a private chapel by old Governor Stuyvesant (p. 19), and opened for worship as a public church in 1779. In the graveyard in which the venerable structure stands, Stuyvesant is buried, the stone marking the site where he lies being in the east wall of the church. It was from this graveyard that the body of A. T. Stewart was stolen (p. 164).

NEW YORK HISTORICAL SOCIETY, No. 170 Second Avenue.—Open daily, except Sunday and in August, 9 A. M. to 6 P. M. Admission on presentation of a card from a member. The New York Historical Society was founded in 1804, and at once took measures to secure books, manuscripts, statistics, newspapers, pictures, antiquities, medals, coins, and specimens of natural history relating to the United States, thus instituting in a comprehensive manner a library and museum of such objects, always, however, keeping as its main purpose the collection and preservation of material relating to the history of New York. As a result it has a library containing some 75,000 volumes of books, and 2,700 bound volumes of newspapers issued in America from 1704 to the present time; a large collection of manuscripts, public and private documents from the earliest colonial period to the Civil War, and it is exceptionally strong in works relating to American history and genealogy. Here the American in search of a family tree can find a whole forest and select as fine and varied a line of ancestors as that purchased by *Major-General Stanley* in the "Pirates of Penzance." The Society also has a large permanent picture gallery, and while many of the paintings are portraits which have only local interest, many others are valuable works of art. It owns the Abbott collection of Egyptian antiquities, well-known to Egyptologists through the studies of distinguished scholars, and the Lenox collection of Assyrian sculptures, consisting of thirteen large marble slabs excavated by Layard from the ruins of Nineveh. These are in the basement of the building. The library, art, and Egyptian galleries are on the floors above, the entrance to the library being on the second floor.

The walls of the stairway are lined with paintings which have not found accommodation in the gallery proper, and on the landing of the first story at the entrance to the library is a nude, finely modeled figure of an Indian, a replica by Thomas Crawford from his "Progress of Civilization in America," a group executed by order of the National Government for the Capitol at Washington. The art gallery and the collection of Egyptian antiquities are reached from the library. A catalogue is loaned by the librarian.

Egyptian Antiquities.—Conspicuous in the Abbott collection of Egyptian antiquities are: 1—A colossal head in sandstone, the face painted red, being a portion of a statue of Thothmes III, who, according to Sir Gardner Wilkinson, was the Pharaoh of the Exodus, 1491 B.C. This Pharaoh wears the white crown of Upper Egypt, with the sacred serpent, the emblem of royalty, in front. 43—A small coffin in unbaked clay. This illustrates a curious usage among the Egyptians. At the entertainments of the rich just as the company was about to rise from the repast, a small coffin was carried round containing a perfect representation of a dead body, the bearer exclaiming: "Cast your eyes on this figure. After death, you, yourself, will resemble it. Drink then, and be happy!" 44, 45, and 46 are bricks without straw, possibly made by the children of Israel. 140—

11

Three wooden cats with glass eyes, from the cat tombs of Sakkaron. One has its face gilded and contains the mummy of a cat. 152—Three large mummies of the Sacred Bull, Apis, found in the Tombs of Dashour. These are perhaps the most valuable exhibits in the collection, as these mummies are very rare. It is said no other museum possesses a specimen. On the back of the middle bull may be seen a net of rope used for the purpose of carrying objects between two persons, a stick being passed under the two pieces of wood, and supported on the shoulders of the carriers, together with a large rope bag found in the pit with the bulls, and supposed to have been used by their attendants to carry the food for the sacred animals. Two skulls of the sacred bull are found in the same case. 234—Papyrus in the Hieratic character 36 feet long, and in such perfect preservation that it does not require to be stretched on paper. 460—A beautifully executed spoon in hard wood, representing a Nubian woman swimming, sustaining in her extended arms a duck or goose which is hollowed out and forms the bowl of the spoon. 554—An iron helmet with a neck-guard in chain armor, found at Thebes, with the fragment of a breastplate (575) made of pieces of iron in the form of scales, one of which is the cartouche of the Egyptian king Shishak, who invaded Jerusalem 971 years B.C. 743—A caricature painted on a fragment of limestone, representing a lion seated on a throne as a king, and a fox as high priest making an offering of a plucked goose and a feather fan. 766—A funereal papyrus 22 feet long, exquisitely written in very small hieroglyphics and finely illuminated, being perfect both at the commencement and the end, the illustrations representing the most remarkable events in the life of the deceased. 1,050—A gold signet ring bearing the name of Shoofoo, the Suphis of the Greeks, 2,325 B.C., a fine piece of antique gold weighing nearly three sovereigns; hieroglyphic details minutely engraved and beautifully executed. Found in a tomb at Ghizeh. 1,052—Two ear-rings and a necklace found in a jar at Dendera. They are made of gold leaf, have three pendants of lapis-lazuli, and two beads of blue glass attached to the centre, where there is also an oval amethyst bead capped at each end with gold. The name of Menes, the first Pharaoh of Egypt, who reigned 2,750 B.C., is stamped upon the ear-rings, and upon eight oval plates of the necklace.

Picture Gallery.—The picture gallery embraces the entire collection of the old New York Gallery of Fine Arts, which contains the Luman Reed collection. In 1867 the Bryan Gallery of Christian Art, and in 1882 the Dürr collection were donated to the Society. From 1 to 175, the paintings in the gallery are chiefly by early American artists, representing John Trumbull, C. W. Peale, Rembrandt Peale, Benjamin West, Stuart, A. B. Durand, Elliott, Jarvis, Vanderlyn, Mount, Morse, Inman, Cole. 175—*Gainsborough,* Landscape. Names of old Italian masters are found in the Bryan collection which runs from 176–556. Several, however, are but indifferently authenticated. 178—*Guido of Sienna,* "Virgin and Child with Four Saints." From the collection of Artaud de Montor. 183—*Simone Memmi,* "The Last Judgment." This is the picture of which Michaels wrote a graphic description in the *Gazette de France.* 197—*Perugino,* "Adoration of the Infant Christ." 198—*Leonardo di Vinci,* "St. John Weeping." 200—*Raphael,* "Birth and Resurrection of Christ." The authenticity of this and the last-named picture rests entirely upon critical opinion. 208—*Titian,* "The Repose in Egypt." The authenticity of this replica is argued from the absence of some figures in the background and the introduction of a rivulet in the foreground, and a butterfly upon a flower in the right corner, it being presumed that a copyist would have made an exact copy. 214—*Paul Veronese,* "Abraham Discarding Hagar and Ishmael." 220—*Andrea Montegna,* "The Crucifixion." The Jewish type is preserved in the features of many of the figures, and in this crowded canvas no two pieces of offensive or defensive armor are alike, which is worthy of particular remark, as Squarcioni, the master of Montegna, had the largest and most varied collection of ancient arms which existed in his day. 222—*Correggio,* "The Virgin and Child, Mary Magdalene and St. Jerome." The original is at Parma. The authenticity of this replica is argued from differences in minor points, as the work of a copyist would probably have reproduced the original with all possible fidelity. 232—*Domenichino,*

"St. Paul borne to Heaven by Angels." 242—*Salvator Rosa*, "Landscape," with historical figures.

Among examples of the *Dutch School* are: 259—*Jan Beerestraten*, "Winter Scene," a fine example of this master. 289—*Douw*, "The Artist in his Studio." 291—*Jan van Eyck*, "The Crucifixion." 328—Portrait signed with R. (Rembrandt). 334–338—*Rubens*, the authenticity of 337 has been denied by critics of authority. 343 and 344—*Jacob Ruysdael*. 349—*Jan Steen*, family scene. 351—*David Teniers, the younger*, "Incantation Scene."

Early German: 375—*Dürer*, "St. George and the Dragon." 377 and 378—*Holbein*.

Spanish School: 383-386—*Velasquez*. 387-390—*Murillo*.

French School: 398-402—*Nicholas Poussin*. 403-405—*Guaspare Poussin*. 421-423—*Antoine Watteau*. 436-441—*Greuze*. 444 and 445—*Vernet*. 567-574 are Indian portraits by St. Memin, and 578-591 is a collection of paintings of the Incas of Peru.

The Dürr collection embraces Nos. 634-812. 634 and 635—*Murillo*. 643—Attributed to *Titian*, "Martyrdom of St. Lawrence," signed. Possibly the first of three pictures on this subject which Titian painted. 644—Attributed to *Titian*, "Aretino the Poet." This picture was found in the wagon of a vivandiere named Machau, who was killed at the battle of Marengo, and finally passed into the private cabinet of Denon, director of the Musée Napoléon. There are many examples of the Dutch school in the Dürr collection, among them, 736—"Combat of Cavalry," attributed to Rembrandt.

Returning to Broadway and continuing up that thoroughfare the first structure of interest is the large iron building bounded by Ninth and Tenth streets, Broadway and Fourth avenue, and occupied by the dry goods house of E. J. Denning & Co., successors to A. T. Stewart, the famous "merchant prince," and the pioneer among the great retail dry goods dealers of the city. Alexander T. Stewart was born in Lisburn, near Belfast, Ireland, on the 20th of October, 1823, died in New York April 10, 1876. Having studied for the ministry he came to New York in 1823, where he taught school for a short time, soon afterwards returning to Ireland to secure the moderate fortune left him by his father. He invested it in a stock of Belfast laces and linens which he brought with him to this country, opening in 1825 a store at 273 Broadway. The venture was successful and his business grew to extraordinary dimensions. He erected the store at Ninth and Tenth streets and Broadway in 1862. His fine marble residence on the northwest corner of Thirty-fourth street and Fifth avenue, now occupied by the Manhattan Club, was for many years the most conspicuous private house in the United States. Where Broadway verges toward the northwest is Grace Church.

GRACE CHURCH.—Open daily (9 A. M. to 5 P. M.). Hardly any building in the city occupies so advantageous a position from an architectural point of view, for it faces obliquely down Broadway, effectively ending off the vista from down town. The first Grace Church was built in 1755, on Broadway near Trinity Church; the present in 1846. It is a fine example of ornamental Gothic. The parsonage and the structure joining it to the church, known as Grace House, are in the same style. In front of the parsonage is a pretty garden, with well-kept lawn, flower-beds and shrubbery, the whole forming a most picturesque break in the line of business houses. All the windows of the church are stained-glass memorials. The large chancel window illustrates in 15 separate pictures the Te Deum. In the left transept window are the Patriarchs and Prophets, in the right the Saints. Connected with the church is a pretty little chantry, in which services are held daily, at 4.30 P. M. The congregation is very wealthy and fashionable, and there is an idea prevalent that it is a self-satisfied collection of worshipers, partaking of religious stimulants in commodious and elegant quarters, and not caring very much what becomes of the souls of the rest of the world. As a matter of fact, however, Grace Church does a vast amount of arduous mission work, having a chapel on East Fourteenth street, between Third and Fourth avenues, a mission house at 540 and 542 East Thirteenth street, a summer home at Far Rockaway, a library and reading room in Grace House, on the church premises, and a Memorial House at 96 Fourth avenue, where an immense amount of industrial and mission work is accomplished. A pretty feature of this is a day nursery where working women may leave their children for the day, the little ones being entertained and fed by the good people of Grace Church at a charge of only five cents to the mothers.

UNION SQUARE.—Broadway is intercepted at Fourteenth street by Union Square, one of the prettiest public parks in the city, covering about 3½ acres, and extending from Fourteenth to Seventeenth street, and from Broadway to Fourth avenue. It is laid out in lawns, with shrubs, shade-trees and flowers. In the center is a pretty fountain with water plants, and on the east side, near Sixteenth street, a drinking fountain. At the north end of the Square is a broad space for parades and reviews. A cottage within the park faces this plaza and has a balcony for reviewing officers, and along the southern end of the plaza in front of the cottage is a long row of ornamental colored lamps. The Square is illuminated at night by a cluster of brilliant electric lights on a tall pole near the center of the park.

There are three statues on Union Square: In the south-east quarter a bronze equestrian statue of Washington of heroic size, by H. K. Browne, one of the finest monuments in the city; opposite Broadway, at the southern end of the park, Bartholdi's graceful statue of Lafayette, erected in 1876 by French residents of the city "In remembrance of sympathy, 1870–1871"; in the southwest quarter a bronze statue of Lincoln, by H. K. Browne.

The Square is surrounded by important business buildings. The most attractive is that occupied by Tiffany & Co., the famous gold and silversmiths, on the southwest corner of Fifteenth street, a visit to which should be made, as its contents form a veritable museum of jewelry and allied arts. Between the Livingston Building and Tiffany's is Brentano's, a noted periodical and book store. The music trade also has its head-quarters at and near Union Square. The most conspicuous building on the northern side of the Square is that partly occupied by the Century Company, which publishes the *Century* magazine and *St. Nicholas.* Adjoining this on the corner of Fourth Avenue is the

Everett House. Fourteenth street to the west is given up to a great variety of retail business, including several piano warerooms, while to the east of Union Square on the same thoroughfare are numerous concert halls and restaurants, Steinway Hall, the headquarters of the piano manufacturing house of Steinway, and on the corner of Irving Place and Fourteenth street the old Academy of Music, once famous as the home of Italian opera, and in days gone by graced by the most fashionable audiences of the city, but now given over to theatrical purposes of a different order. Next to it on the east is Tammany Hall, the headquarters of the famous local Democratic organization. The most noted German theatre in the city, Amberg's, stands at the corner of Irving Place and Fifteenth street. Irving Place ends at Twenty-first street with Gramercy Park. This comprises about an acre and a half, but is not open to the general public, being reserved for those living in the neighborhood. At Sixteenth street and Stuyvesant Square is St. George's P. E. Church (open all day) and its fine parochial house, the headquarters of a vast amount of mission work.

Young Women's Christian Association.— On Fifteenth street, between Union Square and Fifth avenue, is the fine building of the Young Women's Christian Association, an organization which accomplishes an immense amount of good in its special field of work. This was founded in 1870 and incorporated in 1873, and its advantages are offered more especially to those young women who are dependent upon their own efforts for support. There is a circulating library of some fifteen thousand volumes of miscellaneous reading matter, open daily from 9 A. M. to 5 P. M. and from 7 to 9 P. M; a reading-room open daily during the same hours; an employment bureau open from 9 A. M. to 5 P. M.. which secures employment for girls with the exception of domestic service; a boarding house directory, open from 10 A. M. to 1 P. M. and from 7 to 9 P. M., which directs applicants to boarding places, more particularly with private families, thus securing for them as near an approach to home surroundings as possible. Concerts and lectures are also given during the winter and spring, and there is Bible instruction every Sunday on the premises. Admission to the lectures is by ticket obtained on personal application at the building. The support of the association is by voluntary contributions.

On the south side of Sixteenth street, between Union Square and Fifth avenue, is the free circulating library and reading-room of the General Society of Mechanics and Tradesmen, an institution generally known as the *Apprentices' Library*, free to all persons presenting a certificate approved by a member of the society, which has meeting rooms on the second floor. Connected with the society is a free school of mechanical and free-hand drawing, which is conducted in the basement. On this same block, and adjoining the Apprentices' Library, is the etching and engraving store of F. Keppel & Co. Similar establishments in this neighborhood are Klackner's on the north side of Seventeenth street, between Union Square and Broadway, and Wunderlich's on the east side of Broadway, between Seventeenth and Eighteenth streets. On the same block, but on the west side of the street, is "Huyler's," a noted candy store.

Broadway, between Union Square and Twenty-third street, is one of the great shopping districts of the city, and all the establishments mentioned below are worth visiting, as business is carried on there on a colossal scale. On the block between Eighteenth and Nineteenth streets are, at 877, A. A. Vantine & Co., whose store is a museum of oriental goods; and, adjoining this, the dry goods store of Arnold, Constable & Co. Opposite this is the great carpet warehouse of W. & J. Sloane, filled with articles of domestic and foreign manufacture from the cheapest priced to the most costly. Between Nineteenth and Twentieth streets are, on the west side, the Gorham Mfg. Co., silversmiths, and the dry goods house of Lord & Taylor. The northeast corner of Broadway and Nineteenth street, which is not yet occupied by a business building, and affords the curious sight of a private residence in spacious grounds in the line of the rush and turmoil of traffic, belongs to the Goelet estate, and will doubtless in time be given over to commerce. On the northwest corner of Twenty-first street is the china store of Davis, Collamore & Co. At Twenty-third street Broadway crosses Madison Square.

CHAPTER VIII.

FIFTH AVENUE.

FROM WASHINGTON SQUARE TO CENTRAL PARK.

In order to gain a comprehensive idea of Fifth avenue, which Broadway crosses at Madison Square, it is necessary to proceed down "the Avenue" to its beginning at Washington Square.

WASHINGTON SQUARE.—Washington Square, originally a Potter's Field, is a public square of about nine acres, bounded on the north by Waverley Place, on the south by West Fourth street, on the east by University Place, and on the west by Macdougal street. Washington Square separates the most fashionable from one of the least fashionable quarters of the city; though one does not now, as formerly, in crossing Washington Square, pass from the abode of wealth to the abode of poverty and vice, for the southerly neighborhood has been greatly improved. It still harbors a large colored population and the "French quarter."

The most noteworthy building on the south side of Washington Square, is the Adoniram Judson Memorial Church and Mission, built in memory of the well-known Baptist missionary to Burmah. It stands on the corner of Thompson street. On the east side, between Washington Place and Waverley Place, is the castle-like structure of the University of the City of New York.

NEW YORK UNIVERSITY.—This institution of learning originated in the action of a number of citizens who met December 6, 1829, and considered the establishment of an university, the plan being to add a graduate course to the regular college curriculum. Instruction began in 1832. In 1841 a Medical School was added, and in 1859 a Law School. In 1886 the graduate division of the School of Arts and Sciences was greatly extended, so that the institution is now really deserving of the name University. The School of Arts and Sciences and the Law School occupy the building on Washington Square, the erection of which was begun in 1832. It contains, besides the regular recitation rooms and laboratories, the council-room, and an excellent law library. Among the distinguished members of the faculty have been Prof. Samuel F. B. Morse, who in a room in the south tower carried on experiments which resulted in the invention of the telegraph, and Prof. John W. Draper's experiments in photography were carried on in what is now the library.

The Medical School occupies a building on East Twenty-sixth street, between First avenue and the East river, opposite Bellevue Hospital. Here a course of two years enables the student to acquire, on satisfactory examination, the degree of M. D., provided he has studied medicine for an additional year. Part of the structure used for laboratories in chemistry, physiology, biology, pathology, and materia medica is the Loomis Laboratory, the money to build and equip it having been given through Dr. Alfred L. Loomis, the donor remaining anonymous. The last matriculation in this department amounted to 633, and included besides many New Yorkers and students from other parts of the country, natives of Norway, Turkey, Russia, France, Canada, Persia, Chili, Hungary, Mexico, Germany, Central America, Austria, Bulgaria and Poland.

In the University building Robert Winthrop laid the scene of his powerful novel, "Cecil Dreeme." Above the University, University Place extends up to Fourteenth street. On the east side of this thoroughfare are at No. 9 the College for Training Teachers, and at No. 21 the Charity Organization Society.

Washington Square, North. — The houses on the north side of Washington Square are examples of the old style New York fashionable residences, of brick with white steps and porticoes, white sills and pediments, and in many instances white doors. Between Fifth avenue and University Place stands a row of these houses in an almost unbroken line, like a company of soldiers. Fifth avenue ends at the north side of this square, but a broad thoroughfare continues it through the park and circling around a basin, about in the centre, winds into South Fifth avenue and Thompson street. East of the basin is a statue of Garibaldi, represented as a hero of the swashbuckler order, erected by Italian citizens of New York in 1888.

WASHINGTON ARCH.—The most conspicuous structure in or about the square will be the Washington Centennial Memorial Arch, built of marble from designs of Stanford White. It will stand 50 feet south of Fifth avenue, 86 feet high with a span 30 feet wide, the piers having a width of 10 feet each. The abutments will be occupied by large rectangular panels, and the architrave festooned with garlands. At the base of the piers are to be figures in statuary. It will be flanked by slender marble columns rising slightly above the level of the imposts of the arch and each surmounted by the figure of an eagle. These columns will support lamps on either side near the ground. The erection of this arch was suggested during the Washington Inauguration Centennial in 1889, when a temporary arch of Mr. White's design was put up at Fifth avenue and Washington Square. The arch is now in course of construction, and certain details of decoration have not yet been decided upon, but it will undoubtedly be one of the noteworthy sights of New York.

A good idea of Fifth avenue may be obtained by taking one of the stages which, starting from South Fifth avenue and Bleecker street, cross Washington Square and then run up Fifth avenue to Eighty-fourth street, near the Metropolitan Museum of Art. Fare, five cents. A number of stages have accommodation for passengers outside. Fifth avenue from Washington Square to Central Park is, however, well worth a trip on foot. It is crossed between these points by several great thoroughfares, among them Fourteenth, Twenty-third and Forty-second streets, and near these it is given over to business. Along the rest of its course, however, it is occupied by fashionable residences, hotels and clubs, and the business conducted on it is mostly of a kind which appeals to people of wealth and fashion.

From Washington Square to Fourteenth street the greater part of Fifth avenue is given up to residences. At Tenth street a detour may be made to the Jefferson Market police court and prison, Tenth street and Sixth avenue. To this police court all the prisoners apprehended in the famous "tenderloin" precinct (p. 152) are brought. The prison itself is built on modern principles, and whoever has been through the tenement house district of New York will probably conclude that the prisoners are much better off as far as light and air are concerned than they were before they were apprehended.*

On the north side of Tenth street, between Fifth and Sixth avenues, is the well known Studio Building, a large brick structure, the earliest built exclusively for studio purposes. The studio of William M. Chase, one of the handsomest in the city, which may be visited Saturday afternoons, is in this building. Other studio buildings are the Sherwood, 58 West Fifty-seventh street, the building of the Y. M. C. A. (p. 174), and the University Building p. 169).

An interesting detour may be made through Fourteenth street to Sixth avenue, both Fourteenth street and the last-named avenue being among the most crowded retail business thoroughfares of the city. The large bazaar of R. H. Macy & Co. stands on the southeast corner of Fourteenth street and Sixth avenue, and is well worth a visit, for under its roof one can purchase the furnishings of a house as well as an outfit for one's self. It is merely a matter of choice whether the visitor will make a short detour up Sixth avenue and visit some of the large retail houses on that thoroughfare, or do so from Twenty-third street.

---

*By taking at this point the cross-town cars which run down West Tenth street to Christopher street ferry, the visitor can reach the piers of the White Star and Inman lines of steamships, and it will be worth while to do so if the *Teutonic*, which holds the record (5 days, 15 hours and 53 minutes), the *Majestic*, both of the White Star line, the *City of Paris* or the *City of New York*, of the Inman line, are in port. The Cunard, Guion and French lines are near here and the Bremen and Hamburg lines in Hoboken are easily reached by Christopher street ferry.

New York Hospital.—On the north side of Fifteenth street, between Fifth and Sixth avenues, and running through to Sixteenth street, is the large building of the New York Hospital, one of the oldest institutions of its kind in the United States, and the oldest in New York, having received its charter from George III, June 13, 1771. During the Revolution, its building, Broadway and Duane street, served for barracks. Not until January 3, 1791, was the hospital first opened to patients. Treatment of patients suffering from mental disorder has always been part of the work of the Society. These were treated in the Hospital until the Society purchased in 1816 a farm at Bloomingdale, where the Bloomingdale Asylum was completed and occupied in 1821.

The present New York Hospital edifice was built in 1877. Besides the reception and private rooms and the wards of the hospital, there are in the building a fine medical library and pathological collection. The total number of patients treated last year was 1,716, of which 306 are to be credited to the Bloomingdale Asylum. where, since 1821, 8,688 patients have been admitted, The original building of the New York Hospital was one of the first structures on Broadway above Chambers street. Although it was not regularly opened as a hospital until 1791, anatomical experiments were carried on until 1788, when a medical student threatened some peeping boys with a cadaver's arm. The frightened boys conveyed the intelligence to others and a mob gathered, upon which the soldiers were compelled to fire before the excitement was quelled.

The large building on the northwest corner of Fifth avenue and Sixteenth street, is occupied by *Judge*, and other publications; and on the south side of Sixteenth street, near Sixth avenue, are the church and college of *St. Francis Xavier*, well-known Catholic institutions.

On the northwest corner of Fifth avenue and Eighteenth street is Chickering Hall, and directly opposite it the residence of the late August Belmont. At 154 Fifth avenue is the large building of the Methodist Book Concern, which also includes the rooms of the missionary society; on the northwest corner the Union Club, the largest purely social club in the city; and opposite it the Lotus Club, which includes a number of literary men, artists and actors among its members; on the southwest corner of Twenty-second street, Boussod, Valadon & Co.'s (Goupil's) art store, where generally a number of fine paintings can be seen on exhibition.

TWENTY-THIRD STREET.—At Twenty-third street, both Fifth avenue and Broadway enter Madison Square. The block bounded by Twenty-second street, Broadway and Fifth avenue, runs here to a narrow point, forming a triangle corresponding to another on the north, but, unlike the latter, occupied by houses. Twenty-third street both east and west of Fifth avenue, is an important thoroughfare. Between Fifth and Sixth avenues it is a crowded retail business block, there being here several of the best known dry goods houses in the city, and also the publishing houses of G. P. Putnam's Sons, and E. P. Dutton & Co.

On the north side is the Eden Musée and on the northeast corner of Sixth avenue and Twenty-third street the Masonic Temple. On East Twenty-third street are, at No. 6, the American Art Galleries, where paintings are generally on exhibition, and on the southwest corner of Twenty-third street and Fourth avenue the building of the Young Men's Christian Association.

YOUNG MEN'S CHRISTIAN ASSOCIATION.—This is virtually a young men's club of a somewhat religious tendency, offering also opportunities for instruction, the club and instruction fees being within the means of nearly every self-supporting young man. The Association offers to its subscribers the privileges of reading-room, parlors, gymnasium, bowling alleys, library and baths, all well furnished. Informal social gatherings take place at stated intervals; there are "member's meetings" and musical and other entertainments, and athletic club, outing, rambling, football and tennis clubs. The Association owns an athletic ground at One Hundred and Fiftieth street, near Mott avenue, and boat-houses on the Harlem river near by. Regular competitive sports are here held in the spring and fall. The educational department carries on its work in a liberal and extended manner, classes and lectures being held chiefly in the evening.

NATIONAL ACADEMY OF DESIGN.—On the northwest

corner of Fourth avenue and Twenty-third street is the National Academy of Design, a building of white and grey marble and blue stone, copied after a Venetian palace, with 80 feet front on Twenty-third street and 99 feet on Fourth avenue. A double flight of steps rises to the main entrance on the Twenty-third street front, and here a massive stairway leads from a vestibule to the third story in which are exhibition galleries lighted from the roof. The Academy was founded in 1826 and is still by virtue of its age, membership and influence the best known institution of its kind in the country. Its membership is composed entirely of artists, known as National Academicians (N. A.), who form the corporate body, and of Associates (A. N. A.). Exhibitions of paintings and statuary are held in the spring and fall, the galleries being then open from 9 A. M. until 10 P. M. Admission, 25 cents.

Connected with the Academy are schools of art, open from the first Monday in September to June 1st following. Those desiring to become students must submit some specimen of their work. Features of the course are the "Harper Fund Lectures," the expenses of which are defrayed by a fund given by Harper & Bros., the publishers.

At 143 East Twenty-third street is the Art Students' League, founded June 2, 1875, instruction being given here by artists identified with the progressive tendency of the Society of American artists. The League is soon to occupy fine quarters in the new building of the American Fine Art Society (composed of the Society of American artists, the American Water Color Society, the Institute of American Architects, and the Art Students' League) on West Fifty-seventh street, between Sixth and Seventh avenues, where the various societies named will exhibit. On the southeast corner of Lexington avenue and Twenty-third street is the *College of the City of New York*, which is under the jurisdiction of the Department of Public Schools, the tuition in it being free. On the southeast corner of Twenty-third street and Fourth avenue is the *New York Society for the Prevention of Cruelty to Children*, an admirable institution.

In its rooms may be seen a collection of implements which cruel parents and others have used in torturing little ones. During its sixteen years of existence it has rescued nearly 28,500 children, besides sheltering, feeding and clothing many more at its room. The President of the Society, Elbridge T. Gerry, was largely instrumental in its founding. The *Society for the Prevention of Cruelty to Animals*, is building a new structure on the southeast corner of Fourth avenue and Twenty-third street. During twenty-years it has prosecuted some 16,000 cases in court, compelled a temporary suspension from work of over 39,000 disabled animals, humanely killed over 29,000 horses disabled past recovery, and removed from the streets in ambulances over 5,000 horses. It has a museum of implements with which animals have been cruelly treated, the stuffed skin of a dog killed at a prize fight, with all its hideous wounds, the stuffed skins of the victor and victim of a cocking main, a victim of rabbit coursing and similar objects.

MADISON SQUARE.—Fifth avenue crosses Madison Square in a straight line, Broadway diagonally, forming with Fifth avenue on the northwest corner a small triangle occupied by a monument to Major-General Worth (see below). At Broadway and Twenty-third street, fronting the Square, is the Fifth Avenue Hotel. Broadway is, from here to Forty-second street, given up largely to fine hotels, theatres, restaurants and shops. In the lines of promenaders who throng its sidewalks there is apt to be a dash of the "off-color" element, which becomes more pronounced as the shades of night deepen, for Broadway, from Twenty-third to Thirty-fourth streets, is the main artery of the "Tenderloin District" (p. 152). A block above the Fifth Avenue Hotel are the Albemarle and the Hoffman House. The Hoffman House Café is elaborately decorated and hung with works of art, among them Bouguereau's "Nymphs and Satyr." On the east Madison Square is bounded by Madison avenue, which runs to the northern end of

Manhattan Island and is almost entirely given over to residences ; on the north by Twenty-sixth street. On the northeast corner of Fifth avenue and Madison Square is the Brunswick Hotel, and diagonally opposite it Delmonico's, the most famous restaurant in the United States.

MONUMENTS.—There are three monuments in Madison Square. On the southwest corner is a bronze statue by Randolph Rogers of William H. Seward, Lincoln's Secretary of State ; on the northwest corner a statue of Admiral Farragut, by Augustus St. Gaudens, presented to the city by the Farragut Memorial Association in May, 1881, and in the northern triangle, formed by the intersection of Fifth avenue and Broadway, the Worth monument.

Farragut Statue.—The Farragut statue is considered the most artistic work of its kind in New York and in fact one of the finest of modern statues. The sculptor has solved the problem of producing a picturesque representation of a man in modern clothing, giving even artistic value to such prosaic articles as trousers. The pedestal also is a noteworthy variation from the ordinary conception of this necessary accompaniment of a statue, and would have been still more striking had the monument been placed on some elevation as the sculptor believed it would be. This pedestal, the plans for which were drawn by Stanford White, is of North River blue stone, and is flanked by a curving wall beneath which is a seat, each of the arms formed by the curved back of a sea fish. Next to the pedestal are allegorical figures; that on the left Loyalty, on the right, Courage. Wavy lines, on the pedestal and over the inscription on the wall, cover the designs and letters like a veil of undulating sea. The inscription on the right wing of the wall is biographical; that on the left is as follows:

"That the memory of a daring and sagacious commander and gentle great-souled man, whose life from childhood was given to his country, but who served her supremely in the war for the Union A. D. MDCCCLXI-MDCCCLXV, may be preserved and honored, and that they who come after him and who will owe him so much may see him as he was seen by friend and foe, his countrymen have set up the monument A. D. MDCCCLXXXI."

The statue which stands upon this pedestal is not a mere portrait study. The pose and features "express the seriousness, the coolness and the moral strength which accompany authority, a boldness of conception and an initiative force, which are peculiar to Americans and of which Farragut was a living example. * * * * * There is the sailor with his simple and well ordered costume, the frock-coat buttoned close, the skirt loose in the wind, the figure well balanced with the legs a little apart as is natural on a moving ground." The whole figure has the solidity of a living person, not the mere avoirdupois of a lump of bronze.

David Glasgoe Farragut was born at Campbell Station near Knoxville, Tenn., July 5, 1801. He died at Portsmouth, N. H., August 14, 1870. He became a midshipman at the age of eleven, his first service being aboard the famous *Essex* during her engagement with the *Alert*, and also when she surrendered to the *Phœbe* and *Cherub* in the bay of Valparaiso, 1814. Commodore Porter commended the gallant behavior of the lad, Farragut, expressing his regrets that he was too young for promotion. In 1823 he took part in the attack on the pirates at Cape Cruz, Cuba. During the next 40 years his promotion was by the slow process of seniority, and when the Civil War broke out he was sixty years old and only a Captain. He was then at Norfolk, Va., on waiting orders, and when Virginia seceded he took his pistols and his family, and hastened north to offer his services to the government. After nine months' idleness at Washington he was ordered to command the expedition for the capture of New Orleans. Here he performed his first great feat of war, which drew the eyes of the world upon him. On the night of April 24, 1862, he passed the forts under tremendous fire and destroyed twenty armed steamers, four iron-clad rams and many fire rafts, silenced the two Chalmette batteries three miles below New Orleans, and at noon the second day had the city beneath his guns. He next passed the fortifications at Vicksburg, but there being no co-operative land force he repassed them and withdrew to Pensacola for repairs. July 11, 1862, he received the thanks of Congress and later was placed first on the list of Rear Admirals. In the autumn he captured Corpus Christi, Sabine Pass and

Galveston. In March, 1863, he got the *Hartford* and *Albatross* past Port Hudson to Vicksburg, establishing communication with the upper Mississippi fleet and blockading the Red River so that no supplies could reach the Confederate forces. Late in May he co-operated at the reduction of Port Royal, and August 5, 1864, he assisted at the capture of Mobile. Here, lashed to the rigging, he dashed to the head of the fleet at the first favorable opportunity. He again received a vote of thanks from Congress and was created Vice-Admiral, and July 25, 1866, Admiral. From 1867 to 1868 he was in command of the European squadron and was received with great honor at every port he visited.

Worth Monument.—The Worth monument is directly opposite the Farragut statue. It is of granite, in the shape of an obelisk. On the south face there is a bronze relief of Worth, mounted, and above it an armorial design; on the east face, cut in stone in a panel of the pedestal, "Ducet amor Patriæ"; on the north face, a coat of arms, and on the west face, "By the Corporation of the City of New York, 1857—Honor the Brave." The names of battles in which Worth was engaged are sculptured on bands around the obelisk.

William Jenkins Worth was born at Hudson, N. Y., 1794; died at San Antonio, Texas, May 7, 1849. He entered the army as a private in 1812, became Second Lieutenant in 1813, and subsequently aide to Generals Lewis and Scott. At the battle of Chippewa he won the brevet of Captain for gallant conduct, and at Lundy's Lane, that of Major. In 1815 he became Captain. From 1821 to 1828 he was instructor of infantry tactics and commander of cadets at West Point. In 1841 he had the chief command in the war against the Seminoles, and in 1842 was brevetted Brigadier-General. He distinguished himself during the Mexican war in numerous battles, especially in storming the City of Mexico. He was brevetted Major-General and received swords from Congress, the State of New York, and his native county. He died of cholera. His remains rest beneath his monument.

MADISON SQUARE GARDEN. — The most conspicuous building in the neighborhood of Madison Square, is the Madison Square Garden, the work of Stanford White, filling the block bounded by Madison and Fourth avenues, Twenty-sixth and Twenty-seventh streets. Its interior is divided into an amphitheatre, entered from Madison avenue, and holding 15,000 people, surpassing the capacity of any other hall in the world; a theatre occupying the northern corner on Madison avenue, with a beautifully decorated interior; a ball-room, the most elaborately decorated room in the building, in the style of Louis XVI, accommodating 1,500 people; a restaurant; and an open air garden on the roof, which will hold from 3,000 to 5,000 people, and is lighted by a maze of electric lights. On the southeast corner of the building is the tower, reached by elevator, 300 feet above the street, the only point of observation in the upper part of the city from which a view of New York and its environs may be had. Directly opposite the Madison Square Garden, southeast corner of Madison Square and Madison avenue, is the University Club.

Returning to Fifth avenue, there is at No. 204 the art store of William Schaus, and at 226 that of Reichard & Co., where pictures may usually be seen on exhibition; on the southwest corner of Twenty-eighth street, No. 246, the bric-à-brac and antique store of Sypher & Co.; at No. 254, the foreign (chiefly French) book-store of Christern; on the northwest corner of Twenty-eighth street, one of the Collegiate Reformed Dutch churches (p. 124), with a tablet reciting its history; on the opposite corner, the fine building of the Calumet Club, and between Fifth and Madison avenues, on the north side of Twenty-ninth street, the Protestant Episcopal Church of the Transfiguration, standing back among well-kept grounds, a most picturesque break in the line of houses, and popularly known as "the little church around the corner," from which so many actors have been buried. Joseph Jefferson relates in his "Autobiography" the circumstances from which it derived its name and its popularity with the dramatic profession. When George Holland, the actor, died, Joseph Jefferson, with a son of the deceased, called upon the pastor of Mrs. Holland's sister, who, however, upon hearing that Holland had been an actor, declined holding service at the church, adding "There is a little church around the corner where you may get it done." "Then, if this be so, God bless 'the little church around the corner,'" exclaimed Jefferson.

At the northeast corner of Fifth avenue and Thirty-second street is the *Knickerbocker Club*, the most exclusive social club in the city. The block on the west side of Fifth avenue, between Thirty-third and Thirty-fourth streets, belongs to the Astor estate. On the corner of Thirty-third street William Waldorf Astor, the present head of the house, is erecting a hotel. The fortune of the Astor family is chiefly in real estate. It is valued at about $150,000,000 and yields an annual income of about $13,000,000. The estate is said to own some 2,700 dwelling-houses.

John Jacob Astor, the founder of this great estate, was born at Waldorf, near Heidelberg, July 12, 1763; died at New York in 1848. He was the fourth son of a butcher, and worked for his father until he was sixteen years old. He then joined a brother who was working for an uncle in the piano and flute factory of Astor & Broadwood, London. In 1783 he sailed for Baltimore, with an invoice of musical instruments, but conversations which he had on shipboard with a furrier caused him to enter the fur business in New York. He was not long in setting himself up in business on his own account as a furrier, and at the same time acted as agent for Astor & Broadwood, being the first regular dealer in musical instruments in the United States. He married Sarah Todd. By 1800 he had accumulated a fortune of $250,000, and then, for the first time, established himself in a dwelling separate from his store. In 1811, he founded Astoria, at the mouth of the Columbia river, Oregon, his idea being to go into the trapping and trading business on a huge scale in the far West, but the war of 1812 interfered with his plans. He died worth $20,000,000. He was founder of the Astor Library (p. 155).

The hill which rises from Thirty-fourth street to Forty-second street, is known as *Murray Hill*, and is named after an old family which once owned much of the property. When, after the battle of Long Island, the British were pursuing the Americans, who were fleeing toward the upper part of Manhattan Island, Mrs. Murray entertained the English officers long enough for Burr to conduct a retreating column two miles long unobserved within half a mile of the house. The marble structure on the northwest corner of Thirty-fourth street is now the home of the *Manhattan Club*, which is the representative Democratic club of the city. The building was erected by the late A. T. Stewart (p. 164) as a residence. The house above it is occupied by the New York Club.

UNION LEAGUE CLUB.—On the northeast corner of Fifth avenue and Thirty-ninth street is the fine building of the Union League Club, the representative Republican club of the city, and one of the largest and most important politico-social clubs in the United States. It was organized February 6, 1863, incorporated February 16, 1865. May 12, 1863, it occupied its quarters at No. 26 East Seventeenth street. April 1, 1868, it removed to the house southeast corner of Twenty-sixth street and Madison avenue, now occupied by the University Club, and into its present building March 5, 1881. The club was organized during the darkest hours of the Civil War, "to promote, encourage, and sustain, by all proper means, absolute and unqualified loyalty to the government of the United States." The total membership of the club is limited to 1,600. The admission fee is $300, the annual dues of resident members $75, and of non-resident members $45. The club has exhibitions of pictures in its gallery, and also holds receptions to which ladies are invited. The income of the club, according to the last annual report, was $296,428.46, of which $133,950 was from admission fees and annual dues. The receipts from the restaurant amounted to $62,174.32; for wines, $20,601.45; for liquors, $19,651.54; and for cigars, $32,494.58. The payments for salaries and wages to employees aggregated $56,476.73. The architects of the building were Peabody & Stearns, of Boston. It is in Queen Anne style, of Baltimore pressed brick, with brownstone trimmings and ornaments of moulded brick, occupying 84 feet on Fifth avenue and 132 feet on Thirty-ninth street.

The reading-room on the first floor, which runs the entire length of the Fifth avenue side and is decorated in Pompeiian style, has on each side four pillars with Corinthian capitals, with reading-stands for periodicals running to the wall and forming pleasantly secluded niches. The stairway to the second floor has a carved oak balustrade and at the first landing there is a great arch of oak, behind which there is a large stained-glass window. The hall of the second floor is vaulted in Moresque style, studded with opalescent glass. On the Fifth avenue side is the well stocked library. Over the north alcove hangs Carpenter's picture of the Inauguration of Lincoln. The dining-room occupies the greater portion of the Fifth avenue side of the fourth floor, being 30x80 feet. The decorations are by La Farge. The large dormer window, already referred to, opposite the door, is a rose window studded with brilliant glass. The walls are paneled in oak in English seventeenth century style. The center of the ceiling rises to a sharp Gothic roof and is decorated in gilt, blue and green.

At the southeast corner of Fortieth street is Frederick W. Vanderbilt's house. The reservoir on the west side, extending to Forty-second street, is a good example of Egyptian architecture. It was part of the old system of waterworks and is practically no longer in use. To the west of it, bounded by Fortieth and Forty-second streets and Sixth avenue, is Bryant Park.

METROPOLITAN OPERA HOUSE.—A detour may be made down Fortieth street to Broadway, on the west side of which, between Thirty-ninth and Fortieth streets, stands the Metropolitan Opera House, and on the southeast corner of Thirty-ninth street and Broadway the Casino, a fine example of Moorish architecture. The Metropolitan Opera House has the largest auditorium of any opera house in the world, and its stage is exceeded in size only by that of the Imperial Opera at St. Petersburg and the new Opera at Paris. It is built of yellow brick in the style of the Italian Renaissance. The auditorium is divided into a parquet, two tiers of boxes, dress circle, balcony and gallery. It is calculated that the house can be emptied in three minutes. The auditorium is decorated in yellow, which is relieved by the red upholstery of the boxes. The usual proscenium is omitted, its place being taken by paneled pilasters. In the center, above the opening for the stage, is Lathrop's "Apollo Crowned by the Muses," and among the decorations of the pilasters are Maynard's figures of the Chorus and Ballet. The boxes are 7 feet front by 13 feet deep, and are intended for six. Broadway above Forty-second street is largely given over to fine apartment houses, as is also Seventh avenue, which Broadway crosses at Forty-second street.

Returning to Fifth avenue and proceeding up to Forty-second street, there is on the north side of Forty-second street and Fourth avenue the *Grand Central Depot*, which extends to Forty-fifth street. This structure, 695 feet long by 240 feet wide, is of pressed brick trimmed with iron painted white. It is used by three railroads—the New York Central and Hudson River, the New York and Harlem, which is a branch of the former, and the New York, New Haven and Hartford. The waiting-room and offices of the last named are on the south side; those of the other two companies on the west. The glass-covered arch from under which all trains start has a span of 200 feet, is 110 feet high and running the entire length of the building, and is capable of accommodating 12 trains of 12 passenger cars each. On the west side is a police station for the officers who are on special duty at the depot. An addition, also extending from Forty-second to Forty-fifth street, and covering about half the block between Fourth and Lexington avenues, is used for incoming trains and there are accommodations here for people who are waiting for trains.

St. Bartholomew Mission.—One of the finest mission houses in New York City stands on the north side of Forty-second street east of Third avenue, covering a lot 75 feet front by a little over 100 feet deep. It is a handsome structure of five stories, after plans of William H. Russell, of Renwick, Aspinwall & Russell. In the basement is a large lavatory with baths and showers, and a plunge 22 feet long by 16 feet wide, into which unfortunates who come to the mission under the influence of liquor are dipped. The center entrance on the ground room leads to the Rescue Mission room, which will accommodate 1200 people. The entrance to the different stories of the building is on the eastern side. In the rooms of these stories a great variety of mission work and instruction will be carried on, a special feature being a kindergarten class. On the fourth floor there is a gymnasium, and a portion of the roof will be made into a summer garden. The house is in the style of the Italian Renaissance. The first story is of Indiana limestone with a granite water table. From the first story cornice to the top there will be light buff brick with terra cotta trimmings. The façade has three bays filled in with cast iron work and mullions forming the frames of the windows. The fifth story, in the cornice, is richly modeled in terra cotta. The mission house belongs to the parish of *St. Bartholomew*, whose church stands on the southwest corner of Forty-fourth street and Madison avenue, and is one of the wealthiest congregations in the city, several members of the Vanderbilt family worshiping there. On the east side of Madison avenue, between Forty-fourth and Forty-fifth streets, is the handsome new building of the Manhattan Athletic Club, and on the northeast corner of Madison avenue and Forty-fifth street the Railroad branch of the Young Men's Christian Association, built from funds supplied by the Vanderbilts.

On Fifth avenue above Forty-second street are many places of worship, as well as fine private residences. The northeast corner of Forty-third street is occupied by the *Temple Emanu-El*, a Jewish synagogue, the property of a very wealthy organization. It is in Saracenic style, the finest specimen of its class in the United States and one of the costliest places of worship in the city. Conspicuous on the Fifth avenue front are two minarets, with artistic open work. The material used in its construction are brown and yellow sandstone, black and red tiles alternating on the roof. (L. Eidlitz, architect). On the southwest corner of Forty-fifth street is the Universalist Church of the Divine Paternity; between Forty-fifth and Forty-sixth streets, on the east side, the Church of the Heavenly Rest; and on the block above, the Windsor Hotel.

JAY GOULD.—On the northeast corner of Forty-seventh street, No. 579 Fifth avenue, is the residence of Jay Gould, a brownstone structure with a mansard slate roof. Jay Gould was born at Roxbury, Delaware Co., N. Y. As a boy he worked on his father's farm, and to defray the expenses of his tuition at Hobart Academy he became book-keeper for a blacksmith. Subsequently he made surveys of Ulster, Delaware and Albany counties, and organized surveying parties for two counties in Ohio and one in Michigan. From the profits of this work he saved $5,000. In 1856 he published a "History of Delaware County." After a year in the lumbering business, he put all his money into bonds of the Rutland and Washington R. R. at 10 cents on the dollar, and so successful was he in this and similar enterprises, that he became in 1859 a broker in New York, investing heavily in Erie Railway stock, becoming president of the road, a position he held until 1872. He has since then acquired immense Western railroad interests, and is the controling personality in Manhattan (N. Y. City) Elevated Railway and in the Western Union Telegraph Co. March 13, 1882, rumors that he was financially embarrassed having been circulated, he summoned several men of high standing to his office and exhibited $53,000,000 in securities in his own name, offering to produce $20,000,000 more if they so desired.

On the southeast corner of Forty-eighth street is the residence of Ogden Goelet, whose brother, Robert Goelet, resides on the southwest corner of Forty-ninth street. The Goelets are, next to the Astors, the largest private holders of real estate in New York City, the annual income from their estate having lately turned the $2,000,000 point. The northwest corner of Forty-eighth street is occupied by another of the Collegiate Dutch Reformed churches (p. 124). It owns the bell presented by Minuit (p. 19) to the first congregation in New Amsterdam. On the east side, between Forty-ninth and Fiftieth streets, is the Buckingham Hotel and its adjunct, the Belgravia.

Columbia College.—On the east side of Madison avenue, occupying the entire block bounded by Madison and Fourth avenues, Forty-ninth and Fiftieth streets, is Columbia College, the greatest educational institution in the city and in the front rank of the educational institutions of the country, a position it has attained within recent years, during which, under the last part of the administration of President Frederick A. P. Barnard and his successor, Seth Low, it has been fulfilling its mission as a great university.

History.—Columbia College was chartered as King's College October 31, 1754. In December, 1746, money for it was raised by public lottery and vested, in November, 1751, in ten trustees. Episcopalians predominating among these and Trinity Church having made a liberal grant of land to the College, there was great opposition to the chartering of the institution, it being looked upon as a design to introduce a church establishment into the province. This opposition being, however, in a great measure surmounted, Dr. Samuel Johnson, of West Haven, Conn., became president, and in July, 1754, in a room in the school-house belonging to Trinity Church, commenced the instruction of a class of students.

In 1755 Trinity Church granted land to the college bounded by Church, Barclay and Murray streets and running down to the North River, the condition being that the president should always be a member of the Protestant Episcopal Church, and that prayers should be drawn from the Protestant Episcopal prayer-book. The consideration paid was 12 shillings and the annual rental of a pepper-corn. The trustees held their first meeting May 17, 1755. The Governors built a structure 180 feet long by 30 feet deep at the foot of Park Place. In 1763 Dr. Johnson resigned the presidency and was succeeded by Rev. Dr. Myles Cooper, of Oxford. In 1777 a medical department was added. Dr. Cooper was a violent loyalist and during the excitement of a Liberty meeting a mob approached the college for the purpose of laying violent hands on its Tory president. In order to delay them longer and enable Cooper to escape, Alexander Hamilton, then a student at the college, mounted the college steps and began haranguing the mob, while another student warned the president. Cooper ran off only half-dressed, clambered over the college fence, dashed down to the shore of the Hudson and trotted along the river bank until near morning, when he found shelter "in the house of his friend, Mr. Stuyvesant," remaining there for that day, and on the following night taking refuge on board the *Kingfisher*, a British sloop-of-war. During the Revolution the college was used for military purposes.

In May, 1784, the corporate title was changed from King's to Columbia College. In November, 1813, in consequence of the establishment of the College of Physicians and Surgeons in New York, the medical school was discontinued, but in 1860 the College of Physicians and Surgeons was merged into Columbia College as its medical department. The Law School of Columbia College was established in May, 1858 ; in 1863, the School of Mines, certainly a misnomer for an institution in which a full scientific course is carried on ; in 1880 a School of Political Science, and in 1890 a School of Philosophy. The college was removed from its old site to the block which it now occupies in 1857. It derives its large income, not any too large, however, for the vast amount of work it carries on and the benefits which accrue to its students at a very moderate fee, from the rental of buildings on the land granted to it by Trinity Church, and also on a tract of land of about 20 acres between Fifth and Sixth avenues, from Forty-seventh to Fifty-first streets, the latter granted by the State to the College in 1814 and valued at the time at only $5 000. The professors and other instructors of Columbia College are probably the best paid in the United States. In 1874 a new building for the School of Mines was erected at a cost of $150,000, and in 1879 a new building (Hamilton Hall), after the plans by C. C. Haight, for the School of Arts. Dr. Barnard became president in 1864 and held the office until his death in April, 1889. It was about 1880, during his presidency, that the College began to be regenerated, and the work inaugurated by Dr. Barnard is now being carried out by Seth Low, who was elected president in October, 1889. In May, 1890, the trustees adopted a plan for university instruction in connection with the College, created a new faculty styled the Faculty of Philosophy, placed all university work in mathematics and the natural and applied sciences under the charge of the faculty of the School of Mines, and constituted a University Council to have general supervision of the work of the University as a whole.

Departments.—Columbia College employs a president and 204 professors, instructors and assistants, and has in all the departments 1,648 students, who are stimulated in their work by numerous valuable scholarships and fellowships, many of them founded by private endowment. The term college has almost become a misnomer for the institution, its work having expanded so enormously during recent years. Columbia seems destined to have a great future as a university, both because of its resources and the learning of its various faculties, and its location in the chief scientific, art, and literary center of the New World. Free tuition is given to deserving young men under certain conditions, and several free scholarships have been established. The departments of instruction in the *School of Arts* embrace elaborate courses in the classics, literature and studies pertaining to the usual college curriculum, with many elective studies. There is a course of post-graduate instruction in the higher branches of the studies pursued in the under-graduate department, with degrees of Master of Arts, Doctor of Philosophy, Doctor of Letters, and Doctor of Science. The system of instruction in the *School of Mines* embraces a full scientific curriculum, including Architecture, with post-graduate courses in Electrical Engineering, Sanitary Engineering, and for the degree of Doctor of Philosophy. There are also special higher courses of all studies taught in the school. The *School of Law* exceeds in reputation any law school in the United States. The *School of Political Science* gives a complete general view of all branches of internal and external public polity, from the threefold standpoint of history, law and philosophy. The *School of Philosophy's* course of study embraces the higher branches of several of the studies pursued in the School of Arts. For *School of Medicine* see page 200.

The students and graduates of Columbia College have the use of a library containing over 100,000 volumes, and subscribing to more than 500 different serials. There are also in the various departments cabinets and collections of specimens and models, and the various laboratories are fully equipped.

The block on Madison avenue above Columbia College is occupied by a group of buildings resembling a Florentine palace, one of the most striking blocks of residences in the city. Among its residents are such well-known citizens as Whitelaw Reid, editor of the *Tribune*, and Edward D. Adams.

ST. PATRICK'S CATHEDRAL.—The entire block bounded

by Fiftieth and Fifty-first streets and Fifth and Madison avenues is occupied by St. Patrick's Cathedral, considered the largest and the finest church building in the United States. Open every day.

The corner-stone of this noble structure was laid August 15, 1858, by Archbishop Hughes, some 100,000 people having gathered to witness the ceremony. May 25, 1879, the Cathedral was dedicated by Cardinal McCloskey, surrounded by 36 archbishops and bishops, and more than 400 priests.

Exterior.—The building, after plans of James Renwick, is a fine example of decorative and geometric style of Gothic architecture. The architecture of the residences of the archbishops and canons, in the rear of the Cathedral, harmonizes with that of the main structure. The dimensions of the Cathedral are: Length, 306 feet; height of side aisles, 54 feet; breadth of nave and choir with the chapels, 120 feet; length of transept, 140 feet; height, 108 feet. Above the base course, the whole exterior is of white marble. The principal front on Fifth avenue consists of a central gable 156 feet high, with a tower and spire on each side reaching to a height of 330 feet. In the towers 110 feet above the grade of the avenue is a fine chime of bells, the heaviest in the country, weighing 30,000 pounds as against Trinity's 15,000.

Interior.—The interior of the Cathedral is cruciform, and is divided into a nave, two transepts, and a choir or sanctuary. The nave is 164 feet long, 96 feet wide between the side aisle walls, and 124 feet broad if the side aisle chapels are included. It is divided by columns into seven bays, each bay being 23 feet in length, with the exception of the first one, which is 26 feet long. It is cross-sectioned into a center aisle, 48 feet wide and 110 feet to the apex of the groined ceiling; two side aisles 24 feet wide and 54 feet high, the chapels under the window sills at the side aisles being 14 feet wide by 18 feet high, transepts 144 feet long, choir or sanctuary 95 feet long, having three bays, and being terminated at the east end in the central aisle by the semi-decagon apside. The columns which divide the central aisle

ST. PATRICK'S CATHEDRAL.

from the side aisles are of white marble, 35 feet high, and consist of four main columns and eight others clustered to a central shaft, the combined diameter being 5 feet; the arches between the columns rise to 54 feet; the treforium is 15 feet high, and is covered by the roof of the side aisle. A passage 56 feet above the floor of the Cathedral leads through the treforium all around the building. The third story windows are a continuation of the tracery of the treforium. The spring line of the ceiling of the central aisle is 77 feet from the floor. The seating capacity of the floors of the naves and transepts is about 2,500, divided among 408 pews from 8 to 11 feet in length. The sanctuary floor is raised six steps above the main floor, and the high altar is three steps higher, the steps being of gray marble, and the platform in front of the altar of richly colored marble. All the woodwork is of white ash.

Altars.—The high altar stands at the east end of the structure in the center aisle of the choir. The reredos, 23 feet wide and 50 feet high to the top of the center pinnacle, was carved at St. Brieuc, France, in Poitiers stone, and was presented by the clergy of the diocese. In the center tower of the reredos is a niche, containing a statue of the Saviour, the two flanking towers bearing statues of St. Peter and St. Paul, the towers being crowned with pierced spires of open tracery work. The three niches between the central and corner tower on either side contains angelic figures bearing emblems of the Passion. The altar proper and the lower division of the reredos are of purest Italian marble inlaid with alabasters and precious marbles, and were constructed in Italy. Niches and panels in the front of the bottom part of the altar contain respectively statues of the Evangelist, and bas-reliefs of the Last Supper, the Carrying of the Cross, and the Agony in the Garden, all of the purest Carrara marble. The tabernacle on the altar is of marble decorated in Roman mosaics, and flanked by columns of rare marbles. Its door of gilt bronze is set with emeralds and garnets, and was the gift of Cardinal McCloskey. A crypt or vault of sufficient capacity to contain 42 coffins and intended for the entombing of the archbishops of New York, is under the floor of the sanctuary.

Other altars are: The Altar of the Blessed Virgin, at the eastern end of the north side aisle of the sanctuary, of French oak and white marble; the Altar of the Sacred Heart, in the south transept, of bronze; the Altar of the Holy Family, in the north transept, of Caen stone, the gift of Joseph Donohue of San Francisco; St. Joseph's Altar, in front of the west walls of the sacristy, of bronze and mosaic. This altar and the window of St. Agnes, above it, are gifts of Mrs. Agnes Maitland.

The *Archbishop's Throne*, of carved French oak, is erected against the first column inside the sanctuary. The superb Gothic canopy over it is supported by columns and crowned by octagonal lanterns of fine design. The sanctuary rail of polished brass branches out from the first column in the form of an elliptical curve. The *Pulpit* at the first column outside the sanctuary of the main altar on the epistle side is of Gothic style and is the gift of the clergy of the diocese over which Cardinal McCloskey presided when he was archbishop, and a memorial of the fiftieth anniversary of his ordination to the priesthood.

Windows.—There are in all seventy windows in the Cathedral. Thirty-seven of these represent scenes from Scripture and the lives of the Saints and have been donated, and form a rich collection of stained glass. The two windows of the transept are the most elaborate. The six-bayed window over the south transept door is the titular window of the Cathedral, being the window of St. Patrick, consisting of eighteen scenes from the life of that saint, the series beginning at the base of the left-hand bay and running upward in lines of three each. In the center of the tracery St. Patrick's coronation in heaven is represented. Around it in a circle hover angels (after Fra Angelico), each holding a scroll on which the line of a hymn is inscribed, all the scrolls together constituting the entire hymn. This window is the gift of old St. Patrick's Cathedral to the new, and, like all the other stained-glass windows of the Cathedral, was executed in France. Located over the north transept door is the window of the Blessed Virgin, the gift of the Albany diocese. It is in nineteen scenes, which are read from left to right in lines of six each, the coronation being represented in the tracery window.

The windows of the sanctuary, six lateral windows, three on each side, relate to sacrifice: and the five windows of the apse contain subjects from the life of Christ. On the last of the sacrificial windows on the south side, the "Sacrifice on Calvary," the gift of John Laden, the kneeling figure before the altar is Cardinal McCloskey, and his offering is the Cathedral itself. The windows in the Chapel of Our Lady represent the Presentation of the Blessed Virgin in the Temple, John Kelly; the Adoration of the Child Jesus, Thomas H. O'Connor; the Virgin Exposing to Veneration the Infant Jesus after His Birth, Mrs. Julia Coleman. Opposite this window on the south aisle of the church are the Death of St. Joseph, Joseph Florimond Loubat, St. Alphonsus Ligouri miraculously giving Speech to a Dumb Youth; in the right-hand bay St. Susanna, and in the left-hand bay St. Theresa, Susan Elizabeth Loubat, in memory of Theresa Aimee Loubat, Countess of Comminges Guitaut. In the center of the next window is a life-size figure of St. Agnes; in the right-hand bay the apostle St. James the Greater, below this the Blessed Virgin appearing to him at Saragossa, in Spain; in the left-hand bay, St. Thomas the apostle, and below, St. Thomas touching the wound in the side of the Saviour, Mrs. Agnes Maitland. In the southern arm of the transept is the window of St. Louis, King of France, Henry L. Hoguet; adjoining this the window of the Sacred Heart, Mrs. Elenora Iselin; on the same line in the north transcept St. Paul's window, Eugene Kelly, in memory of Rev. John Kelly; adjoining this, the window of St. Augustine and St. Monica, representing St. Augustine at the death-bed of his mother, Mamie and Lena Caldwell, in memory of their parents; on the east side of the north transept door, St. Matthew's window, Andrew Clark; on the west side, St. Mark's window, Bernard McGuire; on the west side of the south transept door, St. Luke's window, Denis J. Dwyer; on the east side, St. John's window, William Joyce; on the west wall of the north transept, the window of St. Charles Borromeo, showing the cardinal during the plague of Milan, Lorenzo Delmonico; on the west wall of the south transept the window of St. Patrick, preaching to an assembly of Irish peasants, James Renwick. The scene underneath shows the architect submitting his plan to Archbishop Hughes. Cardinal McCloskey stands in the foreground. There are ten aisle windows, beginning on the north or gospel side. At the angle of the transept there are: St. Bernard preaching the Second Crusade, Diocese of Rochester; The Martyrdom of St. Lawrence, Diocese of Ogdensburg; The Papal Approbation of the Constitution of the Brothers of the Christian Schools, by Benedict XIII, January 26, 1725, The Christian Brothers; St. Columbanus Administering to Thierry II, King of Burgundy, the Rebuke which led to his Conversion, Jeremiah and William Devlin, in memory of Daniel Devlin; The Three Baptisms—in the center our Lord's baptism by St. John, the baptism of water; to the right a martyrdom, the baptism of blood; to the left, a solitary reclining figure, consumed with the desire of baptism, the baptism of desire, James McKenna. On the south aisle: St. Vincent de Paul, the saint in the central division, habited in stole and surplice; on the right hand, the saint undergoing punishment on behalf of a prisoner who is seen going on his way rejoicing; on the left, the saint holding an infant in his arms and directing a sister of charity to another infant asleep on the pavement, James Olwell. The window of St. Elizabeth, St. Andrew and St. Catherine,—St. Andrew in the center taking upon himself the cross; beneath, the scene of his execution; on the right, St. Catherine, leaning upon the wheel with which her cruel torture and death were inflicted; below, the nuptials of St. Catherine to our Lord (after Rubens); to the left, St. Elizabeth bearing bread to the poor, which turned into flowers when her unjustly suspicious husband insisted upon seeing what she was carrying so carefully concealed, J. A. and Eliza O'Reilly. The Annunciation, William and John O'Brien; St. Henry in the battle against the Slavonians, the most spirited window in the series, Henry J. Anderson. The Immaculate Conception, commemorating the proclamation of this dogma by Pius IX, the pontiff standing on his throne in the act of giving the apostolic benediction after having proclaimed the dogma. Above the head of the Pope is a figure of the Immaculate Conception. The statues of St. Peter and St. Paul on either side are copied from the statues in the entrance to St. Peter's,

Rome, Diocese of Newark. The organ gallery between the front towers is 46 feet wide, 28 feet long, and capable of accommodating a choir of 100 singers. Access to it is had by a spiral staircase situated in the south lobby of the Fifth avenue entrance, which also leads to the passage around the treforium. The organ has four manuals and a compass of two and one-half octaves in the pedals.

Roman Catholic Orphan Asylum.—Two large blocks bounded respectively by Fifth and Madison avenues, Fifty-first and Fifty-second streets, and by Madison and Fourth avenues and the same streets, are devoted to the purposes of the Roman Catholic Orphan Asylum, the asylum for boys occupying the Fifth avenue block, and that for girls the Madison avenue block. The latter is a comparatively new building, and admirably arranged. There are an average of 400 children in each of the buildings, the choir of the cathedral being drawn from the boys' asylum. Neither girls nor boys are required to wear a uniform, and are not brought up with the idea that they are dependent on charity, the course of instruction aiming to make them independent men and women. It includes a common school education, music and singing for both the boys and the girls, and sewing, crocheting, cooking and housekeeping for the girls, and trade instruction for the boys. Each building has a large playground, and a feature of the Madison avenue structure is a beautiful chapel 145 feet in depth. The best time to visit the Female Orphan Asylum is on Wednesday between 12:30 and 2:30 P. M., when the girls are instructed in calisthenics; the boys' asylum, Tuesdays and Thursdays at 3 P. M., when they go through a regular military drill under the command of a militia officer. On state occasions they are uniformed and fully accoutred. The Asylum was organized in 1817, and incorporated under its present name in 1852.

VANDERBILT HOUSES.—On the west side of Fifth avenue, between Fifty-first and Fifty-second streets, are the residences erected by the late William H. Vanderbilt, the southerly building being occupied by his widow, the northerly by his son-in-law, W. D. Sloane. On the north side of Fifty-second street opposite the Sloane residence is the residence of Wm. K. Vanderbilt. Cornelius Vanderbilt resides on the northwest corner of Fifty-seventh street. The "Vanderbilt houses," as the two brownstone buildings between Fifty-first and Fifty-second streets are popularly spoken of, were first occupied in January, 1882, Mrs. Vanderbilt throwing them open to her friends on the 17th of that month. They were built, furnished and decorated by Herter Bros. in a little more than two years. Their architecture has been severely criticised, but this makes them none the less objects of interest to the curious.

The houses are connected by a vestibule in the middle of the block. The doors leading into Mrs. Vanderbilt's house are reduced copies of the Ghiberti gates in Florence. The main hall, carried up to the full height of the house, is surrounded by galleries from which the private living rooms are entered. On the ground floor is a high wainscoting of English oak, square columns of dark red African marble supporting the first gallery. Facing the entrance is a large fireplace with a full-sized bronze female figure in relief on each side, and massive sculptured marble chimney-pieces. On the east side is a door flanked by carved oaken seats. This leads to the drawing-room. The woodwork of this room is a maze of carving, gilded and glazed with warm tints. The walls are hung in pale red velvet embroidered in foliated and floral designs, crystal being sprinkled among the leaves and flowers to represent dew-drops. At the northern end of this room a door leads to the library, the decorations of which are conspicuous for the beautiful effect produced by antique Greek patterns in mother-of-pearl and brass on mahogany and rosewood, the furniture being designed to harmonize. South of the drawing-room is the Japanese parlor, which is modeled and furnished in free Japanese fashion. A ceiling of bamboo with its pole rafters, a rich low-toned tapestry with panels of velvet, a low cabinet in imitation of lacquer work with innumerable shelves for bric-à-brac running around the room, a large open fireplace with a seat covered with uncut velvet, are features of this apartment. The dining-

VANDERBILT HOUSES.

room is finished in the style of the Italian Renaissance, an arrangement of glass-faced cases supported by rich consoles resting on a beautiful wainscot of rich golden-hued English oak, delicately carved. The ceiling is elliptically arched with oblong panels carved in designs of fruits and foliage in various tints of gold, and frescoed with hunting scenes by Luminais. The main staircase, which rises from the north of the main hall, is lighted by nine stained windows by Lafarge.

The entrance to the picture gallery is from the west end of the hall, but there is a separate entrance from Fifty-first street. The picture gallery is, of course, a strictly private one, but artists of recognized rank and connoisseurs who apply through acquaintances of the family have little difficulty in obtaining admission to it. On a niche of the broad arch over the entrance from the house is *Alma Tadema's* classic "Entrance to a Theatre." Opposite, before the fireplace recess, hangs *Detaille's* famous painting showing two wounded French officers carrying a mortally wounded comrade out of a shattered church between two lines of Prussians who have fallen back on either side to make way for them. As the arrangement of the pictures is changed from time to time as accessions are received, the exact order of their hanging cannot be given. The collection embraces *Vibert's* capital "Cardinal and Monk Destroying Forbidden Books," the Cardinal, however, first gorging himself on the contents. *Villegas'* "Royal Christening," the baby shrieking lustily, much to the consternation of all concerned; the same artist's picture of a Turk sensuously outstretched on a divan listening to the music of a fair almond-eyed slave; *Fortuny's* "Dancing Arabs," five wildly whirling figures, two of them discharging their firearms, watched by their motionless comrades, wrapped in the folds of their white burnous; five *Millets*: a peasant girl of sturdy frame carrying water; peasant mother teaching her daughter how to knit; woman emptying a pail into a glass jar just outside the door, near which are ducks and geese; shepherdess wrapped in a cloak knitting; two hunters in a snowy wood. *Van Marcke's* cattle collected outside a thatched stable in an orchard. *Meissonier's* picture of a commandant in a green buff coat, white trousers and top boots, straddling pompously before an open fireplace, puffing at his pipe, and frowning over a dispatch handed to him by a soldier, while a brother officer in scarlet lounges on an easy chair. The same artist's picture of troops halting while officers question a peasant. *Gerome's* "Sword Dance" of a beautiful slave before an Oriental dignitary, and an Oriental soldier leaning against the pillar of a courtyard and raising an earthen cup to his lips. *Zamocois'* "King's Favorite"; *Roybet's* "Florentine Dames and Cavaliers at a Concert"; *Breton's* Peasant Girl busy at her distaff, seated on a large stone, with shore and sea for background; *Bouguereau's* "Italian Flute Player"; *Frère's* "Two little Water Carriers in a snowy street". The girl has set down her pitcher to rub her chilled hands. *Daubigny's* "Cattle on the Shore of a Quiet Lake"; *Rosa Bonheur's* "Huntsman," leaning against a tree, dogs resting, and four horses awaiting their riders, the whole canvas flooded by a beautiful light. In the smaller adjoining room is *Meissonier's* portrait of William H. Vanderbilt showing him in an upright position in an arm-chair, his right hand resting on his knee, his left fingering his watch chain; *Meissonier's* "Artist and Wife" viewing the former's work; *Diaz's* "Scene in the Forest of Fontainbleau"; the same artist's "Moorish Children"; *Fromentin's* "Gambling Scene in a Tavern" and "Caravan Crossing a Stream"; *Troyon's* "Cattle"; *Dupré's* "Landscape"; *Detaille's* "Gen. Von Moltke and Staff"; *Rosa Bonheur's* "Sheep"; *Knaus's* "Village Festivity"; *Delacroix's* "Indian Warrior at the Head of his Troops." A number of fine water colors hang in a gallery about this room.

The Vanderbilt family is of Dutch origin. Members of it were settled at Flatbush, L. I., about 1650. In 1718, Jacob Van der Bilt purchased a farm near New Dorp, Staten Island. The family became members of the Moravian Church. Cornelius Vanderbilt (the "Commodore" and founder of the family's wealth) was born near Stapleton, May 27, 1794. He earned his first capital by doing a certain amount of work within a certain time on his mother's farm. His mother, thinking it impossible for him to do the work within the time specified, offered him $100 if he would accomplish the task. He hired a number of boys on his promise to give them free trips in the boat he intended purchasing with the money. The work was done; he bought a boat with the money and started a ferry to New York. Nineteen years later he was able to build a stately residence at Stapleton. He became a captain and later an owner of steamboats, subsequently owning steamships. He foresaw the prominent part railroads were destined to play in the development of the country and abandoned water traffic for railroad investments. The family now control the New York Central and Hudson River Railroad and many connecting lines. (See also p. 200).

On the northwest corner of Fifth avenue and Fifty-third street is *St. Thomas' Protestant Episcopal Church*, a wealthy congregation which does a large amount of charitable work. The chancel contains a representation in bronze of the Adoration of the Cross, by Lafarge. To the left hangs Lafarge's picture of the Resurrection; to the right Mary meeting the Shining Angels in the Garden, also by Lafarge. The entire block on the west side of Fifth avenue between Fifty-fourth and Fifty-fifth streets is taken up with St. Luke's Hospital. On the northwest corner of Fifth avenue and Fifty-fifth street is the Fifth Avenue Presbyterian Church, of which Rev. Dr. John Hall, one of the most noted Presbyterian divines, is pastor. On the southwest corner of Fifth avenue and Fifty-seventh street is the residence of ex-Secretary William C. Whitney, on the southeast corner that of Collis P. Huntington, on the northwest corner that of Cornelius Vanderbilt. Central Park begins at Fifty-ninth street, the open space beginning at Fifty-eighth street being the Plaza. Fifty-seventh street is one of the finest residence streets in the city, and it is well worth the vistor's while to make a short detour through it in either direction from Fifth avenue. At the southeast corner of Fifty-seventh street and Sixth avenue is the Sherwood Studio building, and between Sixth and Seventh avenues the Fine Arts Society's building. On Fifty-ninth street, between Sixth and Seventh avenues, are the series of apartment houses known in the aggregate as the "Central Park," but separately named after cities of Spain. They form an enormous pile of buildings, and show, perhaps, the largest scale upon which structures of this kind have been planned in New York.

The visitor interested in seeing another typical structure of this class will find the Dakota, a yellow brick pile, on Seventy-second street and Eighth avenue, of interest. It is visible from many points in Central Park, and in fact is so conspicuous an object that it often looms up in the landscape of the upper part of the city.

At Ninth avenue and Fifty-ninth street is the fine church and school of the Paulist Fathers, and opposite it the Roosevelt Hospital, one of the greatest institutions of its kind in the city (p. 60).

COLLEGE OF PHYSICIANS AND SURGEONS.—Here also is the College of Physicians and Surgeons of Columbia College, a group of buildings which are a donation from the late William H. Vanderbilt and his family, and from William D. Sloane, Mr. Vanderbilt's son-in-law. They consist of the school building proper, the Vanderbilt clinic, and the Sloane Maternity Hospital. On the second floor is a fine pathological collection, including the Swift Physiological Cabinet, and a large laboratory. The fourth floor, which is lighted entirely from above, and illuminated by electricity at night, is devoted to dissecting. It is fitted up with thirty-six tables, at which one hundred and thirty-eight students can dissect simultaneously. Smaller rooms for private dissection, and for the teaching of operative surgery upon the cadaver, are grouped around this apartment. The northern portion of the building is devoted nearly entirely to laboratory purposes. The Vanderbilt Clinic, endowed by sons of the late William H. Vanderbilt as a memorial, contains a fully equipped dispensary, and, in connection with the school, serves as a field for extended clinical instruction. It contains a theatre for clinical lectures, illustrated by practical work, which accommodates an audience of nearly four hundred. The Sloane Maternity Hospital, at the corner of Fifty-ninth street and Amsterdam avenue, adjoining the clinic, has a capacity of thirty beds.

In the vicinity of Central Park and Fifty-ninth street are a number of riding schools, the ride through the Park being a favorite jaunt for equestrians. The most convenient of these schools for strangers to visit are Durland's, situated at the Grand Circle, near the Eighth avenue entrance to Central Park; and Dickel's Riding Academy, the oldest in the city, at 124 West Fifty-sixth street, near Sixth avenue. Between Fifth and Madison avenues, running through from Fifty-eighth to Fifty-ninth street, is the four-story brick structure of the Riding Club, a private association with a membership of about 500, being the largest and most exclusive organization of its kind in the country. The club building has accommodations for 200 horses, and a ring 100x105 feet; initiation fee $20; annual dues $100.

In and near Central Park are three of the greatest institutions in the city. The Metropolitan Museum of Art in Central Park, near Fifth avenue opposite Eighty-third street; the Lenox Library, on Fifth avenue between Seventieth and Seventy-first streets; the American Museum of Natural History in Manhattan Square, between Seventy-seventh and Eighty-first streets, separated from Central Park only by Eighth avenue. The visitor who wishes to see these institutions thoroughly cannot do so by making them incidental to a tour of Central Park. They are, therefore, described at this point, the tour of Central Park being given in Chapter X.

CHAPTER IX.

METROPOLITAN MUSEUM OF ART.

Open every week-day 10 A. M. to 6 P. M., and Tuesdays and Saturdays 8 P. M. to 10 P. M. Admission free except Mondays and Tuesdays 25 cents, Tuesday nights, however, being free. The Metropolitan Museum of Art, situated in Central Park near Fifth avenue and Eighty-first street entrance, is a plain but substantial building leased to the Museum by the city.

HAND-BOOKS.—The collections are not yet completely catalogued. There are a brief general guide (10 cents); three hand-books of the paintings (10 cents each); a hand-book of the drawings, water-colors, photographs and etchings (10 cents); of the Oriental Porcelains (10 cents); and of the Johnston Collection of Engraved Gems (15 cents). Many of the important exhibits in the various uncatalogued collections are, however, fully labeled.

HISTORY.—The first attempt to found the institution which has developed into the Metropolitan Museum of Art, was made at a meeting of the Union League Club, in February, 1869. The matter was referred to the Art Committee of the club, which, November 23, 1869, called a meeting at the Academy of Music. A committee of fifty was appointed, which subsequently was enlarged to 116. Subsequently a provisional constitution was adopted, and at an executive meeting May 14, 1870, a special charter which had been secured from the Legislature, April 13, 1870, was presented, and a permanent constitution adopted. John Taylor Johnston, a well-known art connoisseur, was elected president. He has been a valued adviser and friend of the museum, and is now its honorary president. In April, 1871, the Legislature passed the Act by virtue of which the Metropolitan Museum of Art occupies its present quarters, where it may continue as long as it complies with the terms of the lease, but which it is at liberty to leave upon giving due notice.

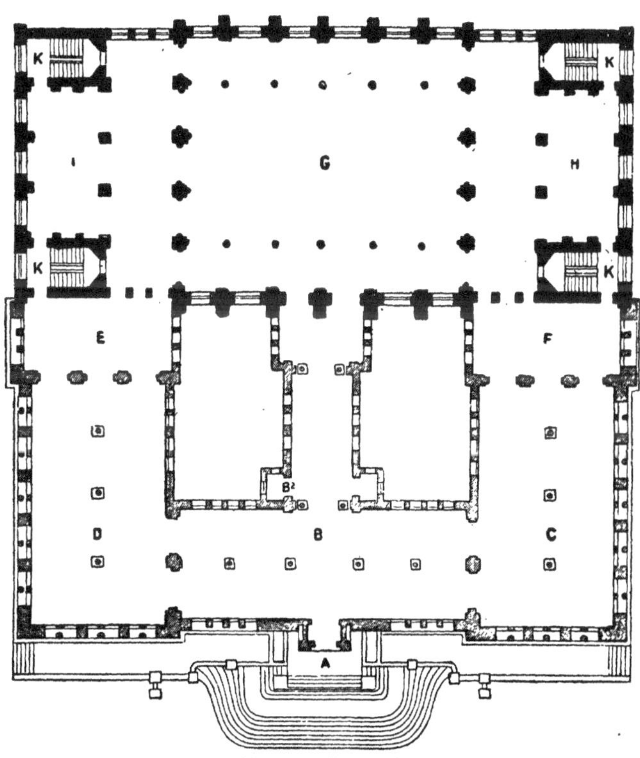

FIRST FLOOR.

METROPOLITAN MUSEUM OF ART.

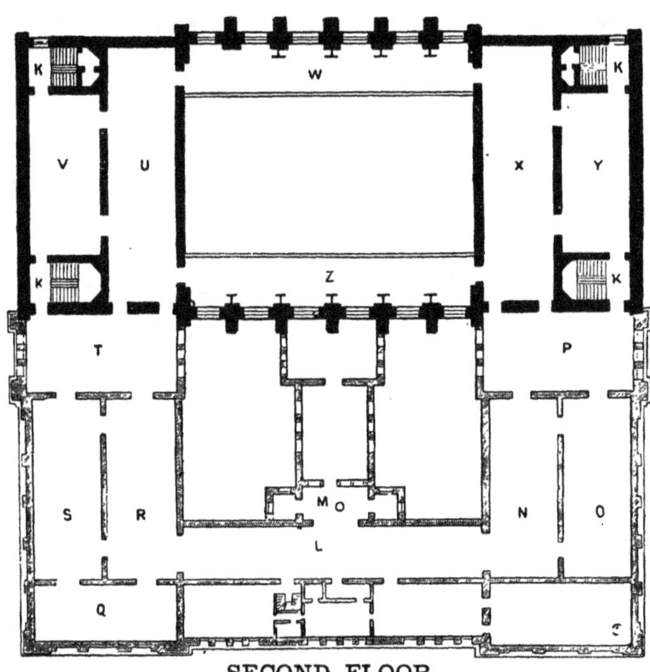

SECOND FLOOR.

METROPOLITAN MUSEUM OF ART.

It moved into this building during March and April, 1879, having previously occupied buildings respectively on Fifth avenue, between Fifty-third and Fifty-fourth streets, and on the south side of Fourteenth street, between Sixth and Seventh avenues. During the removal to the present structure, the trustees carefully superintended the packing of the various objects, doing much of the work with their own hands, a fact which illustrates the deep interest they take in the welfare of the institution. In December, 1888, the first extension to the building was opened, and, as the collections in the museum are growing at a remarkably rapid rate, another is now being erected.

MEMBERSHIP.—The contribution of $1,000 or more to the funds of the Museum at any one time entitles the donor to be a Patron. Such person enjoys a Patron's right in perpetuity for each sum of $1,000 so contributed, and has the privilege of appointing his successor. The contribution of $500 at one time entitles the donor to be a Fellow in perpetuity, who also has the right to appoint his successor. The contribution of $200 at one time entitles the donor to be a Fellow for life. Persons may become Annual Members at a subscription of $10. Patrons, Fellows, and Members are entitled to certain desirable privileges. The present officers of the Museum are: President, Henry G. Marquand; vice-presidents, William C. Prime and Daniel Huntington: treasurer, Salem H. Wales; secretary, L. P. Di Cesnola; librarian, William N. Andrews. L. P. Di Cesnola is director; Isaac H. Hall, curator of the Department of Sculpture; John A. Paine, curator of the Department of Casts; George H. Story, curator of the Department of Paintings; and Arthur L. Tuckerman, manager of the Art Schools.

The Metropolitan Museum of Art is the most important institution of its kind in the United States. In wealth and variety of collections it cannot, of course, compare with the British Museum, or with several others in foreign countries. But when it is considered how recent a creation it is, its growth to its present dimensions is most remarkable. Moreover, it has proceeded upon the admirable plan of making such collections as it possesses complete of their kind, and it therefore, in some details, surpasses all other similar institutions. The Cesnola collection, the glass and gem collections, and the collection of Egyptian textiles, for instance, are unrivaled; the collection of mummies, though small, is varied, and each specimen in it is very fine and interesting; the collection of Indian idols from New Mexico is unique, and the collections of paintings by Dutch masters and of the work of the most distinguished modern painters are large and important.

The diagrams show the general arrangement of the building.

THE COLLECTIONS.—The entrance (A) leads into the *Hall of Casts of Ancient Sculpture* (B). Here are reproductions of the most noted remains of ancient Greek, Roman, Assyrian and Egyptian sculpture, all the objects being labeled. On the floor of the larger portion of the hall, running east and west, are statues of ancient sculpture. Around the wall at the top, beginning on the west side of the principal entrance, are reproductions of famous friezes. Directly opposite the principal entrance (A) is a passage connecting this hall (B) with the Hall of Architectural Casts (G). In the alcove (B2) is a collection of Renaissance wrought iron. Against the pier at the north end is the "Assumption of the Virgin," by *Luca della Robia*, and on the sides of the pier are photographs of several works of the Della Robias. The "Assumption," a fine example of Luca della Robia's work, was originally in the mortuary chapel of the Prince of Piombino and was presented to the Museum by Henry G. Marquand, who is also the donor of the wrought iron in the alcove.

Hall of Architectural Casts (*G*).—The central exhibit in the Hall of Architectural Casts into which this passage leads is the superb pulpit from the Cathedral at Sienna, the work of Nichola Pisano, 1268 A. D. Facing it from the south is the elaborate façade of the Guild of the Butcher's House at Hildesheim, 1529 A. D. Facing it from the north is a one-twentieth reproduction of the front of the Cathedral Notre Dame, Paris. To the right of the pulpit is a superb reproduction of the Parthenon exterior and interior with the frieze and sculptures of the pediment colored. To the left of the pulpit are, among other objects, Bay of Cloisters, St. John Lateran, Rome,

Twelfth Century A. D.; Shrine of Saint Sebaldus, Nuremberg, Peter Vischer & Sons, 1519 A. D.; Standard Bearer from the plaza of St. Mark's, Venice; Alessanndro Leopardi, 1505 A. D.

On the north face of the gallery of this hall and continued over the eastern half of the south face are casts from the frieze of the cella of the Parthenon, arranged so that the center of the eastern frieze of the Parthenon forms the center of the north face of the gallery, the whole corresponding as nearly as possible to the position of the original on a line from this center. All the architectural casts in this hall are purchases made with a fund bequeathed to the Museum in 1884 by Levi S. Willard.

The object in this room which will probably strike the general visitor as most interesting is the large canvas, "Diana's Hunting Party," by *Hans Makart*, on the west wall. It was presented by Mrs. Ellen Josephine Bancker. It is 31 feet in length by 14 feet in height and has become familiar through frequent reproductions. Diana and her train have reached the rocky shore of a lake in full pursuit of a deer, which has just plunged into the water. In spite of the many and important accessory figures Diana remains the central object of interest. She stands firmly posed upon a rock, her lance poised for the throw. Her face, crowned with auburn hair, is beautiful, but lighted up with the fierce joy of the hunt. Of the six nymphs in her train all but one seem impelled by the same savage spirit, the one exception being the nymph at Diana's left, who looks up to the goddess with a pitying glance, as if pleading for the hunted animal. Between the deer and its pursuers seven naiads have swum protectingly, one of them—the chief figure in this group—rising far out of the water, with her auburn hair streaming down her back and her arms high uplifted as if protesting and exposing her own fair body to Diana's weapon. The nude forms of these naiads follow in their lines the sweeping undulations of the waves which dash up into the rocky cove.

Over this canvas and also over the canvases on the other walls are tapestries by Furguad de Lavergne dated 1788. The paintings on the east wall are *Benjamin Constant's* "Justinian in Council," presented by G.

Mannheimer; *Ludwig Knaus'* "Peace," and *Gustav Richter's* "Victory," the last two presented by Jacob F. Schiff,

Egyptian Antiquities.—The visitor should now proceed to the Hall of Ancient Sculpture and Egyptian Antiquities (C) and view the mummies and other Egyptian antiquities in this hall and in the room of Ancient Terra Cottas (F), and then continue his study of the forms of ancient burial, as shown in the cases of Egyptian mummies, by inspecting the fine sarcophagi in the Hall of Ancient Statuary, Inscriptions and Bronzes (H). The mummies are in two lines of cases, beginning on the floor on the west side of the Hall of Ancient Sculpture and Egyptian Antiquities (C). The specimens are varied and mostly in a fine state of preservation. Many of them are from the sealed tomb of Gourmet-Mourrai, discovered by Maspero in 1886. The student can here see the mummy swathed in mummy cloth; the cartonage which, consisting of some 15 to 20 strips of linen gummed together, was pressed over the body and thus made to reproduce its contour and even the features of the face; the first casket into which the mummy and cartonage were placed, and the outer case into which the smaller one was set. Indeed one exhibit shows even a third case. (See below.) The caskets were shaped to conform with the figure of the deceased and the carved features on the upper lid were a representation of the face of the dead. The cases are fully labeled.

One of the finest caskets in the collection is in case 83, which is the first in the line of cases to the left on entering from the Hall of Casts of Ancient Sculpture (B). This is made of cedar probably from Lebanon, and certainly not from a less distance than the Taurus range. Case 79 forms with case 77, and the casket standing on the top of case 68, the most complete exhibit in the collection, 79 showing the inner casket and mummy of Khelshire from Gebelin, 77 containing the outer casket and cartonage, the latter finely preserved, of the same mummy, and a second outer casket standing on the top of 68. We have, therefore, here a complete example of the Egyptian mode of preserving the dead. On the upper shelf of 78 are mummied feet and heads from Thebes, showing the appearance of the features and the feet several thousand years after they were embalmed. Though the features can be easily traced the heads are ghastly objects after all, and one cannot help thinking that it is preferable to change into a plain white skeleton rather than to remain a brown and shrunken mummy. In 75 are the mummy, cartonage and the wooden figure of Iounofirte, who, to judge from the hierogliphics on the casket and the carved features, must have been a young woman of beauty and wealth. Case 73 contains, beside an inner casket and mummy, three closets for the preservation of funerary statuettes, and two boxes divided within into four compartments for the protection of funerary jars.

The collection of miscellaneous Egyptian antiquities begins at case 48 on the west wall of the Hall of Ancient Sculpture and Egyptian Antiquities (C). This contains one of the largest known collections of funerary statuettes ("respondents") of porcelain, clay, wood and terra cotta. These were buried with the deceased in mummy cases and closets, such as are exhibited in case No. 73 above. Those in blue porcelain are from the remarkable discovery of tombs of kings and princes of the twenty-first dynasty at Deir-El-Bahari. These statuettes hold in their hands hoes and picks and have baskets slung over their shoulders. The belief was that when the deceased entered the Elysian Fields and work was demanded of him by the supernatural authorities there, these statuettes would rise up and perform the labor required of the deceased. This collection of statuettes extends through cases 48 to 53 and are from the Maspero collection. Other collections represented in the Egyptian antiquities are those of J. W. Drexel, Jas. Douglass, and Farnham. Besides the statuettes referred to, there are: In 49 a statuette of an Egyptian gentleman, a wooden head-rest showing that the Egyptian gentleman had very uncomfortable sleeping accommodations; a mummified Osiris on a block containing the mummy of a sparrow; in 51 to 53, besides funerary statuettes, the fine Egyptian bronzes of the Drexel collection, there being on the floor of 51 a statuette of Osiris standing upon a hawk-shaped coffin containing the mummy of a hawk (the gift of R. M. Laimbeer); in 66, top shelf, several mummies of cats, and in other parts of the case bricks, with and without straw, stamped with the cartouche of the rulers, chiefly of the eighteenth dynasty, during which the Children of Israel were captives in Egypt, the inference being that some of these bricks were made by them. A collection of ancient Egyptian textile fabrics will be found in standards in the Hall of Ancient Statuary and Egyptian Antiquities (C) and in the Hall of Ancient Statuary and Inscriptions and Bronzes (H). Many of the specimens are woven in colored patterns and comprise articles of apparel, both plain and ornamental, and mummy cloths, with designs or attached borders, which were found at Sakkarah, Faiyum and Ahkmyn. They date chiefly from the second to the eleventh century of the Christian era. The most interesting standards are those in the Hall of Ancient Statuary, Inscriptions and Bronzes (H), which were presented to the Museum by George F. Baker, who purchased them of Emile Brugsch Bey, curator of the Boulek Museum, now at Gizeh, Cairo. No 1210, in the southwest standard of H, shows what may be the earliest pictures of episodes in the life of Christ, as they date from the third century A. D. These standards, with those in the Hall of Ancient Sculpture and Ancient Antiquities, form the most complete collection of its kind in the world.

Greek Vases.—There are two small but excellent collections on this side of the first floor to be inspected before taking up the sarcophagi chiefly from the Cesnola collection, to which all the other objects in the rooms on this side of the building belong, and which, therefore, should be considered together. The first of the small collections referred to consists of very fine specimens of Greek vases contained in four large table-cases standing on the floor of the Room of Ancient Terra Cottas (F). These were discovered at Alexandria, and are admirable specimens of Greek art in Egypt. They were probably mostly made and sold as water jars (hydriae), but, as the Greeks cremated their dead and no other strictly funerary jars could be obtained, hydriae were used for cinerary purposes and inscribed in ink or scratches with the name of the deceased and the date of his death.

On the west center pier between this room and the

Hall of Ancient Statuary and Egyptian Antiquities is the Ward collection of clay tablets from Assyria and Babylonia, a small but excellent cabinet.

Hall of Ancient Sculpture, Inscriptions and Bronzes (H).—The *Sarcophagi* in this hall form an interesting continuation of the mummy series. No. 6, which stands against the east wall in the passage between the Room of Ancient Terra Cottas (F) and the Hall of Ancient Statuary, Inscriptions and Bronzes (H), is a superb marble sarcophagus of Roman workmanship dating from 1 or 2 A. D., discovered near Rome, the sculpture being of the vigorous Roman type. 5 is a Greek sarcophagus from Tarsus, presented by Abdodebdas. It is of Roman style of the time of the Roman Empire. One side is unfinished, showing that it was intended to rest against the wall of the tomb. 3 is the casket of a king of Cyprus, who reigned about 600 B. C., found at Golgos in Cyprus. On the southern end of this casket is a representation (sculptured) of the myth of Perseus and Medusa. Perseus has cut off the Medusa's head and is making off with it in his wallet. Pegasus and Chrysaor spring from the neck of Medusa. Perseus and Medusa are of Assyrian features and in Assyrian garb, showing the Assyrian origin of a myth which has always been attributed to the Greeks. The east side of the casket is pure Greek, but is evidently copied, because, although it represents only a hunt, those engaged in it are fully armed for battle. One of the most interesting of all the specimens of sarcophagi is No. 1, as it shows quite a remarkable combination of various styles of art, and seems to reflect the conflux of nations which, from time to time, inhabited Cyprus. It was discovered at Amathus, a Phœnician city of Cyprus, in a tomb 55 feet below the surface of the soil. A large part of the cover is missing, but the rest is in an excellent state of preservation. The friezes show not only the Egyptian lotus, but also the egg and tongue design of Greek origin. The borders at each end are Phœnician, as are the panels, the south end showing the Cyprian Venus, a nude figure, excepting for the necklace, in her characteristic attitude supporting her breasts with her hands. The Sphinxes on the pediments are again Greek, as they have female heads. There are also Greek figures on the sides, among them being warriors in chariots; the number of spokes in the wheels of the chariots differing, thus contradicting the theory which was once ingeniously advanced that it would be possible to determine the relative age of sculpture containing chariots by the number of spokes in the wheels, the suggestion being that the fewer the spokes the more ancient the piece of sculpture, as it would show ruder and more primitive methods of manufacturing chariots.

On the east wall of the northern end of this hall are panels of ancient figures and glazed Persian tiles. Against the east wall in the north corner are the fragments of the bronze crabs taken from the base of the obelisk (Cleopatra's Needle) now in Central Park.

Cesnola Collection.—Having disposed of the other collections and miscellaneous objects on the eastern side of the first floor, it is now possible for the visitor to view systematically the Cesnola collection of Cypriot antiquities. Cyprus is one of the largest islands in the Mediterranean, the Kittim of the Bible. Its first colonists were probably the Phœnicians of Tyre; and the most ancient antiquities in the Cesnola collection are objects of Phœnician make. There were two Egyptian occupations, and the island at various times paid tribute to Persia and Assyria, so that we have among the antiquities coming immediately after those of Phœnician origin, Egyptian and Assyrian relics. From about 333 B. C. until 58 B. C. the island was held by the Ptolemies and was then reduced to a Roman province. The antiquities of these epochs are Archaic Greek, pure Greek and Græco-Roman. The various divisions of the collection are arranged to show the progression from the Phœnician through the Egyptian and Assyrian, Archaic Greek and Greek to the Græco-Roman. These antiquities were discovered by General Louis Palma Di Cesnola, while U. S. Consul at Cyprus. Soon after he had settled in the consulate at Larnaca he became impressed with the thought that as Cyprus had been the great central meeting point of the ancient races above mentioned, relics of these races might be discovered, and he decided to institute excavations, which he conducted with great tact and perseverance.

The objects excavated were remarkably well preserved, owing to the fact that the Cypriots built their walls of mud. In 1874, after the Metropolitan Museum of Art had in 1873 acquired the collection of Cypriot antiquities made by Cesnola, up to that year, he continued his explorations on the site of ancient Curium. Discovering the mosaic pavement of a temple in that ruined city, he sank a shaft some 20 feet below it. Here he found a vaulted passage leading to a door, on breaking through which he entered the treasure chambers of the temple, four vaulted rooms containing objects in gold, silver, pottery, alabaster and bronze. Piles of silver dishes which had become attached to each other by oxidation, gave evidence of the richness of the room. These objects had great inherent value, but they were even more valuable as an illustration of art history, which had been a sealed book heretofore. The temple of Curium was destroyed certainly as early as 6 B. C., possibly earlier. It is at about this time that the history of Greek art commenced, and as the treasures of this temple dated back to an earlier period, it will be seen that the discovery was of importance from an historical point of view, affording as it did a knowledge of Greek art older than any yet known. In fact, when Gen. Di Cesnola opened the doorway at the end of this vaulted passage, he opened the entrance to an art history and a history of man and of civilization preceding the earliest known history of Greek art, and leading back to the source of Greek civilization. Indeed, in the light thrown upon the origin of Greek art by this collection, the Greeks appear as inspired adapters of the art of earlier civilizations, rather than as originators. The valuable Curium treasure was also obtained by the Museum. The authenticity and integrity of the Cesnola collection was attacked and vindicated in court in what is known as the Feuerdent-Cesnola trial, which lasted through November and December, 1883.

Statuary, Inscriptions and Bronzes.—Arrranged in the Hall of Ancient Statuary, Inscriptions and Bronzes (II) against the piers on the west side and on the center piers, beginning with case 10, is a collection of statuary illustrating the various epochs of art represented in the Cypriot discoveries—Phœnician to Græco-Roman; No. 16, in case 11, is an Assyrian statue in a remarkably fine state of preservation; No. 19 is a statue, probably of

Heracles, with a lion's skin for a cloak and head-dress; No. 22, in case 13, an Assyrian head with wonderfully fine sculpturing of the hair, was borrowed and copied by Ruskin. In the east wing of this hall are cases of Phœnician, Cypriot and Greek inscriptions. On the north wall are the bronzes discovered among the Curium treasure, including large cauldrons with ornamental handles, vases of great beauty, mirrors, weapons of various kinds, tripods, the bit from a bridle, and the candelabra of a temple.

Terra Cottas.—In the Hall of Ancient Terra Cottas (F) beginning on the north wall, against which stand cases 1 to 6, are the terra cottas of the Cesnola collection, a large number of pieces of great interest to students. The pieces from 1 to 82 are various representations of Venus, beginning with the Semitic Venus or the Venus of Cyprus, a nude female figure supporting her breasts with her hands (the first examples having animal heads), and running the ethnological gamut to pure Greek, 82 being a graceful little figure of a Greek Venus with a child, very much like a sculptured representation of a Madonna and child. Then comes a series of statuettes of musicians, probably of the temples. The little group, 120, seems to represent a judge (in the center) watching a sentence executed upon a thief, the lamb held by the man on the right probably being the object stolen. In the lower part of cases 1 to 6 are larger objects of statuary, including 248, a finely preserved Phœnician head as shown by the pointed features; and 268, a woman's head in pure Greek style. The terra cotta heads in these cases are unique as far as size is concerned. The cases continue from 7 to 13 along the east wall of this room. There are, beginning on the upper shelf, horsemen from the rudest kind of Phœnician art, showing the giraffe-neck horses such as are found in the early pottery of the Cesnola collection, to the fine figure 418, and the elegantly sculptured horse's head beside it. Six pieces, 334 A–F, found in one tomb, evidently illustrate the funeral procession of the person buried there. In the cases around the piers are a large number of terra cotta lamps.

Sculptures.—The Cesnola collection continues in the Hall of Ancient Sculpture and Egyptian Antiquities (C).

There is a line of seven floor-cases on the east side of the hall. Remarkable in case 2 is 183, a colossal Assyrian head. It was claimed in the Feuerdent-Cesnola trial that the nose was added to this statue, and this poor Assyrian gentleman was submitted to the indignity of having a hole drilled in his nasal organ. No. 157, in case 13, in the line ranged against the east wall, is the most famous exhibit in the Feuerdent-Cesnola trial. It was claimed that General Di Cesnola had attempted to palm this off as a figure of Venus holding a mirror, and that the mirror had been taken from some other statuette and patched upon 157. A sculptor testified that the restorer had been so enthusiastic in his work that he had added a sixth toe to one of the feet, but this was afterward shown to be the string of a sandal. In case 30 are various representations of the god Pan. The contents of 31 to 32 are chiefly Archaic Greek and Greek heads of Artemis. The objects in 33 and 34 are Græco-Roman; in 35, unclassified. The marbles of the Cesnola collection are in 43 and 44, the latter containing a large votive ship, from which men are being cast overboard to sea monsters, found at Tarsus in 1876 and presented by John Todd Edgar. Case 45 contains fine alabasters from Phœnician, Egyptian and Greek tombs at Cyprus, chiefly from the Curium treasure. In 46 are various articles in serpentine and in 47 several green-glazed terra cottas, the collection extending to 57, inclusive.

Pottery.—In order to continue the inspection of the Cesnola collection it is necessary to cross the Hall of Casts and Ancient Sculpture (B) to the Hall of Glass, Laces and Ancient Pottery (D). The collection of pottery begins in the northwest corner of the Hall, being arranged in wall and floor cases, the latter containing large vases. The gem of the collection is the large vase on the top shelf in floor case 7. This it from the Curium treasure, and is known as the Great Vase of Curium. It is of brown clay, and covered from top to bottom with decorations. In shape it is unique in the collection, being the only jar on a high foot, and the only vase with four handles. The lid is crowned with a little hydria. From its size and profusion of decoration this vase is one of the finest specimens of its class, and in its early days must have been a superb work of art.

Cases 8 and 9 around the northwest pier, and also 10 against the west wall, contain small objects, among them numerous whorls from Cyprus spindles. On the second shelf of 11 is an object looking like a cluster of small salt cellars. This was probably used for partridge eggs, which are still sold as a delicacy in Cyprus in little wickers closely resembling in shape this article of ancient pottery. In 12 are milk pans; on the third shelf of 18 near 19 and in 19 several infants' feeding-bottles, perforated so that they could be hung around the neck by a string. On the top shelf of 20 are two vases which are filled through a hole in the bottom, a funnel extending to within a very short distance of the top. In 21 and 22 are probably the first objects in the collection made with the potter's wheel. Two little vases in 25 are arranged to show how the trefoil mouth, which has been so much praised in Greek vases, originated in Oriental art. No. 2,300 is a small vase of exquisite shape crowned with an ox head. If this ox head were to be cut in two horizontally, the snout, ears and back of the head would form a trefoil, and in order to show this more clearly a pretty little trefoil vase is placed next to it. On the first shelf of 26 and extending along the corresponding shelf to 30, is a series of vases having for nozzles a pitcher or jar held by a female figure leaning against the neck of a large vase. No. 2,283 B in 29 shows three cups on a hollow pipe at different heights, so that water will run from the highest into the other two and lastly from the nozzle. Case 30 contains a vase, the top of which is modeled after the head and bust of a woman. In 34 are vases on which are rudely painted human heads with mouths for nozzles; in 37, vases with trefoil mouths, the perfect development of which by the Greeks may be seen in case 43; in 38 a number of cups, the adaptation of whose shape by the Greeks may be seen in 44. One of the gems of the collection, a lovely slender amphora, stands upon the middle of the fourth shelf in 41. Cases 45 and 46 contain some specimens of Italian pottery presented by Gen. Cesnola to the Museum.

Glass.—Most of the pieces in the Museum's unequaled collection of ancient glass belong to the Cesnola collection. No other museum contains glass dating back to 800 B. C. like the specimens of Assyrian, Phœnician and Egyptian glass in case 59, against the eastern center pier of the room. The gem of the ancient glass collection is in 47. It is of unrivaled iridescence, supposed to have been caused by the liquiescence of the bodies in the tombs in which the glass was found. There are other fine examples of iridescence in the collection. The glass, excepting the cabinet dating back to 800 B. C., is mostly from 1 B. C. to 1 A. D. The Marquand collection of Græco-Roman glass begins at floor case 62 on the east side of this hall. Probably the most valuable piece in this case is a yellow cup conspicuous on the top step, which bears an inscription and also shows figures of warriors. On the fourth step of case 64 is an exquisitely shaped blue vase. In the lower parts of these cases are specimens of mediæval French glass, the finest specimen being a cup with a crown and fleur-de-lis as a cover, on the west side of case 63. Cases 65 and 66 contain the Jarves collection of Venetian glass. Case 65 dates from 1560 to 1600, the finest specimen being a large yellow vase standing upon the coil of a sea serpent. Case 66 dates from 1600 to 1700. In it is a superb toilet cabinet entirely of glass. Case 67 dates from 1700 to 1750 and shows a falling off in the grade of workmanship. Case 68 dates from 1750 to 1800, the most interesting objects in it being two candelabra.

Miscellaneous.—Down the center of this hall are standards containing a collection of laces, one standard presented by Mrs. Robert L. Stuart, and another by Mrs. John Jacob Astor. On the center pier between this hall and the Room of Carved Wood and Musical Instruments (E) is a case of shrines, a bequest of Mrs. A. M. Minturn. The Room of Carved Wood and Musical Instruments contains a remarkable exhibition of the latter, composed of the Joseph W. Drexel and J. Crosby Brown collections, consisting of antique and modern musical instruments of great variety in construction and nationality, many of them Oriental and aboriginal, all of them being ethnologically arranged, and thoroughly labeled. Besides the instruments there are in this room a finely carved clock of English work, dated 1640, a valuable cabinet inlaid with Oriental porcelains, and a case of drawers and shelves, to which a gold medal at the Centennial Exhibition of 1876 was awarded, it being mentioned in the Committee's report as the most elegant piece of wood carving and designing in the Exposition. It was presented by August Pottier. North of this room is the Hall of Modern Sculpture (I), which contains several notable examples of the work of American and European sculpture, among them a cast of Barye's "Lion and Serpent."

STAIRCASES.—There are staircases (K) at either corner of the Hall of Ancient Statuary (H) and of the Hall of Modern Sculpture (I). These latter are respectively the southwest and northwest stairways. The southwest stairway is hung with Fagnani's pictures of the Nine Muses, which are portraits of New York women, and with ten other paintings, of which 19 is *Murillo's* "Holy Family," the picture known as the "Brevoort Murillo," presented by the late John Jacob Astor Bristed. The southeast stairway has, among a number of old masters, a fine example of *Antonio Pollajuolo* (Florentine School, 1433 to 1498), "St. Christopher and the Infant Christ" (110), cut from the walls of the chapel of the Michelozzi Villa and presented to the Museum by Cornelius Vanderbilt, and the "Head of a Cherub," by *Correggio* (111). Among the paintings on the northeast stairway is *Ruben's* "Lions Chasing the Deer" (120).

PAINTINGS.—The fine collection of paintings by both old and modern masters which is owned by the Museum, is distributed through various galleries on the second floor, and in arranging the descriptions thereof, it has been thought best to conduct the visitor consecutively through the galleries in which are hung the modern paintings (the most interesting to the general public) and then through those which contain examples of the old masters. The visitor will find the most noted of the modern paintings in the old western gallery U, which is reached from either of the staircases on the western side. The southern end of this gallery is filled with 78, the "Horse Fair," by *Rosa Bonheur*, presented by Cornelius Vanderbilt, in 1887. It was first exhibited at the Paris Salon in 1853, but it did not find a purchaser. In 1855 she offered to sell it to Bordeaux, her native town, for 12,000 francs ($2,400). The town refusing to purchase it, she sold it to Gambert for 40,000 francs, painting for him a quarter-size replica, from which Thomas Landseer made the famous engraving. Gambert sold the original in 1857 to William P. Wright, of New York, for 30,000 francs. In 1870 he offered to re-purchase it for 50,000 francs, but the offer was refused. When the Wright collection was sold the picture was bought by A. T. Stewart, and at the sale of his collection it was purchased by Mr. Vanderbilt for $53,500. The replica from which the engraving is made, is now in the National Gallery at London. A second, still smaller replica, brought on its last sale $20,000, and a still smaller water color drawing of it, $12,000. Another of the modern masterpieces in this gallery which is among the first pictures of the collection to be sought out by visitors, is 71, *Meissonier's* "Friedland, 1807," which hangs between the doors of the west wall. It was presented to the Museum by Henry Hilton, in 1887, having been purchased by him for $66,000 at the Stewart sale. The beholder can hardly fail to be impressed with the magnificent swing of horses and riders as the regiment of cuirrasiers dashes past Napoleon I in review on its way to battle. The horses seem almost as if they might leap pell mell from the canvas into the open. Meissonier writing to Mr. Stewart, January 7, 1876, says:

"I did not intend to paint a battle—I wanted to paint Napoleon at the acme of his glory—I wanted to paint the love, the adoration of the soldiers for the great Captain in whom they had faith, and for whom they were ready to die. * * * As to the execution, only a painter (and one of great experience) can say what time labor and patience have been brought to bear upon this work to produce a single whole out of so many diverse elements. The growing wheat is even proof of the difficulties I have encountered in covering it with the dust which hides so many things."

A third work apt to attract attention is 93, *Detaille's*, the "Defence of Champigny," a spirited battle scene, for, although the enemy is not visible, his nearness is felt. Groups of officers and soldiers, sappeurs making embrazures in the wall, barricadiers, artillerists placing guns in position, and the spirited detail on the balcony, all combine to make this a notable canvas full of the fierce energy and action of war. It was also presented by Mr. Hilton. There are several other notable paintings in this gallery, among them *Fortuny's* portrait of "A Spanish Lady in Black," a picture of surpassing grace and a model of portraiture, on the west wall between the door and the north wall. Next to it is 76, *Dannat's* "Un Quatuor" (A Quartette), a capital work, presented by Mrs. Wm. H. Dannat. The oldest of the singers, evidently the basso, sits on a bench singing away in an unemotional style, as if his duty consisted solely in producing a certain amount of sound. A handsome young girl beside him, though evidently weary, is trying to force a professional smile. The tenor standing behind leans gracefully against the wall, and tenor-like is smiling while singing as if flirting with some fair listener. 128, at the southern end of the west wall, *L'Hermitte's*, "The Vintage," presented by William Schaus, shows a robust young woman resting her kindly look upon a vigorous boy half recumbent upon the ground devouring grapes, while a bronzed man and a hale old woman are busy cutting bunches from the vines. The broad, vigorous treatment of the figures and vineyard is admirable. About opposite this is *Baixeras's*, "Boatmen at Barcelona" (105), presented by George I. Seney, a group of gossiping old salts, so true to life that you can even picture the features of the one whose face is turned away. 89 and 96 are capital little sheep scenes by Mauve, the wool being delightfully thick and soft looking, while 86, *Clairin's* "Moorish Sentinel," bequeathed by Stephen Whitney Phoenix, may be pointed out as a fine example of rich coloring. From this gallery the visitor should pass into V to the west. The most striking canvas in this gallery hangs on the north wall, 41, *Francois Auguste Bonheur*, "Woodland and Cattle," with its flood of beautiful light, presented by James Clinch Smith and his sisters. Next to this in interest is 32, *Lerolle's* "Organ Rehearsal," presented by George I. Seney, a large canvas, which has all the disenchantment of a peep behind the scenes. Among other pictures in this gallery is *Piloty's* "Thusnelda at the Triumphal Entry of Germanicus into Rome," painted to order for the late A. T. Stewart and presented by Horace Russell. Before being sent to this country it was exhibited in Berlin at the request of Emperor William I, and a large replica of it hangs in the Munich Gallery. The principal figure is the proud Thusnelda, with her little son.

From this gallery the visitor should proceed to the

galleries containing the Catharine Lorillard Wolfe collection of paintings (S and R), which are reached through the Gallery of Memorials of Washington, Franklin and Lafayette.

Miss Wolfe, who bequeathed the collection to the Museum, was the daughter of John David Wolfe, who at the time of his death was President of the American Museum of Natural History in New York. Beginning in Gallery S the most noteworthy canvases are: 1—The fine portrait of Miss Wolfe by *Cabanel,* painted from sittings at Paris in 1876, showing an intellectual face set upon a slender, aristocratic figure. 15—*Bonnat,* "Egyptian Fellah Woman and Child," a woman with a wonderfully pathetic face, bearing upon her shoulders a sleeping child whose head rests on hers. 16—*Breton's,* "Returning from the Christening." 18—*Munkacsy,* "A Pawnbroker's Shop." 19—*Vibert's* "The Reprimand," full of the painter's capital humor. 20—*Bargue,* "A Bashi Bazouk," a fine example of rich though subdued coloring. 22—*Troyon,* "Holland Cattle." 25—*Merle,* "Falling Leaves," a lovely figure of a girl half draped in black gold striped gauze. 27—*Rosa Bonheur,* "Weaning the Calves." 28—*Kaulbach,* "Crusaders Before Jerusalem," an allegorical painting, the intention of the artist being to express symbolically the idea that Christianity is the religion of the universe. 30—*Lefebvre,* "Graziella, a Girl of Capri." 32—*Kaemmerer,* "Study of a Girl's Head," full of this artist's characteristic chic. 33—*Madrazo,* "Girls at a Window," a coquetish bit. 36—*Piloty,* "Parable of the Wise and Foolish Virgins." 44—*Schreyer,* "Arabs on the March." 45—*Le Roux,* "Roman Ladies at the Tomb of their Ancestors," a strong little canvas. 48—*Gérôme,* "Prayer in a Mosque; old Cairo." 51—*Cot,* "The Storm," a powerful canvas, showing sheep huddling together in a wild winter storm. 53—*Rousseau,* "River Landscape." 60—*Corot,* "Ville d'Avery." 61—*Troyon,* "Study of a White Cow."

Gallery R: 63—*Meissonier,* "The Brothers Adrian and William Van de Velde." 64—*Gérôme,* "Boy of the Bischari Tribe." 68—*Breton,* "A Peasant Girl Knitting." 69—*Couture,* "The Idle Student." 74—*Breton,* "Religious Procession in Britany," perhaps the most interesting painting in the collection, with spare, wiry figures of peasants, wearing the trunk hose of the sixteenth century, their features thin yet bronzed and strong; and lines of peasant women and girls looking on as the procession passes. 76—*Defregger*, "German Peasant Girl." 79—*Bouguereau*, "Brother and Sister." 84—*Meissonier*, "A General and Adjutant." 92—*Dupré*, "The Old Oak." 94—*Detaille*, "Skirmish between Cossacks and the Imperial Body Guard, 1814." 95—*Vernet*, "Horses." 101—*Vibert*, "The Startled Confessor." 102—*Henner*, "A Bather," one of this artist's characteristic nudes. 106—*Max*, "The Last Token," the popular painting, familiar from numerous reproductions, of a young girl about to suffer Christian martyrdom in the Colosseum looking up as if to discover whose friendly hand dropped the flower that has fallen at her feet. 111—*Cabanel*, "The Shulamite Woman," full of eager expectation. 113—*Meyer Von Bremen*, "The Letter." 115—*Knaus*, "Repose of the Holy Family in Egypt." 116—*Roybet*, "The Game of Cards." 118—*Willems*, "Preparing for the Promenade." 119—*Berne-Bellecour*, "Soldier in the Trenches." 122—*Falero*, "Twin Stars." 123—*Doré*, "The Retreat from Moscow." 136—*Bida*, "The Massacre of the Mamelukes." 137—*Leloir*, "Wandering Minstrel, Old Nuremburg." 138—*Meissonier*, "The Sign Painter." 140—*Leloir*, "In His Cups." 141—*Boughton*, "A Puritan Girl," the last-named painted on wood, the preceding three being water colors.

In order to continue with the collections of modern paintings, the visitor should next proceed to Gallery X. Among the paintings hung here are usually such as are loaned to the Museum, which may be either old or modern. Some very noted pictures have, from time to time, been loaned to the Museum. The last most notable collection hung in this gallery was that loaned by H. O. Havemeyer, consisting of fourteen masterpieces, including three portraits by Rembrandt, among them the famous "Gilder." Among modern paintings belonging to the Museum in this gallery are: 34—*Bastien Le Page*, "Joan of Arc," one of the most notable modern canvases in the Museum, showing Joan of Arc before she became her country's savior, her face that of a homely peasant girl, but lighted up with the fire of exaltation and the spirit of prophecy, while in the background are the shadowy figures of her future; 57—*Messerschmitt*, "Wallenstein's Camp," a scene in the spring of 1635, representing an episode in the war of the Reformation in Austria and Hungary; 64—*Brozik Vacslav*, "Columbus at the Court of Ferdinand and Isabella," a large canvas presented by Morris K. Jesup, it being most fit that it should hang in this Museum, as it represents the beginning of American history, showing Columbus after his repulse by other European States resorting to the Court of Spain, where Isabella offers her jewels to defray the expense of the expedition, the Moorish wars having exhausted the Spanish treasury. The contract between Ferdinand and Columbus is about to be signed.

To the east of this gallery is Gallery Y, which is devoted to the fine collection of old masters, chiefly Dutch, which extends into Gallery O. Most noteworthy in Gallery Y are: 4—*Greuze* (early French), Study for a Head in the "Father's Curse." 5—*Karel De Moor*, "The Burgomaster of Leyden and his Wife." 7—*David Teniers*, the younger, "The Marriage Festival," a small canvas containing no less than seventy-three figures. 11—*Trumbull*, "Portrait of Alexander Hamilton," presented by H. G. Marquand, an excellent example of this early American painter's work, and considered worthy by the curator of being hung among portraits by Dutch masters. 13—*Adrienne De Vries*, "Portrait of a Dutch Gentleman." 23—*Aart De Gelder*, "Portrait of a Dutch Admiral," full of healthy vigor. 30—*Sir Joshua Reynolds*, "Portrait of the Honorable Henry Fane and his Guardians, Inigo Jones and Charles Blair." This fine example of the great English portrait painter's work was presented by the late Junius S. Morgan, of London. 35—*Bonifacio*, "The Musical Party," a decorative canvas of the Venetian School, looking as if intended for part of a frieze; presented by Morris K. Jesup. 48—*Jordaens*, "The Visit of St. John to the Infant Jesus," one of the most notable canvases in the Museum, being among the finest known paintings by this artist. It is wonderfully rich and glowing in color, a style for which Jordaens was noted. The babies are chubby, healthy and very Dutch looking. 51—*Franz Hals*, "Hille Bobbe

Von Haarlem," a vigorous little canvas. 52—*Rubens*, "Portrait of the Artist's Wife." 68—*Gilbert Stuart*, "Portrait of John Jay," an interesting example of the early American School. 77—Attributed to *Caravaggio*. Italian School of the seventeenth century, "St. Francis of Assissi," notable for the beautiful light on the upturned face. 78—*Van Dyck*, "St. Martha interceding with God for a cessation of the plague at Tarascon." 92—*Nicholas Poussin* (French), mythological subject. 93—*Gilbert Stuart*, "Washington," painted at Washington, D. C., 1803; presented by Henry O. Havemeyer.

To reach Gallery O, in which the balance of this collection is hung, it is necessary to cross the Gallery of American Antiquities (P). The paintings in O were presented by Henry G. Marquand. Most notable are: 3—*Terburg*, "Portrait of a Gentleman." 4—*Velasquez*, "Olivares," a three-quarters left portrait of a man in black, a fine example of this great Spanish artist. 14—*Velasquez*, a fine portrait of himself, three-quarters left with black hair, dark habit, and narrow linen collar. 19—*Gainsborough* (English), "Landscape." A broad, luminous, richly wooded landscape glowing with color and animal life. 20—*Leonardo da Vinci*, "Portrait of a Lady." 21—*Rembrandt*, "Portrait of a Man." A head or three-quarters portrait of a man wearing a black slouched hat and dressed in a rich golden brown gabardine, the entire figure standing out softly yet plainly on a luminous background. A mellow brown light is diffused over the whole canvas. 22—*Franz Hals*, "The Smoker," executed in the same bold and impressionist style as 51 in Gallery X. The numerical sequence is here broken by the hanging next to 22 of 43, *Franz Hals*, "Portraits of Two Gentlemen," a most beautiful piece of portraiture, very different in treatment from No. 22, and its companion-piece, showing great refinement of workmanship, the canvas being a model of its kind. 23—*Rubens*, "Susanna and the Elders." Susanna, half nude, is seen in a crouching attitude near a fountain. The Elders, one of them climbing over a stone balustrade, the other holding on to the branch of an apple tree, gaze eagerly upon the alarmed maiden. The Susanna is a portrait of Rubens' second wife, Helen Fourment, whom he frequently used as a model. She is also shown in 52, Gallery Y. 25—*Hogarth* (English), "Miss Rich Building a House of Cards," the portrait of a charmingly frank looking young girl dressed in white. 27—*Ruysdael*, "Landscape," in subdued yet rich colors. 28—*Velasquez*, "Portrait of Baltasar Carlos," eldest son of Phillip IV. 29 and 30—*Rembrandt*, 29, the "Portrait of a Man;" 30, the "Adoration of the Shepherds," a picture similar to that in the National Gallery, London, with, however, a few differences. 31—*Gainsborough*, "A Girl with a Cat." 32—*Turner* (English), "Saltash," painted about 1812-14, showing the River Tamar in the foreground, with a barge moored at a dock on the left, and on the right a boat drawn on shore. On the wall at the right of the large beer-house, shown in the picture, is scrawled: "England expects every man to do his duty." Through a square gateway in the building a street is seen. The canvas is enlivened by groups of men, women, children, sailors and horses. 33—*Reynolds*, "Lady Carew," a charmingly simple and delightful portrait of a maiden in a grayish white dress open at the neck, her head turned three-quarters to the left, her hair arranged in a coil. 35 and 36—*Rubens*, "Pyramus and Thisbe" and "Portrait of a Man." 37—*Constable*, "A Lock on the Stour," a capital example of this English painter. 38—*Van Dyke*, "James Stuart, Duke of Richmond and Lennox," probably as fine an example of Van Dyke's style of portraiture as can be found, and worthy of prolonged study. 39—*Constable*, "The Valley Farm."

Drawings and Etchings.—Gallery O leads through Gallery N into Gallery L and its alcove M, containing drawings, water-color paintings, photographs and etchings. The collection of drawings is composed of two portions: the first, Nos. 1 to 670, was begun in the latter part of the last century by Count Maggiori, of Bologna, a learned scholar and connoisseur and a member of the Academy of Sciences in that city, and has been gradually increased by additions from collections of Senior Marietta, Professor Angelini, Doctor Guastalla and Mr. James Jackson Jarves, from whom it was purchased in 1880 and presented to the Museum by Cornelius Vanderbilt. The other portion, Nos. 671 to 851, was collected by Cephas G. Thompson and by him presented to the Museum in 1887. The whole forms a very fine collection of its kind. Many of the drawings are small, some of them perhaps nothing more than sketches for larger works or of works which were never carried out, but each will well repay study. Here are found many names of old masters—*Caravaggio, Andrea Pozzo, Carlo Lotti, Raphael, Benvenuto Cellini, Salviati, Michael Angelo, Leonardo da Vinci, Andrea del Sarto, Mantegna, Domenichino, Caracci, Guercino, Guido Reni, Salvator Rosa, Paul Veronese, Titian, Tintoretto, Rembrandt, Van Dyke, Rubens, David Teniers,* younger and elder, *Durer, Murillo, Correggio, Velasquez, Cortese, Watteau, Callot, Claude Lorraine* and *Greuze.* The collection is arranged in standards and also along the wall, beginning on the northwest wall. Above them, on the wall opposite the alcove, is a sketch of *Chavannes'* "Symbolical Figure of the Sorbonne." The water-colors in the alcove are by William P. Richards, and there are besides these a collection of steel engravings and etchings, the latter extending into the main room, and a case of war medals and decorations. With this gallery and its alcove the collection of paintings, drawings and prints is ended and there remain now the miscellaneous collections on this floor.

ENGRAVED GEMS, ETC.—Gallery Q contains the fine *King-Johnston* collection of *Engraved Gems* (presented by John Taylor Johnston), which is arranged in cases along the west wall, the collection of Assyrian cylinders with an impression of each along the north wall between the doors. On the east wall is the fine *Moses-Lazarus* collection of fans, snuff-boxes, painted medallions, etc., and against the south wall the *Curium Treasure* discovered by General Di Cesnola in the Temple at Curium, Cyprus. In the center of the room in eight large cases is the collection of *Mediæval and Historic Engraved Gems* loaned by Maxwell Somerville. A series of wall cases above the Curium treasure contains a collection of *Ancient and Mediæval Spoons* loaned by Mrs. S. P. Avery, and following these is a cabinet containing largely *Jewelled Watches* presented by Mrs. Lucy W. Drexel. In the northeast corner case is, besides the Bryant vase, a fine specimen of Tiffany's workmanship, presented to the poet on his 80th birthday, a gold medal struck by the King of Italy in 1882 in honor of General Cesnola; in the northwest corner case, a cabinet of objects from the celebrated Demidoff Collection, also the *Battersea Enamels*, presented by Henry G. Marquand, and gold and silver South American relics; in the southwest corner case, two large Sevres vases, which the unfortunate Louis XVI of France sold through Gouverneur Morris to Doctor Hosack; in the southeast corner case, silver objects from the Cesnola collection and pieces of Peruvian silver from the spoils of the Pizarro conquest. The Curium treasure along the south wall brings the Cesnola collection to a rich and fitting close: Case 1—Gold cups in Phœnician, Assyrian and Grecian style. Case 2—Silver and gold-plated bracelets, ear-rings, dagger hair-pins and necklaces. Case 3—Gold necklaces and bracelets. Case 4—Gold ear-rings and rings. Case 5—Gold ear-rings, brooches and various mortuary and votive ornaments. Case 6—Seal rings with engraved gems.

Gallery T contains a large number of interesting memorials of Washington, Franklin and Lafayette; Gallery Z, a remarkably choice and varied collection of Japanese and Chinese objects of art, the most important of them being labeled. Part of the collection was loaned by Rufus E. Moore, the other part bequeathed by Stephen Whiteney Phœnix. The general visitor will probably be most interested in the superb cabinet of swords, which stands against the balustrade of the gallery. Gallery W contains a large collection of Oriental porcelain, chiefly Chinese. The choicest pieces are in cases against the balustrade; the rest in wall cases. Gallery N has reproductions of gold and silver work, chiefly from the treasures of St. Petersburg.

American Antiquities.—In Gallery P, is a collection of American antiquities. The table cases on this floor hold a unique collection of Indian idols, obtained in New Mexico, by L. Bradford Prince. The idols on the west side are still in use among the Indians of New Mexico, and it is considered a death offense to betray their secrets, so that Mr. Prince had to pledge himself never to divulge the name of the person or persons from whom he obtained these idols and the secret of their worship. It has always been supposed that since the

Spanish conquest the Indians of New Mexico have been good Christians, but here we have evidence of idolatry flourishing in secret among them. These deities are arranged in groups of seven each, each group representing a family of gods. For instance 24 and 26 are husband and wife, while the five smaller objects, 30 to 37, are their children.

LENOX LIBRARY.

Admission free. Open every week-day, except Monday, from 11 A. M. to 4 P. M. On Fifth avenue between Seventy and Seventy-first streets. Endowed by the late James Lenox, a bibliophile of rare taste and an art connoisseur. It was incorporated in 1870, and the massive limestone building in classic style was first opened to visitors in January, 1877. The general visitor will probably be most interested in the picture gallery on the second floor. A catalogue of the collection is on sale at fifteen cents. Directly opposite the entrance to the gallery on the north wall hangs the most conspicuous portrait in the collection, No. 70, *Gilbert Stuart's* portrait of George Washington, a full-length painted for Peter Jay Monroe in 1799. Washington is standing. He is clad in black. The fingers of his right hand rest firmly on a table. His left foot is slightly forward. The pose is strong and dignified. Grouped around this portrait are: 56—*James Peale*, half-length portrait of Washington in uniform; 84—Portrait of Washington copied from the portrait by *Charles Wilson Peale* in Arlington House, painted in 1772. 85—*Rembrandt Peale*, Portrait of Washington. Besides these Washington Portraits, there hang in this group: 65—*Gilbert Stuart*, Head of Mrs. Robert Morris. 64—*Sir Joshua Reynolds* (English), Portrait of Edmund Burke (probably a copy). 99—*S. B. Morse*, Portrait of Lafayette, painted in Washington from sittings in the month of February, 1825, presented by Wm. H. Osborn. 74—*Charles R. Leslie*, Portrait of Washington Irving. 147—Portrait of John Milton, formerly in the possession of Chas. Lamb, presented by Robert Lenox Kennedy. 73—*Landseer*, "Study of a White Horse." 137—*Jimenez*, "A Spanish Café." Noteworthy pictures on the right of this group are: 52—*Horace Vernet*, "Siege of Saragossa," a powerful canvas. 52—*Fred. de Braek-*

leer, the elder, "Mid-Lent in a School." 59—*Salentin*, "The Reception of a Young Prince," the contrast between the diffident curiosity of the lads and the assurance of the young prince being capitally brought out. The most conspicuous painting on the north wall is, 146—*Munkacsy*, "Milton Dictating Paradise Lost to his Daughters," too well known through its reproduction as an etching, and in various periodicals, to require description. Presented by Robert Lenox Kennedy. It is flanked on the left by 148—*Henry Raeburn*, Portrait of a gentleman; on the left by 103—*Sir Joshua Reynolds*, A charming picture of a boy in a red velvet dress leaning forward on a green cushion, holding pen and paper in his hand. From the collection of Philip Metcalf, Reynold's executor. Other noteworthy paintings on this wall are: 83—*Hubner*, "The First Grandchild." 92—*Daniel Huntington*, after *Trumbull*, Alexander Hamilton. 43 to 47—Sketches by *Sir David Wilkie*. 97—*Daniel Huntington*, Christopher Columbus. On the south wall is 101—*Sir Joshua Reynolds*, Mrs. Billington as St. Cecilia, a beautiful full-length portrait of this famous singer with a choir of angels fluttering around her and singing to the music of her voice. Mrs. Billington had a great admirer in Haydn. On seeing this picture in Reynold's studio as it was nearing completion, the great composer, eyeing it critically, remarked: "You painted it wrong." Mrs. Billington looked annoyed, and the artist, greatly displeased, asked: "In what respect?" "Why," said Haydn, "the angels should have been listening to Mrs. Billington, instead of Mrs. Billington listening to the angels." Upon this, Mrs. Billington jumped up and gave the composer a hug and a kiss. Next to this picture hangs on the right, 34—*J. M. W. Turner*, "Staffa, Fingal's Cave," a canvas most characteristic of this master, especially in the wonderful confluxion of the waves in a heavy sea. It was bought from the artist for Mr. Lenox in August, 1845. On the left, 32—*J. M. W. Turner*, "A Scene on the French Coast," with an English ship-of-war stranded, in which a gorgeous sunset is represented in the smooth mirror-like wet sand and water. Other paintings on this wall are: 100—*Sir Joshua Reynolds*, Portrait of Miss Kitty Fisher, with doves. Miss Kitty's attitude is charming as she holds out her hand for another dove to alight. 143—*Sir Henry Raeburn,* Portrait of Lady Belhaven; and 105—*Gilbert Stuart Newton,* "The Dull Lecture." On the west wall over the door is 138—*Valati,* "A Boar Hunt on the Campagna." To the left of the door, 118—*Escosura,* "The Parrot Dealer at the Chateau of Blois," time of Louis XIII. 133—*Samacois,* "The Court Fool," a portrait of the painter. 110—Original sketch of part of the "Blind Man's Buff," *Sir David Wilkie.* To the right of the door, 86—*Andrea del Sarto,* "Tobit and the Angel," one of the most noteworthy canvases in the collection. A collection of sculptures is in the vestibule.

The collection of rare books in the hall to the north of the vestibule, on the ground floor, is the richest in this country, and is especially noteworthy in Bibles, many of these being Incunabula, or specimens of the first products of the art of printing. There are also remarkable collections of Shakespeareana, Miltoniana, and editions of *Bunyan's* "Pilgrim's Progress," and of Eliot Indian Bibles. On the extreme right of the south wall is the alcove of porcelains. Adjoining this and extending to the doorway are, in three small cases, nine copies of the first edition of *Milton's* "Paradise Lost," with variations in the title; the first edition of *Milton's* "Comus," "Lycidas," and "Poems"; and his polemic "Pro Populo Anglicano Defensio et Eikonoclastes," and the proclamation of the King, dated August 13, 1660, directed against this work. In the doorway itself are six small cases containing choice works. Arranged in three cases along the southern wall of the room, to the right of the door on entering, are rare editions of *Shakespeare,* in the first case, two copies of the *First Folio,* with two titles, respectively 1622 and 1623, the latter being the so-called Litchfield copy mentioned by Dibdin; beginning in the first case, and extending through the second, seven copies, each with variations of the *Second Folio,* 1632; in the third case, two copies of the *Third Folio,* 1663-64, and two of the *Fourth Folio,* 1685. In all the cases are early editions of single plays.

The collection of *Bibles* is contained chiefly in two rows of four cases each, placed back to back, extending from the extreme left down the middle of the room to a point opposite the entrance. In the first case is the "*Mazarin*" *or* "*Gutenberg Bible,*" printed by *Gutenberg*, probably with the assistance of Fust, at *Mainz*, 1450–1455, and probably the first book printed from movable type, a work valued at about $30,000. Among Latin Bibles, in case 2 is one printed at *Nuremburg* by *Antonius Koberger*, 1477, with commentaries, emendations, and interlineations in the handwriting of *Melanchthon*; in case 4, *Coverdale's Bible* (1535), the first complete Bible printed in England; in case 1, at the head of the north line, a Bible printed by *Johann Zainer, Ulm*, 1450, the first with summaries at the heads of chapters; in case 2, *Block Bibles* and other block books (printed from carvings in wood), among the Bibles the first and second editions of *Biblia Pauperum*, the only known examples of Italian xylographic work. In this case is also the only perfect copy of the *sixth* and *rarest edition* of "Sancti Johannis Apocalypsis," consisting of forty-eight leaves of xylographic printing. In case 4, New Testament, *London*, by *Robert Barker*, the first 12-mo edition of King James' version, and the only copy of it known; *Tyndall's* "New Testament," 1536, the first portion of the Scriptures in English printed on English ground; and *Coverdale's* "New Testament," the first edition separate from the Bible.

The Bibles are continued in the alcove of the middle of the north wall. In the second case is, "Torquemada on the Psalms," *Mainz, by Schoeffer*, 1476, the first book printed with a date; in the third case the "*Wicked*" *Bible, London*, 1631, and the *German* "*Wicked*" *Bible, Halle*, 1731, both open at the page showing the version of the 7th Commandment to which they owe the epithet "Wicked"; the *first edition* of the "Pilgrim's Progress," part 1st, *London*, 1678, only one other copy being known; also the *first edition* of the second part; the earliest extant edition of the "New England Primer," *Boston*, 1727; and the only known copy of the *first edition* of the Psalms in "Meeter" by *Rous, London*, 1641, a work which Scottish writers have declared never existed; fourth case, a superb manuscript on vellum, propably the finest in the collection, entitled, "Giulio Clovio Christi Vita Ab Evangelistis Descripta." This manuscript is beautifully ornamented with six full-page paintings; six miniatures of the Evangelists; eight historiated borders and four headings with figures for intitulations, all heightened with gold in the best style of Italian art by Giulio Clovio. It is bound in crimson velvet with a patent lock and key, was executed for Alexander, Cardinal Farnese, and presented to Pope Paul III.

In the middle of the alcove, out on the floor, are two cases, that on the east side containing a complete collection of *John Eliot* Indian Bibles, and others of *Eliot's* works, together with an autographic letter of Eliot, and letters of other early New England colonial worthies; the letters presented by Robert Winthrop, of Boston. In the west case are "Doctrina Christiana," *Zumarraga, Mexico*, 1543–44, one of the earliest productions of the press in America, it being a fact worth noting that printing was done in Mexico earlier than in the colonies; "Bay Psalm Book," printed by *Stephen Daye, Cambridge, Mass.*, 1646, the first book in the English language printed in America; "Laws and Acts of New York," *William Bradford, New York*, 1693–1694, the first book printed in the city or province of New York (p. 95); Petrus de Alyco (Pierre d'Ailly), "Imago Mundi," about 1483, supposed to have directed Columbus to the possible existence of a Western Continent.

In a case against the wall east of the alcove, and in each of two cases placed back to back along the center of the floor east of the door, are books relating to the discovery of America, among them the rare account of the third voyage of Vespucius; four of the famous Columbus letters, one of which was certainly printed by *Stephen Plannck*, at *Rome*, 1493; a complete series of the Cortez letters, several autograph letters by Diego Columbus, who succeeded his father as Admiral of the Indies; "Cosmographia Introductio," 1507, in which the word "America" occurs for the first time; one of the earliest maps of America, *Vienna*, 1520, and "Conquesta de Peru," *Francisca de Xeres, Salamanca*, 1547.

In the third case, down the middle of the room, in the south line east of the door, are: The first German Bible, printed by *Henry Eggestein, Strasburg*, about 1466, and the first edition of the Bohemian Bible, *Prague*, 1480. At the east end of the center line of cases, on the north side, is a case containing chiefly Aldine classics, and next to it examples of Caxton's works, among the latter the "Breeches Bible," *Westminster*, 1484, so-called because of the use of the word, "breeches," Genesis, iii, 7.

The library proper in the south wing numbers about 50,000 volumes and is especially rich in works of early American history and belles-letters, and in works relating to Shakespeare and biblical literature, and contains the large musical library of the late Joseph W. Drexel. A carefully selected library of English and French literature was recently bequeathed to it by Felix Astoin.

AMERICAN MUSEUM OF NATURAL HISTORY.

The American Museum of Natural History is situated in Manhattan Park, which extends from Seventy-seventh to Eighty-first streets, between Eighth and Ninth avenues. It is governed by a board of twenty-five trustees, and its privileges are extended upon the same terms as those of the Metropolitan Museum of Art, excepting that the tickets carry with them the further privilege of utilizing the study collections which are not on exhibition to the general public. The city furnishes the building, the Museum occupying it under a lease similar to that of the Metropolitan Museum of Art. The Museum is open every week day from 10 A. M. to 4:30 P. M., and also Wednesday and Saturday evenings. The institution is still in the early stages of its development, its plan being to gradually extend its collections until it can offer every facility for the study of natural science. Its growth has been remarkably rapid. It was chartered in 1869. The nucleus of its collections was formed by the purchase of the D. G. Elliott collection of North American birds, to which was soon added the collection of birds and mammals of the late Prince Maximillian of Neuwied; the principal acquisitions since then have been the James Hall collection of fossils, which is the best of American palæozoic forms, and is one of the most important cabinets in the Museum; the Jay collection of shells, presented by Miss Catharine L. Wolfe (p. 219), as a memorial of her father, John David Wolfe, who was the first president of the Museum; the Baily collection of minerals; the Jesup collection of woods; the

Jesup collection of building stones; the Emmons archæological collection of Alaskan objects. The present building being too small for the complete exhibition of the collections of the Museum, the city is now erecting a large addition of brick faced with brownstone at the southern end, which has caused a temporary transfer of the entrance to the northeast side. The corner-stone of the present building was laid by President Grant, June 2, 1874, and the building was formally opened December 22, 1877. The halls in this building are 170 feet long by 60 feet wide, the stories varying in height from 18 to 30 feet. During this year the new addition will probably be completed, when large additions will be made to the exhibits, and their arrangement possibly altered. In the addition is a fine lecture-room already completed, where lectures are delivered under the auspices of the State Superintendent of Public Instruction, and under the special charge of Prof. A. S. Bickmore.

COLLECTIONS.—*Jesup Collections:* The hall on the ground floor is chiefly taken up with the Jesup Collection of American Forestry, and the Jesup Collection of Economic Entomology, both the gift of Morris K. Jesup, the president of the Museum. The Jesup Collection of American Forestry is believed to contain a specimen of the wood of all but twelve kinds of trees in the United States, and is thoroughly arranged in large cases placed at right angles to the walls of the room between the windows, an admirable arrangement for securing perfect lighting, which is followed throughout the building. Each specimen is split about half way down its entire length. The lower half, therefore, which is intact, shows the appearance of the tree with its bark untouched, while the upper split half shows the grain of the wood, beautifully polished. The collection is thoroughly labeled, the cards giving not only the family and species of the tree, but its specific gravity, percentage of ash, coefficient of elasticity, etc. On each label is also a chart showing in green the geographical distribution of the tree. Besides the wood, there are artificially prepared, but none the less admirable, specimens of the leaf and blossom of each tree. An important adjunct of this collection is the Jesup Collection of Economic Entomology. This is exhibited on table cases in the alcoves, and in the middle of the room. It consists of branches, leaves and blossoms of the various trees exhibited, and upon them insects which are destructive to their growth. These, though artificial, are most natural in appearance. The insects, of course, are sometimes of great beauty, such as butterflies and large caterpillars, so that both collections are as beautiful as they are interesting, and are with the general visitor a very popular feature of the Museum. *Mammal Groups.*—In this hall are also a series of cases with bird groups, completely labeled and admirably arranged to show their habits. For instance, in one case are five specimens of Labrador duck. One of them is on a stump upon a snow-covered shore, others stand upon thin ice which extends a little out over the water, another is swimming in the water itself. Other similar groups will be found in the Hall of Birds in the floor above. The groups, unique in this country, are the gift of Mrs. R. L. Stuart.

BIRD HALL.—The hall on the second floor is devoted to the collection of birds and other mammals, although the latter are not very numerous, the chief feature being a fine collection of monkeys. Handbook to this hall, 15 cents. There are about 50,000 birds all told in the Museum, but not all of these are on exhibition, many of them being preserved in the study room on the top floor in moth-proof tin cabinets. Among the study collections is one especially fine of humming birds and a collection of from 10,000 to 12,000 birds' eggs. There is a small exhibition of these latter in the first alcove to the left on entering the Bird Hall. Of the objects, not birds, on exhibition in this hall, those which will probably attract most attention are the stuffed skin and skeleton of *Mr. Crowley*, the famous chimpanzee from the Zoölogical Garden in Central Park; in the middle of the hall the skeleton of *Jumbo*, the famous elephant, loaned by Barnum & Bailey, and at the southern end of the hall the cases containing a fine collection of monkeys.

The birds exhibited in this hall number about 11,000 specimens, of which about 3,000 are North American, 3,000 are South American and 5,000 from the Old World. The North American birds occupying cases from B to F on the east side of the hall, form a faunal collection of birds of the United States and of regions thence northward to Greenland and the Arctic Ocean, nearly every species and sub-species in this great tract of country being represented by one or more specimens. The South American birds occupy the remaining cases F to J on the east side of the hall, and include birds from Mexico, West Indies, Central America and South America. The Old World birds occupy all the cases on the west side of the hall. Each collection is arranged systematically, starting at the north end of the hall with the highest or more specialized group, the song bird, and ending with the lowest, which in the North American birds are the auks, loons, and grebes, and in the South American and Old World birds the penguins and struthuous birds. Many New World birds have been arranged with Old World specimens so that the series on the west side of the hall is within certain limits a general systematic collection of the birds of the world. Besides the birds in the general collection, there are in this hall cases containing the balance of the interesting mammal groups and two cases of birds of brilliant plumage.

On the floor above, a gallery leads around this hall, and suspended on a level with this gallery is a huge war canoe made from one tree by the Bella-Bella tribe opposite Queen Charlotte Island, British Columbia, and presented by Heber R. Bishop. Only the bottom of it can be seen from the Bird Hall, but it is one of the most interesting features to be seen from the Ethnological Gallery.

Ethnological Gallery.—The collections in the Ethnological Gallery on the third floor begin in case A on the east side, with weapons, a full suit of cocoa-nut fibre armor and some very scant articles of wearing appearl, chiefly from Samoa and the Fiji Islands. Case B—Fine collection of hideous masks used in war and sacred dances, and of weapons from New Ireland. C—Beautifully carved paddles from the islands of Mangaia and Maori weapons, carved idols, ornaments and apparel, all of fine workmanship. D—Paddles from New Ireland, and weapons, especially effective-looking short clubs, from the Fiji Islands. E—Long war clubs finely carved, from the Fiji Islands and Samoa. F—Besides war clubs several reed pipes from New Ireland, feather head-gear, baskets and gourds from New Guinea. G—Ferocious-looking shark teeth, weapons from the King's Mill group. H—Several Cava bowls from Tunga Islands. I and J—Weapons and articles of apparel from various Pacific islands. In the middle of the southern end of the gallery is a huge Haida idol from British Columbia. On the east side of the gallery beginning on the southern end with K is an admirable collection of hideous masks from Alaska (Emmons collection). L—Alaskan utensils of wood, and horn spoons, gambling implements, large wooden food dishes almost like troughs and baskets of spruce (Emmons collection). M—Fishing implements and seal-killing clubs from Alaska (Emmons collection). Also cloth, beautifully carved pumpkin vessels, shield, baskets, large water-jars and brass rod vessels and Zulu snuff-boxes, Africa,—several of these objects presented by C. P. Huntington. N—Kaffir weapons, Zulu war shields and basket work, and British North American and other American Indian articles. O—North American objects, among them a mummy discovered in Grand avenue cave, Kentucky, and articles from British Guiana. P—American mound pottery. Q—African articles. R—Central and South American antiquities. T—Skulls and dessicated heads from the Pacific islands, shrunken to a ghastly smallness but preserving the features, the effect being heightened by long, black hair.

Besides the collections on exhibition, there is in the study room up stairs the fine A. E. Douglass collection and library of prehistoric Indian relics, many of these from Florida mounds opened by Mr. Douglass himself. It has a line of perfect pottery and the largest collection of hematite relics known, about 350 very interesting pipe heads, discs for games, perforated gorgets and ceremonial objects.

Geological Hall.—This is on the fourth floor. The collections exhibited consist of a conchological, a mineralogical and a geological collection, the latter embracing a collection of fossil organic remains and other material illustrating the geological formations, principally of this country. (Hand-book, 15 cents.) The conchological collection occupies the two ranges of cases placed on the west side of the middle of the room and is what was formerly known as the Jay collection, made by Dr. John C. Jay, of Rye, N. Y., and purchased with the library pertaining to it by Miss Catharine L. Wolfe, and presented to the Museum as a memorial of her father, John David Wolfe, the first president of the Museum. The collection is thoroughly labeled. The shells most popular because of their beauty, the cypraeas and the cones, will be found respectively in cases 17 and 18 and in cases 19 to 21.

The Mineralogical Collection occupies fourteen desk cases arranged along the east side of the middle hall and is classified according to Dana's system of mineralogy. Commencing at the first case on the east side there is arranged a collection representing the native elements as far as the collection contains specimens. Then follow the different groups. Among the minerals is a fine cabinet of malachites, a group of quartz crystals from Hot Springs, Arkansas, and specimens of exquisitely agatized trees, and the Tiffany collection of gems and gem materials and a special case illustrating the geology of Manhattan Island, among the minerals being a huge garnet.

The Geological Collection occupies the large cases forming alcoves along each side of the room and the alcove cases between them. The cases are mostly either lettered or numbered. The large cases along the sides of the room are lettered on the end of the case under the gas bracket; the alcove cases are numbered on the end. In the ends of the alcove cases is arranged a special series of fossils to illustrate the American portion of "Dana's Manual of Geology," a large part of the species exhibited being the very ones from which the figures in the Manual were taken. On the label will be found the name of the species and that of its author, the page of the Manual where figured, and the number of the figure representing it, the group of plants or animals to which it belongs and the locality whence obtained. There is also a copy of Dana's Manual of Geology kept in alcove No. 2 for the use of visitors who wish to consult its pages. This feature is one never before attempted in any collection or museum. Against the windows are beautifully colored transparencies of localities (chiefly Western) showing interesting geological formations.

The most interesting object in this hall to the general public is the skeleton of the *Mastodon Giganteus*, whose extreme length to the anterior curve of the tusks is 18 feet; to the end of the tusk sockets, 14 feet; height to top of dorsal spine, 8 feet 6 inches; breadth across the hip bones, 5 feet; length of tusk along the outer curve, 7 feet 5 inches. The bones of this skeleton were found imbedded in peaty material on the edge of what was less than fifty years before an open pond, subsequently however drained, in Little Britain, near Newburg, N. Y. Other interesting skeletons are that of the Moa, a fossil bird from New Zealand, which stands in the first alcove to the right of the entrance, and a fossil Irish deer which stands at the southern end of the hall. Among the general collection the visitor will probably find of greatest interest a cabinet of fine gum copals full of insects, and also the slabs in the vestibule and in the southern end of the hall showing the strides of a fossil reptile, *Brontozoum Giganteum*. These were made by a large lizard-like animal having a habit of walking on its hind feet, the strides measuring about 4 feet each. The general collection is thoroughly labeled. The admirable hand-book is indispensable to a proper understanding of the exhibits in this hall.

CHAPTER X.

CENTRAL PARK.

Central Park is bounded south by Fifty-ninth street, north by One Hundred and Tenth street, east by Fifth avenue, west by Eighth avenue. It is an evidence of how human skill, guided by artistic taste, may make glad the waste places. Work upon it was begun in 1857, up to which time the ground now covered by what is considered one of the most beautiful pleasure grounds in the world, was a dreary expanse of rock, brush and swamp. Perhaps the very ruggedness of the original has contributed not a little to the beauty of the finished work; the huge boulders which here and there project from the beautiful lawns, or stand guard on the waters of the lakes and ponds, adding not a little to the impressiveness of the landscape.

General Features.—Central Park is a little over 2½ miles in length, and a little more than half a mile in breadth; its area being 840 acres, with 9 miles of drive, averaging in width 54 feet and extending in places to a width of 60 feet; 5¾ miles of bridle paths averaging 16½ feet in width, and 29½ miles of walks. Some 400 acres are wooded, the trees, shrubs and vines put out since the opening of the park numbering over 500,000. The benches distributed throughout the park, placed as much as possible in secluded nooks and within the sheltering shade of the trees or arbors, have a seating capacity of 11,000. The various drives are usually alive with every variety of fashionable equipages; the main entrance for this picturesque procession being at Fifth avenue and Fifty-ninth street. Those who are interested particularly in fast horses can see these entering the Park at Eighth avenue and Fifty-ninth street. The Park Department has made a grand division of Central Park into the South and North Park, regarding the new Croton Reservoir as the line of division. For the beautiful landscape effects in which the Park abounds, the

MAP OF CENTRAL PARK.

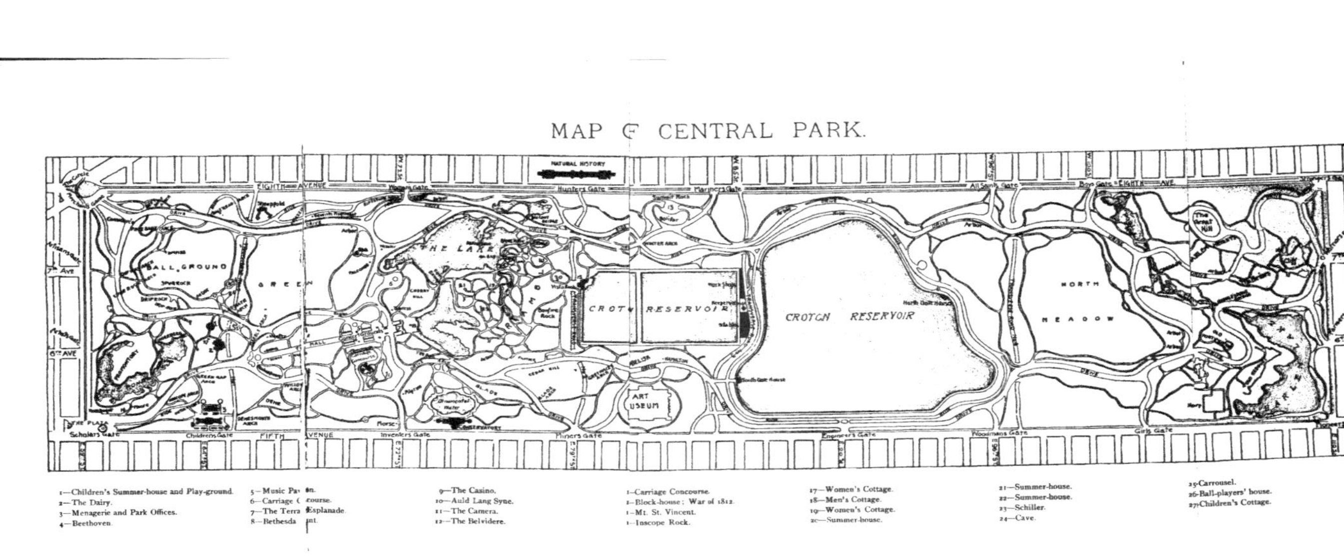

1—Children's Summer-house and Play-ground.
2—The Dairy.
3—Menagerie and Park Offices.
4—Beethoven.

5—Music Pa· on.
6—Carriage C course.
7—The Terra Esplanade.
8—Bethesda nt.

9—The Casino.
10—Auld Lang Syne.
11—The Camera.
12—The Belvidere.

1—Carriage Concourse.
1—Block-house; War of 1812.
1—Mt. St. Vincent.
1—Inscope Rock.

17—Women's Cottage.
18—Men's Cottage.
19—Women's Cottage.
20—Summer-house.

21—Summer-house.
22—Summer-house.
23—Schiller.
24—Cave.

25—Carrousel.
26—Ball-players' house.
27—Children's Cottage.

public is indebted to Frederick Law Olmsted and Calvert Vaux; the architectural features being by Calvert Vaux and the late J. Wrey Mould.

Entrances.—The entrances to the Park, nineteen in number, are called gates, and it is the intention of the Park Commissioners, when sufficient money for carrying out their purpose is on hand, to justify the term by putting up gates of handsome architectural design at the various entrances. The names and locations of the entrances and localities, as officially given, will be found on the accompanying map of Central Park.

Lakes and Reservoirs.—The lakes and ponds in the Park have an area of 43¼ acres. The largest of these is the Lake, whose shores, at about its middle, approach so closely as to virtually form a strait dividing it into two parts. It covers about 20 acres. The Pond, covering about 5 acres, lies in a lovely depression just to the west of the entrance of Fifth avenue and Fifty-ninth street. The Conservatory Water, 2½ acres, is near Fifth avenue and Seventy-fourth street, and derives its name from its vicinity to the site reserved for a conservatory. The Pool, the Loch, and Harlem Meer, are a chain of ponds covering respectively 2 acres, 1 acre and 12¾ acres in the North Park. There are two reservoirs, the older and smaller in the center of the Park, extending from Seventy-ninth to Eighty-fourth street; the newer and larger lying nearly entirely across the Park between Eighty-sixth and Ninety-sixth streets. A walk and bridle path lead around it. The reservoirs have a combined area of 143 acres.

Boats, Goat Carts, etc.—On the Pond are the so-called Lohengrin boats, 22 feet long and holding twelve people and consisting of a catamaran propelled by a stern velocipede, which is concealed in a swan, whence the boats derive their name. Fares: Adults, 10 cents; children, 5 cents; adults, twelve tickets for $1; children, twenty-five tickets for $1. On the Lake are regular row boats. Fares: Circuit of the Lake, 2 miles, one passenger, 10 cents; children under twelve years of age, 5 cents; six adults, 50 cents; six children, 25 cents. Party boats: One person, half hour, 30 cents; each additional person, 10 cents; children, 5 cents. Boats without boatmen can be engaged at the boat house at these rates, but a deposit of $2 is required. Boats can be had until 11 P.M. At the Mall are *donkeys* and *goat* carts, 10 cents; near the ball ground a *carrousel*, 5 cents, and in various parts of the Park *swings*, 5 cents.

Meals. — Meals may be had at the Casino and at McGown's Pass Tavern ; light refreshments at the Dairy, and mineral waters at the Spa. For *Skating* see under Sports, p. 64.

Besides the Metropolitan Museum of Art (p. 202), there are in the Park the Obelisk, a number of statues and groups of statuary and the Menagerie.

OBELISK.—The obelisk is a memorial of one of the most ancient races standing in the chief pleasure ground of one of the youngest of nations. How old it is may be judged from the fact that it was probably gazed upon by Moses.

From Alexandria to New York.—The history of its acquisition by New York City begins with the opening of the Suez Canal in 1869, when the Khedive intimated to William Henry Hurlbert, an American journalist, that it might be possible for the United States to acquire it as a gift. Mr. Hurlbert, on his return to New York, brought the matter to the attention of William H. Vanderbilt, and in October, 1878, the Secretary of State of the United States instructed the United States Consul-General at Alexandria to open negotiations, which resulted favorably. In 1879, bids for its removal from Alexandria and its transportation to New York were advertised for, and Commander Henry H. Gorringe, U. S. N., secured a contract for its removal, transfer and erection in Central Park, for $75,000. England delayed 78 years in transporting to London the twin obelisk of that in New York. The New York obelisk was erected January 2, 1881. Gorringe arrived at Alexandria October 16, 1879. November 6th of the same year he put 100 Arabs at work excavating the pedestal, pushing the work vigorously, as great opposition to the removal of the obelisk had arisen, and he had reason to fear violence. The obelisk was turned and lowered to a horizontal position December 6, 1879. It was then Gorringe discovered, in the foundation and steps, stones and implements of masonic significance, and he carefully noted their position, replacing them exactly when he

OBELISK.

erected the obelisk in New York. He purchased the steamer *Dessong*, and embarked with his cargo of 1,475 tons June 12, 1880, arriving at New York July 20th. The obelisk was disembarked at Staten Island on tracks and cannon balls, and so great interest had been awakened in it that the visitors on one day alone numbered 17,011. It was re-embarked, and on September 16, 1880, drawn from the foot of Ninety-sixth street and East river on tracks with rollers to Greywacke Knoll, a beautiful rise of ground just west of the Metropolitan Museum of Art. On October 9th, 9,000 Free Masons paraded and their Grand Master laid the foundation stone; and January 22, 1881, the obelisk was unveiled in the presence of 20,000 spectators. The total cost of transportation, amounting to $102,576, was defrayed by Mr. Vanderbilt. By a special act of Congress, American registry was allowed the *Dessong*.

Description and History.—The Obelisk is a striking example of graceful and elegant simplicity. Its total height is 90 feet, the height of the monolithic shaft being 69 feet. Its thickness at the base is 8x8 feet, and its weight 448,000 pounds. It is of red syenite from the Assonan quarries. The plinth, of syenite, stands on a base with three steps of hard limestone, the foundation being a mass of concrete, capped with masonry to a level with the pavement. This is the only obelisk, excepting a small one at Corfe Castle, which is accompanied by its original pedestal and steps.

The monolith itself is a quadrilateral shaft ending in a pyrimidion. On this pyrimidion are inscriptions in hieroglyphics which show that the obelisk dates from the reign of Thothmes III, the greatest Egyptian king, 1591 to 1565 B.C., and the inscriptions on the center line of the three sides of the monolith on which the hieroglyphics are still legible, are also dedicated to Thothmes and consist chiefly of his list of titles and of flattering epithets, all the inscriptions being singularly alike. They furthermore show that the obelisk was erected by Thothmes before the Temple of the Sun at Heliopolis. On either side of the center line of inscriptions on each of the three faces are lines of hieroglyphics in which a subsequent king, Rameses II, 1388 to 1322 B.C., glorified himself; and about 933 B.C., another king, Usorkon I, graved his official title near the edges. The obelisk is believed to have been thrown down by Cambyses between B.C. 525 and 521, and it lay prostrate till the Roman Conquest. It is thought to have been removed from Heliopolis to Alexandria by Cleopatra, whence the name Cleopatra's Needle, and to have been erected at Alexandria in front of the Temple of the Cæsars. Its companion, which now stands in London, had fallen, and long lain prostrate in the dust before it had been removed to that city. Ours was still standing, and is the real Cleopatra's Needle, although the name is also given to the obelisk in London.

Bronze Crabs.—At the base of the monolith there were originally four bronze crabs, only two of which, however, remained. These are now in the Metropolitan Museum of Art. They contain Greek and Latin inscriptions which point to the year when the obelisk was re-erected in honor of the Cæsars at Alexandria, the inscriptions reading: "In the year 8 of Cæsar, Barbarus dedicated, Pontius being the architect." This would place the date of its re-erection at 22 B.C. The faces of the obelisk having shown the effects of wear owing to the severity of our climatic changes, have been coated with paraffine.

STATUES AND GROUPS.—The statues and statuary groups in Central Park and their location are in their alphabetical order: *Beethoven*—On the Mall east of the music stand, a bronze bust on a granite pedestal, unveiled July 22, 1884. Looking up toward the bust is an allegorical figure which is only life size, although the bust is "heroic." *Bolivar* (the South American liberator) —On the Summit Rock Concourse on the west side of the Park near the Eighty-first street entrance, an equestrian statue by R. De la Cora, a gift from the people and government of Venezuela, unveiled June 17, 1884. *Burns*—At the south end of the Mall, a bronze statue of the poet by John Steele, Edinborough, presented to the city in 1880 by Scotch residents. *Commerce*—Near the entrance at Eighth avenue and Fifty-ninth street, an allegorical bronze figure eight feet high, presented by Stephen B. Guion. *Eagles and Goat*—East of the Mall, a bronze group by Fratin, presented by Gordon W. Burnham, 1863. *Falconer*—West of the head of the Lake on a high bluff, a graceful bronze figure by George Simonds, presented by George Kemp, 1872. *Halleck, Fitz Greene*—On the Mall, a bronze statue of the poet on a granite pedestal, modeled by Wilson McDonald. *Hamilton, Alexander*—Near the Metropolitan Museum of Art on the west side of the east drive, a granite statue by Conradts, presented by John C. Hamilton, in 1880. *Humboldt*—On the west side of the drive near the entrance at Fifth avenue and Fifty-ninth street, a bronze bust on a granite pedestal, by Gustav Blaeser, presented by German residents September 14, 1869, on the 100th anniversary of Humboldt's birth. *Indian Hunter*—West of the Mall, a spirited bronze figure by J. Q. A. Ward. *Mazzini*—West drive near the Seventh Regiment Monument, an heroic bronze bust by Turini, presented by Italian residents in 1878. *Moore*—On the east shore of the Pond, a bronze bust of the poet by Dennis B. Sheehan, presented May 28, 1880, by the Moore Memorial Committee. *Morse, S. F. B.* (p. 170)—Near the entrance at Fifth avenue and Seventy-second street, life-size bronze statue by Byron M. Pickett, erected in 1871 by an association of telegraphers. *Schiller*—In the Ramble, a bronze bust by C. L. Richter, presented by German residents in 1859. *Scott*—Near the southern end of the Mall, a bronze statue of the novelist and poet on an Aberdeen granite pedestal, copied from the statue by John Steele in Edinborough, presented by Scotch residents in 1872. *Seventh Regiment*—On the west drive near Seventy-second street, a bronze figure of a private soldier, by J. Q. A. Ward, erected in 1874 as a memorial of those members of the Seventh Regiment, National Guard of the State of New York, who fell during the Civil War. *Shakespeare*—At the southern end of the Mall, a gracefully poised bronze statute by J. Q. A. Ward, erected May 23, 1872, the 300th anniversary of the poet's birth. *The Pilgrim*—Near the lake on the crossing of the eastern drive and the roadway leading from the entrance at Fifth avenue and Seventy-second street, a fine bronze statue 9 feet high, by J. Q. A. Ward, a gift of the New England Society to commemorate the landing of the Pilgrims on Plymouth Rock in 1620. *The Still Hunt*—Near the Obelisk on a rock overlooking the east drive, a strong bronze casting by Kemeys, representing a panther crouched for the leap upon its victim. *Tigress and Young*--A short distance west of the terrace, an artistic bronze group put up in 1867. *Webster, Daniel*—At the junction of the west drive and the road from Seventy-second street, a heroic statue of the statesman by Thomas Ball, presented by Gordon W. Burnham.

MENAGERIE.—The Central Park Menagerie, a fair collection, is situated at Sixty-fourth street and Fifth avenue. It occupies about 10 acres of ground. The location is a temporary one, it being the purpose to eventually remove the collection to one of the new parks situated on the north side of the Harlem river. Signs are attached to the cages giving the common and scientific name of the animals, family to which they belong, habitat and name of donor. The carnivora are fed at 2½ P. M.; sea lions, pelicans, etc., at 9 A. M.; monkeys at 9 A. M. and 3 P. M. The first paddock met with on the walk from Fifty-ninth street contains deer. 2. Monkey house. 3. Small house adjoining monkey house contains numerous specimens of birds. 4. The large stone building is used for the offices of administration of the Park and the Park Police. It was erected in 1851 for use as a State arsenal. In the building is to be seen a colossal marble statue of Columbus, carved by Miss Emma Stebbins. 5. The large building in the rear of the arsenal building contains the larger carnivora, such as lions, tigers, leopards, jaguar, puma and hyaena, also a splendid specimen of two-horned rhinoceros from Africa, the only living specimen in this country. 6. To the north of this building is the tank for hippopotami, the youngest of which was born in the Menagerie October 4, 1890, being the first one ever raised in America. 7. To the south of the carnivora building are a number of cages containing small black bears, and a tank in which are sea lions from the Pacific Ocean, and numbers of water fowl. 8. The next building is occupied by antelopes. 9. In the rear is the elephant house, containing four specimens of the Indian species. "Tip," the largest, is 8 feet 9 inches in height, weighs 9,000 pounds, and is 23 years old. This animal formerly belonged to the King of Italy, Victor Emanuel, and after his death was purchased by Adam Forepaugh, and

MENAGERIE.

subsequently presented to the Menagerie. It is at times very unruly, having killed six men before it came into the menagerie. Paddock in the rear. 10. In the rear of the elephant paddock is the prairie dog inclosure. 11. Further up the hill are several cages containing foxes, raccoons, etc., and the bear pit, with Polar, grizzly and large black bears. A walk leads around this pit to the top, where the visitor can look down on the animals. From this point also a good view is obtained of the grounds of the Menagerie. 12. Continuing down the steps there is reached a straight walk with several paddocks on each side, containing the American bison or buffalo (the bull a remarkably fine specimen), African buffalo, zebra from India, llamas from South America, avudads or Barbary wild sheep from Africa, and the camels. All of the latter were bred in the Menagerie. A wire inclosure contains the emu from Australia, and storks and cranes. 13. The buildings north of the old arsenal are the small mammal house; a variety of small carnivorous animals; the eagle house, and an inclosure containing a variety of water-birds and waders.

General View. — An excellent general view of the Park may be had by those who care to merely skim over it, instead of to study its beauties thoroughly, by making a tour in one of the Park carriages, which are to be found at the entrance at Fifth avenue and Fifty-ninth street. They make the trip up to McGown's Pass Tavern, near the northern end of the Park, and return, at twenty-five cents for each person, children fifteen cents, and stop en route at the various points of interest. Visitors may alight, and by taking a return ticket on leaving the carriage, return by another carriage. The public hacks, which may be found at most of the entrances on Ffty-ninth street, charge about double these rates.

Detailed Tour.—Usually, when visitors have seen the Managerie, the Mall, the Musems and the Obelisk, they think they have made a tour of Central Park. As a matter of fact, they may be said to have only just skimmed over it, for Central Park, while beautiful as a whole, is most exquisite in its various details. There are paths, nooks, arbors and vistas which have endeared themselves to all who are familiar with this wonderful pleasure ground, details of which strangers, merely going over the ground as most strangers do, have no knowledge whatsoever. The Park being long and narrow, it is easy to start in at either end and make a reasonably thorough tour of it without retracing one's steps.

After entering the Park at Fifth avenue and Fifty-ninth street the visitor should linger and watch the wonderful procession of carriages of all descriptions. He should then take the first path to the left and descend to the beautiful little sheet of water called the "Pond," whose wavelets ripple up towards the weeping willows overhanging the rocky shores. The path along the southern shore leads to the wharf where the Lohengrin boats are anchored. Besides these boats, black swans glide in and out of the numerous bays which penetrate into the shore. After passing the wharf the path rises toward the Sixth avenue entrance to a rocky eminence. Further on, it leads to a much higher mass of rock, Copcot Rock, on which there is a large rustic summer house, shady, cool and inviting and affording glimpses of the west drive to which a path descends. It is preferable, however, to continue on around the "Pond." The path leads to a superb rise of pine-crowned rock called the "Promontory," and passing behind this crosses a little bridge spanning a miniature strait, which toward the north broadens out again. A little beyond the bridge the paths separate, that to the south leading over to the Menagerie, while that to the north rises again to the main drive with its brilliant throng of vehicles. Taking the latter and proceeding along the drive, over the bridge which crosses the equestrian path, the visitor reaches a small path on the left which descends to a romantic dell, from which glimpses of the northern extremity of the pond are had, and leads up again to the Kinderberg (Children's Hill), a rustic arbor of great beauty large enough to accommodate several hundred people. This arbor is loveliest of a spring or autumn day when the vines are rustling in the breeze and glints of sunshine are dancing over the floor. Many children are usually gathered in this arbor, for near it are the swings and the Dairy and by crossing the drive to the west by the path which descends from this arbor the Carrousel (Merry-Go-Round), another set of swings, and the Ball Grounds are reached. A fine view is had of the latter. Umpire Rock rises at the southwestern end. West of the drive, a little to the north of the Ball Grounds, there is a path leading through what is known as the Marble Arch to the Mall. This path is deeply shaded and its level is far below that of the drive, and, after passing under the Marble Arch, it rises by a flight of steps to the Mall. The effect of the beautiful vista which bursts upon the view as one emerges from the Arch is one of the great triumphs of architecture and landscape gardening in the Park. After taking a general view of the Mall, peering down its colonnades of stately trees, and obtaining glimpses of the Green—a tree-dotted stretch of meadowland to the west, with a fine flock of sheep—it is practicable to make a detour from the Mall to the Menagerie (p. 244), and, after one has exhausted the sights there, to retrace one's steps to the Mall, but over a different path, which leads through a very romantic section of rocks and trees and small open passages of meadow called the Dene. This path, after crossing the main drive, rejoins the Mall at the concert grounds; but the Casino Concourse, the Casino, and the Pergola can be included.

The Mall is, however, worthy of a stroll along its entire length. It is about one-third of a mile in length, beginning at the Marble Arch and extending to the *Terrace*, which commands a view of the ***Esplanade*** and ***Lake***. Concerts are given at the music stand near the northern end Wednesday and Sunday afternoons during the summer. It is a beautifully shaded stretch of ground, rows of stately trees forming green arched colonnades, and between the main walk and the side paths and drives are beautifully laid out lawns. At the southern end are the statues of Halleck, Scott, Shakespeare and Burns. Around the band stand are ornamental benches and the Beethoven statue stands in an open space to the right. On days when concerts are given the Mall is so crowded as to be practically impassable. The *Terrace*, at the northern end of the Mall upon high ground, is built of yellow stone and from it three stairways lead down to the Esplanade, the central stairway being sunk under the road and leading through a brilliantly tiled and ornamented arch, or, perhaps, more properly speaking, hall, with niches on either side. The two side stairs are open, the sides bearing stone panels with delicately carved designs of birds, animals and fruits. The view from the edge of the Terrace is exceedingly picturesque. On the *Esplanade*, which runs to the edge of the Lake, is the *Bethesda Fountain*, with its sparkling jets and silvery drip from the upper to the lower basin. Across the Lake is its bold northern shore, with grey rocks, whose ruggedness is softened by deep foliage; then comes the green of the Ramble, with the grey tower of the Belvedere in the background, the whole being half framed in by the soft green mounds that rise on either side of the Esplanade. In the main basin of the *Bethesda Fountain* are a number of rare water plants. These are all completely labeled and include the Lotus, the beautiful, flesh-colored India water lily, the Papyrus plant and the beautiful South Americal floating pond-weed.

The Bethesda Fountain is a representation of the story of the Pool of Bethesda, St. John (5, 2–4). Its crowning feature is the figure of an angel who appears to have just alighted on a mass of rock, and extends her hands as if blessing the waters which gush from it into the upper basin of the fountain, overflowing this and dripping into the lower basin, throwing a silvery veil over four figures symbolic of Temperance, Purity, Health and Peace. The fountain was designed and the figures were executed by Emma Stebbins.

A tour in and out among the bays and under the bridges of the *Lake* in one of the boats is quite necessary to a thorough appreciation of the beauties of the Park. A stranger should also not fail to take the path which leads along the Lake around to the boat house and past it over the high ground to the north to some of the most romantic portions of the *Ramble*, over rocky hills and down into surprisingly beautiful glens, finally crossing the graceful Bow Bridge, which spans the Lake at its narrowest point. Taking the road to the west of this bridge the Cherry Hill Concourse is reached, a point to which people in carriages drive, as it commands a superb view of the Lake and its shores. Then, leaving the Concourse and following the path along the drive to

TERRACE AND ESPLANADE.

the west, and passing the Webster statue one has a continuous view of the western end of the Lake which is much larger than the eastern division. At the extreme northwestern end is Bank Rock Bay, named from its bold rocky shores. It is crossed by a bridge at its point of entrance into the Lake and taking this bridge and following the path to the right, one reaches—through what seems a natural cleft in the rock shutting out every sign of civilization—the *Cave*. This is one of the most romantic parts of the Park, for after emerging from the *Cave* and ascending a flight of narrow stairs hewn out of the solid rock, one can take a wild and rocky path along a little stream called the Gill and thus pass through some of the most beautiful parts of the *Ramble*, which, as a whole, is probably the most secluded part of the Park, being rocky, well wooded and having here and there little clearings like meadows on a mountain side. Here, in fact, one is shut out from absolutely any suggestion of the city which lies at either side.

Emerging from the Ramble over Vista Rock, one reaches at the southern end of the old receiving Reservoir, the *Belvedere*, a pretty granite building, from whose tower, 50 feet high, an excellent view of the Park and its surroundings is had. A path leads from the Belvedere to the east to the *Obelisk* (p. 240) and to the *Metropolitan Museum of Art* (p. 202), and to the west of the entrance at Eighth avenue and Seventy-ninth street opposite the American Museum of Natural History (p. 231).

Proceeding from the Obelisk to the new receiving Reservoir, which lies like a great lake almost across the entire Park, one can take a walk which leads all around it and enjoy the fresh breeze as it blows over the water. It is worth while to inspect the South Gate House. After reaching the North Gate House, at the northwestern extremity of the Reservoir, it is best to take the path which leads down to the North Meadow, a broad stretch of tree-dotted grass where the tennis grounds are.

From here walks lead across the extreme westerly drive to the *Pool* which lies far down below the drive and is the first of a series of lakes and water courses which terminate at the extreme northeasterly part of the Park in *Harlem Meer*. The road not only goes around the Pool, but leads from it under a ridge of natural rock along the little stream which connects the *Pool* with the *Loch*. At the head of the *Loch* a beautiful little brook comes trailing down among the rocks from the North Meadow and the path itself, after leaving the *Loch*, follows another stream until the visitor find himself at *Harlem Meer*. To his right is a high promontory and by ascending this to a point which is known as the *Old Redoubt*, he can obtain a fine view of the Meer. He then, instead of doubling his steps, can proceed from the Redoubt in a southerly direction towards McGown's Pass Tavern, across the drive and take a path which will bring him to the head of the *Loch*. This he crosses by a bridge and then ascends the high and densely wooded westerly shore of the Loch. Reaching the westerly drive, he can cross it to what is known as Harlem Heights, or he can keep to the right and plunge into a maze of woodland and rocks rising to the height on which the old *Block House* stands, whence he can descend and leave the Park at One Hundred and Tenth street.

To the west of the northern end of Central Park is Morningside Park, rising toward Bloomingdale Heights. A conspicuous feature of this view will be the great Protestant Episcopal Cathedral of St. John the Divine, to be built on the Heights, near Morningside Park.

CHAPTER XI.

EAST, WEST AND NORTH OF CENTRAL PARK.

East, West and North of Central Park are several club houses and armories and many of the great charitable institutions of the city.

EAST OF CENTRAL PARK.—There is a perfect cluster of these and of other public institutions east of Central Park from Sixty-fifth street to Seventieth street, extending west as far as Madison avenue, and east to Third avenue. Among these are the Armory of the famous Seventh Regiment, a brick building with granite trimmings, 200 feet by 405 feet, occupying the entire block bounded by Fourth and Lexington avenues, Sixty-sixth and Sixty-seventh streets, with a fine drill hall (200 feet by 300 feet), staff, reception and company rooms, a library, gymnasium, and rifle range, 300 feet long; Mt. Sinai Hospital, Lexington avenue and Sixty-sixth street (p. 60); Association for the Improved Instruction of Deaf Mutes (p. 61); Foundling Asylum, Sixty-eighth street and Third avenue (p. 61); Presbyterian Hospital, Madison avenue and Seventieth street (p. 60); Normal College, Fourth avenue and Sixty-eighth street (p. 150). On Sixty-seventh street, between Third and Second avenues, is the handsome structure of the New York Turn Verein. On Sixty-seventh street, between Fourth and Third avenues, are the headquarters of the *New York Fire Department.* Connected with this is an engine house and a drill yard, and this is the best place for the visitor to study the operations of the famous New York Fire Department, and to inspect its apparatus. The force is under the supervision of a Board of three commissioners. The active force, uniformed, is divided into a Chief of Department, 2 Deputy-chiefs, 12 Chiefs of Battalion, 83 Foremen, 90 Assistant Foremen, 136 Engineers of steamers, and 678 Firemen; making a total of 1,002. The stables for training horses until they become so expert that as soon as they hear the signal they leave their stalls and take their places at the shafts, the harness dropping upon them by an automatic arrangement, is in West One Hundred and Thirty-ninth street, between Columbus and Amsterdam avenues. The pay-rolls for 1889 aggregated a little over $1,605,000. There are 56 engines, two of them vessels for work in quenching fire along the water front or among shipping, and 20 hook and ladder companies. The average number of alarms responded to by each company during last year was 116; the average number of fires at which each company performed duty, 50; there having been 2,834 fires; the total loss being $4,142,777.

Fifth avenue continues to the Harlem river, its course, however, being interrupted from One Hundred and Twentieth to One Hundred and Twenty-fourth streets by Mount Morris Square. The Harlem river, which begins at One Hundred and Twenty-seventh street and East river, flows for its greater length northwest and north, thus causing the sudden narrowing of the island at the north. There is nothing in which the stranger will be particularly interested in the east side of the city, between Central Park and the Harlem river. The Harlem is crossed by a railroad bridge at Second avenue, connecting the Harlem river branch of the New York, New Haven & Hartford road and the suburban rapid transit system with the Second avenue branch of the Manhattan elevated railroad; at Third avenue by a bridge for foot passengers and vehicles; by a railroad bridge connected with the Grand Central Depot system at Fourth avenue; by a bridge for foot passengers and vehicles at Madison avenue; by what is known as the McComb's Dam Bridge or Central Bridge at McComb's Lane; by a bridge connecting the New York & Northern R. R. with the Manhattan elevated road at Eighth avenue; by High Bridge (p. 256), Washington Bridge (p. 256), and King's Bridge, and by a railroad bridge at the point where Spuyten Duyvil creek enters the Hudson. In the annexed district, as so much of the city as lies above the Harlem river is called, are a number of new parks which, when fully laid out, will add greatly to the beauty of this part of the city; the Catholic Protectory at Westchester; St. John's College, Fordham, a notable Catholic educational institution, and Woodlawn Cemetery.

West and Northwest of Central Park.—A new section of the city has been springing up west of Central Park and on the narrow northern end of Manhattan Island during the last ten years. This promises to be the most beautiful quarter for residences on Manhattan Island, for the houses have been built since modern ideas of beauty and fitness have come into vogue. As a result there are entire blocks where houses are built in architectural harmony and monotonous rows of brown stone or brick are not to be seen here. This section of the city also has the additional advantage of a number of broad, well laid out thoroughfares (see Driving, p. 65).

Riverside Park.—On this western side of the city is Riverside Park, which runs along the bluff above the river from Seventy-second to One Hundred and Twenty-ninth street a distance of nearly three miles, the average width being about 500 feet. It is really little more than a broad avenue laid out with a road, sidewalk and bridle path, the slope to the New York Central & Hudson River track being in a somewhat wild, unfinished state. A striking feature of the Park are the beautiful views of the river which it affords. West End avenue, running parallel with it on the east is being built up with handsome residences, and it is believed by real estate experts that the future home of fashion will be on these two avenues, it being the opinion that business will drive fashion eventually out of Fifth avenue.

Grant's Tomb.—Near the upper part of Riverside Park is the tomb of General Grant, who was buried here August 8, 1885, with the honors of war, the procession being the finest and the crowd of people the greatest ever seen or gathered in New York before the celebration of the Washington Inauguration Centennial. The tomb is now a plain vault, but the committee having in charge the monument to General Grant have chosen a design by John H. Duncan. This will be an imposing architectural memorial, having a square base 100x100 feet at the ground line and a height of 160 feet in the base line. The lower part of the structure is to be of the Doric order and the upper of the Ionic. It is to be crowned by a dome supported by four arches, under which are galleries, from which a superb view up the river and of the surrounding country may be had. The dome will be pyramidal and surmounted by a group of statuary. In the crypt, which will be of white granite, and will be reached by rear stairways and protected from intrusion, are places for the display of banners, relics and personal souvenirs of Grant. The crypt is in an apse, so that the memorial hall, which is the main room on this floor, may be utilized for patriotic or civic gatherings. Directly in front of the main entrance there is to be an equestrian statue of Grant. The entire work will cost $500,000.

At the end of Riverside Park is Claremont Hill. The Claremont, a restaurant with excellent service, occupies the former residence successively of Viscount Courtenay (Earl of Devon) and of Joseph Bonaparte. Between the tomb and Claremont, right on the bluff, is a little marble headstone marking the grave of a child. On account of its quaintness it has been allowed to remain there by the city authorities, and it will form a touching contrast to the grand structure of the Grant monument. It bears the inscription: "Erected to the memory of an amiable child, St. Claro Pollock. Died 15 July, 1797, in the 5 year of his age." A road descends from the Park to One Hundred and Twenty-seventh street, from which One Hundred and Twenty-fifth street, the main thoroughfare between the eastern and western extremity of the city at this point, is reached. Between the upper part of Riverside avenue and Morningside Park, which latter runs from One Hundred and Tenth street, at a point a little west of the northwestern extremity of Central Park to One Hundred and Twenty-third street, are on One Hundred and Twelfth street the site of the old Leake & Watts Orphan Home, whose ground is to be occupied by the new Protestant Episcopal Cathedral of St. John the Divine, which will probably be the finest church structure in this country, and on spacious grounds bounded by the Boulevard and Amsterdam (Tenth) avenue, One Hundred and Sixteenth and One Hundred and Twentieth streets, the Bloomingdale Insane Asylum, which is a department of the New York Hospital (p. 173). A good view of the upper part of the city, which is here a narow strip of high ground, between the Harlem and Hudson rivers, is obtained by taking the cable road (five cents), which runs from One Hundred and Twenty-fifth street to Fort George, One Hundred and Seventy-fifth street, up New Amsterdam avenue, and then continuing, if the visitor so desires, on foot, crossing King's Bridge, and there taking the New York and Northern Railroad trains, which connect with the rapid transit system of the elevated roads, or the trains of the New York Central and Hudson River Railroad to the Grand Central Station. The various public and semi-public institutions of interest in this part of the city are, besides those referred to, the Convent of the Sacred Heart, a great Roman Catholic educational institution, occupying a large tract of land which begins at St. Nicholas avenue and One Hundred and Twenty-sixth street; the Colored Orphan Asylum in Carmansville, on One Hundred and Forty-third street, between Amsterdam and West End avenues (p. 61); the Sheltering Arms, Amsterdam avenue and One Hundred and Twenty-ninth street (p. 61); Hebrew Orphan Asylum, Amsterdam avenue and One Hundred and Thirty-sixth street (p. 61); Institution for the Deaf and Dumb, Eleventh avenue and One Hundred and Sixty-second street (p. 61); Juvenile Asylum, Amsterdam avenue and One Hundred and Seventy-sixth street (p. 61); the Isabella Home, Amsterdam avenue and One Hundred and Ninety-first street; the Thirty-second Precinct Police Station, Amsterdam avenue and One Hundred and Fifty-third street, where there is an extensive collection of relics of the battle of Harlem Heights; the new cemetery of Trinity church, between Amsterdam avenue and Twelfth avenue, One Hundred and Fifty-third and One Hundred and Fifty-fifth streets, the two sections which are separated by the Boulevard being connected by a bridge. It was especially in the vicinity of Trinity cemetery that the battle of Harlem Heights raged. At One Hundred and Forty-fifth street, a considerable distance back from Amsterdam avenue, stands *Hamilton Grange*, the residence of Alexander Hamilton, which he left on the morning of July 11th, 1804, for Weehawken, to be killed in his duel with Burr. Near the old mansion are the thirteen trees planted in a circle by Hamilton as symbolic of the thirteen original States of the Union. Just above Trinity cemetery is what is kown as Audubon Park, where the distinguished ornithologist Audubon resided, the grounds being now occupied by handsome residences. At One Hundred and Sixty-first street, overlooking the Harlem River, is the old Jumel mansion, which was Washington's headquarters during the battle of Harlem Heights. This mansion was built by Roger Morris, who was struck with the beauty of its situation on his frequent rides to Yonkers, where he was courting the beautiful Mary Philipse, of Philipse Manor, and to this mansion he brought her as his bride in the summer of 1758. Her name has been associated with Washington, whom she is said to have captivated in 1756. The mansion subsequently passed into the hands of the celebrated Madame Jumel, who, after having been twice a widow, married Aaron Burr, then 78 years old.

High Bridge.—On the bold shores of the Harlem river between One Hundred and Seventieth and One Hundred and Seventy-fourth streets is High Bridge Park, in which there is a small reservoir, and a good restaurant. The river is spanned here by High Bridge, now overshadowed as a "sight" by the East River Bridge, but still one of the features of the landscape, along the Harlem. It was built to conduct the old Croton Aqueduct across the river. It is 1,460 feet long, and composed of thirteen arches, the crown of the highest being 116 feet above the river. Foot passengers only can cross the bridge. A fine feature of the view to the north is *Washington Bridge*, which crosses the Harlem river at One Hundred and Eighty-first street. It has two superb central arches of 510 feet span, their crowns being 135 feet above the river. The side arches, four on the west end and three on the east, are of granite faced with pressed stone. Just northwest of High Bridge between One Hundred and Seventy-third and One Hundred and Seventy-fifth streets are the buildings of the *Juvenile Asylum.*

This portion of the city is called Washington Heights, and the station on the New York Central & Hudson River R. R., which runs along the foot of the bluff, Fort Washington. There were earthworks here which the British captured in November, 1776. Fort George, where the cable road stops, derives its name from a redoubt which was here during the Revolution. The upper end of the island is known as Inwood.

Battle of Harlem Heights.—The Battle of Harlem Heights was fought September 16, 1776. Washington, after the battle of Long Island, crossed over to New York and retreating to the upper part of the island made his headquarters at the Apthorpe mansion, which stood at what is now the corner of Ninety-first street and Ninth avenue, until the fall of 1890, when it was torn down to make way for the opening of the street. Washington was here but a short time, and it is said that he had not left it ten minutes to follow his retreating column before Howe and his staff moved in. Washington then made his headquarters at the Morris house, now known as the Jumel mansion (see above). The British were thus in possession of what is now known as Bloomingdale Heights, the Americans intrenching themselves on Washington or Harlem Heights, the battle, however, always being spoken of as the battle of Harlem Heights. This elevation was separated by a ravine from Bloomingdale Heights, and although this district is all built up the depression along the line of the old ravine is still clearly discernible at One Hundred and Fifty-seventh street from the bridge over the Boulevard connecting the two wings of Trinity Cemetery.

The morning of September 16 Washington sent out Colonel Knowlton with 125 men to reconnoitre. Descending a ravine, which led to the river through what is now Audubon Park, Knowlton followed the shore at the foot of the bluff to a point not far from the location of Grant's tomb. He and his soldiers here climbed up the bluff and came suddenly, just as the sun was rising, upon the left flank of the British vanguard, under General Leslie. The British rushed to attack the handful of Americans. Knowlton, waiting till they came within six rods, poured a telling fire into their ranks. After eight rounds, fearing that he might be out-flanked and surrounded, he retreated slowly and in good order down the bluff, retracing his steps along the shore for about two and one-half miles, then, having climbed the west slope of the ravine, faced about, and, sending for reinforcements, stood his ground. Leslie, leaving 300 men in ambush on the river front, led 100 of his men on to the edge of Bloomingdale Heights on the south side of the ravine. Washington ordered Major Leitch with his Virginia riflemen to join Knowlton and to endeavor, with Colonel Reid, to get in the rear of the enemy. The British, seeing a mere handful of Americans, rushed down the slope of the ravine to a fence near a little rivulet, which purled along the bottom of the ravine towards the Hudson. The Americans charged them, and after a sharp skirmish drove them back. By an error, the British reserves were attacked in the flank instead of in the rear, and at a point which is now One Hundred and Fifty-third street in the Boulevard Knowlton was killed, and Leitch also fell. The Americans were then reinforced and drove the British through the woods into a buckwheat field. It was now nearly noon, and Howe and his officers at Bloomingdale, hearing the firing in the direction of Harlem Heights, and becoming uneasy for the safety of Leslie's command, sent some 6,000 picked Highlanders and Hessian troops on the double-quick after him. This detachment encountered Gen. Greene, and from 11 to 2:30 the battle raged over territory extending from Manhattanville or One Hundred and Thirty-fifth street to about One Hundred and Fifty-fifth street. The fiercest conflict of the day was waged on the ground now occupied by Trinity Cemetery. The British were finally driven down Breakneck Hill, a part of the old Kingsbridge Road. There were about 5,000 Americans to 6,000 picked British and Hessian troops, and the result of the battle not only gave Washington an opportunity to withdraw his forces without further molestation, but also inspired his troops, who had found themselves able to cope successfully with the flower of Howe's command, with new courage, and did much to efface the demoralizing influence of the defeat on Long Island. The above is adopted from several greatly varying accounts of the battle of Harlem Heights.

CHAPTER XII.

PUBLIC CHARITIES AND CORRECTION.

PUBLIC CHARITIES AND CORRECTION.—The Department of Public Charities and Correction has its headquarters at 66 Third avenue, where permits to visit the city prisons and other institutions under its jurisdiction must be obtained. Among the prisons, the Tombs (p. 148), and the Jefferson Market prison (p. 172), are the most interesting to visit; and of the other institutions, Bellevue hospital, the Morgue, and the institutions on Blackwell's Island. The permit consists of a printed slip with a list of all the institutions under charge of the Department, but unless the official signing it makes a cross against the insane asylums, the visitor will not be admitted to these. Boats for the various Island institutions which are situated respectively on Blackwell's Island, Ward's Island, Randall's Island and Hart's Island leave foot of East Twenty-sixth street, in the immediate vicinity of Bellevue Hospital and the Morgue at 10:30 A. M. and 1:30 P. M., Saturdays, Sundays and holidays excepted.

Bellevue Hospital.—Bellevue Hospital being situated near the starting point for the various islands at the foot of East Twenty-sixth street, may be visited most conveniently at the time the trip to the islands is made. The entrance to the hospital is at the foot of East Twenty-sixth street. Patients are admitted upon the recommendation of a regular physician, or in case of accidents and sudden illness at any hour of the day or night. Visitors' hours are from 11 A. M. to 3 P. M. The hospital has a capacity of 700 beds. Patients able to pay are charged $3.50 per week. The institution is managed by a board of physicians, which on the last day of every month assigns from its own members the physicians who are to have charge of the various wards for the ensuing month. The grades of junior and senior assistants, house physician or surgeon, the term of service being six months, have been adopted, and in the inspection of the wards the rules of the United States Military Hospital prevail. The annual cost of the institution to the city is about $100,000.

Morgue.—In the Bellevue Hospital grounds are the City's Dead-House and Morgue two of the ghastly sights of New York. In the Dead-House the bodies are cleansed and otherwise rendered as sightly as possible before being exposed in the Morgue. In the latter, which is a low one-story building, the corpses are laid out in an almost nude state on a row of marble slabs upon which jets of water constantly play.

Bodies remaining unclaimed after seventy-two hours are buried in the City Cemetery. Clothes exhibited thirty days, and if not identified, preserved one year. Photographs of the corpse, with the registered number of the grave, also kept.

Blackwell's Island.—Blackwell's Island was bought by Van Twiller, a Dutch Colonial Governor, in 1637. He stocked it with cattle. It subsequently passed into the possession of Capt. Manning, who so ignominiously surrendered New York to the Dutch. After having been publicly disgraced he retired to this island, which he subsequently settled upon his daughter Mary, who married Robert Blackwell, from whom it derives its name. The most southerly building on Blackwell's Island, a granite structure, formerly the small-pox hospital, is the residence for the female nurses of the Charity Hospital. Next to it is the Laundry, where work is done by women from the Work-House. The two wooden buildings just south of the Hospital are pavilions for epileptics. The *Charity Hospital* itself is a 4-story granite building extending across the island, with a frontage of about 500 feet on each branch of the East river. It has a capacity of 1,143 beds, engages the services of 125 attendants, and the average daily number of patients is 1,000. Last year about 8,000 patients were received here, and 7,302 discharged. There were 564 deaths and 376 births. The most interesting department for visitors is the baby ward on the first floor. Every thing here as in the other wards is spick and span, and every effort is made to keep the little ones as happy as possible. Connected with the Hospital is a training-school for female nurses, a library, and rooms for various charitable missions which seek to ameliorate the moral condition of the patients. The medical service of the Hospital is under the charge of a Chief of Staff with some 24 house physicians and assistants, who also perform medical service at the other institutions on the island. The house staff of 8 physicians and surgeons reside in the Hospital, and are appointed after a rigorous examination for a term of 18 months.

North of the Charity Hospital is the *Penitentiary*, which is also the County prison for women, there being no women in the various State prisons; each county being by law compelled to take care of its own female criminals. This is a granite building, 600 feet long, containing 750 cells arranged in tiers. The number of prisoners averages about 1,000 a day, the total for last year being 3,042, of which 396 were women. A card with a record of each prisoner's crime, name, age, date of conviction and arrival, term of sentence and religion is attached to the outside of the cell. The best time to see the prisoners is at 12 o'clock, when they are at dinner, well guarded and compelled to maintain absolute silence. It is also interesting to watch them at work. They are compelled to follow various trades, such as carpentering and tailoring, and they also do a large amount of stone-cutting, there being several quarries on the island, the granite for the large buildings having come from them. The convict labor law does not touch the Penitentiary because all the work here is done for the department itself. There are 50 blacksmiths, 110 shoe-makers and broom-makers and tailors; about 70 carpenters and painters, 2 or 3 upholsterers, 35 tinsmiths and plumbers, 20 clothing-cutters and about 120 stone-cutters. Most of the women are employed in sewing or chamber work in the female prison. Besides this, the Penitentiary furnishes all the unskilled labor for the department. The hours of work are from 7 A. M. to 5:30 P. M. in summer and 4:30 P. M. in winter. In the quarry the men are under a heavy guard, and in case of foggy weather they are massed together and surrounded, in order to prevent their escape by the river. They proceed to or from their work by the lock-step.

The criminal, on entering the Penitentiary, is first taken to the barber shop, where he is shaved and has his hair cut, is bathed, weighed and measured, has his description noted, is dressed in a striped suit and assigned to work. There are good bathing-houses along the river front which the prisoners may use in summer. Books may be taken from the library for two weeks at a time. Prisoners are allowed to receive visitors and write a letter once in four weeks. Besides the guards on the island there are guard-boats constantly patrolling the river. North of the Penitentiary is the Penitentiary farm and the dwelling of the Superintendent. The quarry is at the head of the Penitentiary grounds.

The *Alms House* is next above these. Attached to it is a hospital for females. The old Blackwell homestead is occupied by the Warden. In mild weather the rows of benches under the shady trees are occupied by poor old men and women. Conspicuous on these grounds is the Protestant Episcopal Chapel of the Good Shepherd, erected in 1888 by George Bliss as a memorial of his wife. In the basement of the chapel is a large reading-room. A Roman Catholic mission is also maintained at the Alms House, and various guilds do good work here.

Above the Alms House are the Fire Engine House and the Gas-works. The *Work House* beyond is rather a disagreeable place to visit; its inmates usually belonging to the class known as "drunks," the lowest order of criminals—the very scum and refuse of a great city.

The total admissions for last year were 22,477, of whom 11,706 were males and 10,771 were females. Beyond here is the female *Insane Asylum.*

Ward's Island is more attractive looking than Blackwell's, but not as interesting to the visitor. It contains some 200 acres, and so much of it as is not occupied by buildings is well laid out. The Department of Public Charities and Correction has charge here of the Male Insane Asylum and a Homeopathic Hospital. The Insane Asylum is an imposing structure of brick trimmed with gray stone. Invalid soldiers of the civil war who enlisted in city regiments are provided for in a pleasant home on this island.

Randall's Island, separated from Ward's Island by Little Hell Gate, and divided from the Westchester shore by the Harlem Kills, lies in the mouth of the Harlem river. Under the Commissioners of Public

Charities and Correction are the Idiot Asylum and other institutions provided by the city for destitute children—the Nursery, Children's and Infants' hospitals and various schools. Besides these there is on the southern end of the island a House of Refuge, a fine building under the care of the Society for the Reformation of Juvenile Delinquents; the buildings and grounds, which are finely laid out, occupying about 30 acres. Children sentenced by police magistrates are brought to this institution whose inmates number about 900.

Hart's Island lies between Sand's Point and Pelham Neck on Long Island Sound. Here are a branch Lunatic Asylum, Hospital, Work-House and City Cemetery (the Potter's Field) where about 2,500 unknown and paupers are annually interred. Here are 75,000 drunkards' graves. A soldiers' monument is the only memorial stone in this pathetic piece of ground.

CHAPTER XIII.

ENVIRONS.

The most attractive tours in the vicinity of New York are those of the *Long Island* and *Jersey Coast* resorts, and of the *Hudson River*. *Greenwood Lake* (New York and Greenwood Lake R. R.), partly in New York State and partly in New Jersey, and *Lake Hopatcong* (Delaware, Lackawanna & Western R. R.) in the Highlands of New Jersey are also worth visiting. The *Delaware Water Gap*, though not properly speaking within the environs of New York, should also be mentioned, as it can be reached (Delaware, Lackawanna & Western R. R. ferries from Christopher and Barclay streets) in about three and a half hours and is one of the grandest passages of scenery in the United States.

Long Island.—Long Island is 115 miles long, averaging 12 miles in width. The summer resorts are on the ocean or south shore. A sandy barrier extends some distance out from the main shore nearly the whole length of the island and the ocean penetrating it through narrow inlets has formed several fine bays, the largest of which is the Great South Bay.

Brooklyn.—Brooklyn, the third largest city in the United States in point of population (over 804,000), and the fourth largest in manufacturing and commercial interests, is on Long Island, opposite New York. To strangers the point of greatest attraction in Brooklyn is the United States Navy Yard, on the south shore of Wallabout Bay, best reached by elevated railroad from the East River Bridge. The area of the Navy Yard is 144 acres, with a water front of over a mile. The Yard proper, 45 acres, is inclosed by a high wall. Two dry-docks, one 286 feet long by 35 feet wide at the bottom, and 307 by 98 feet at the top and 36 feet deep, the other 465 feet long by 210 wide, the latter for the docking of the modern war ships of the United States Navy, are among the most conspicuous features of the Yard.

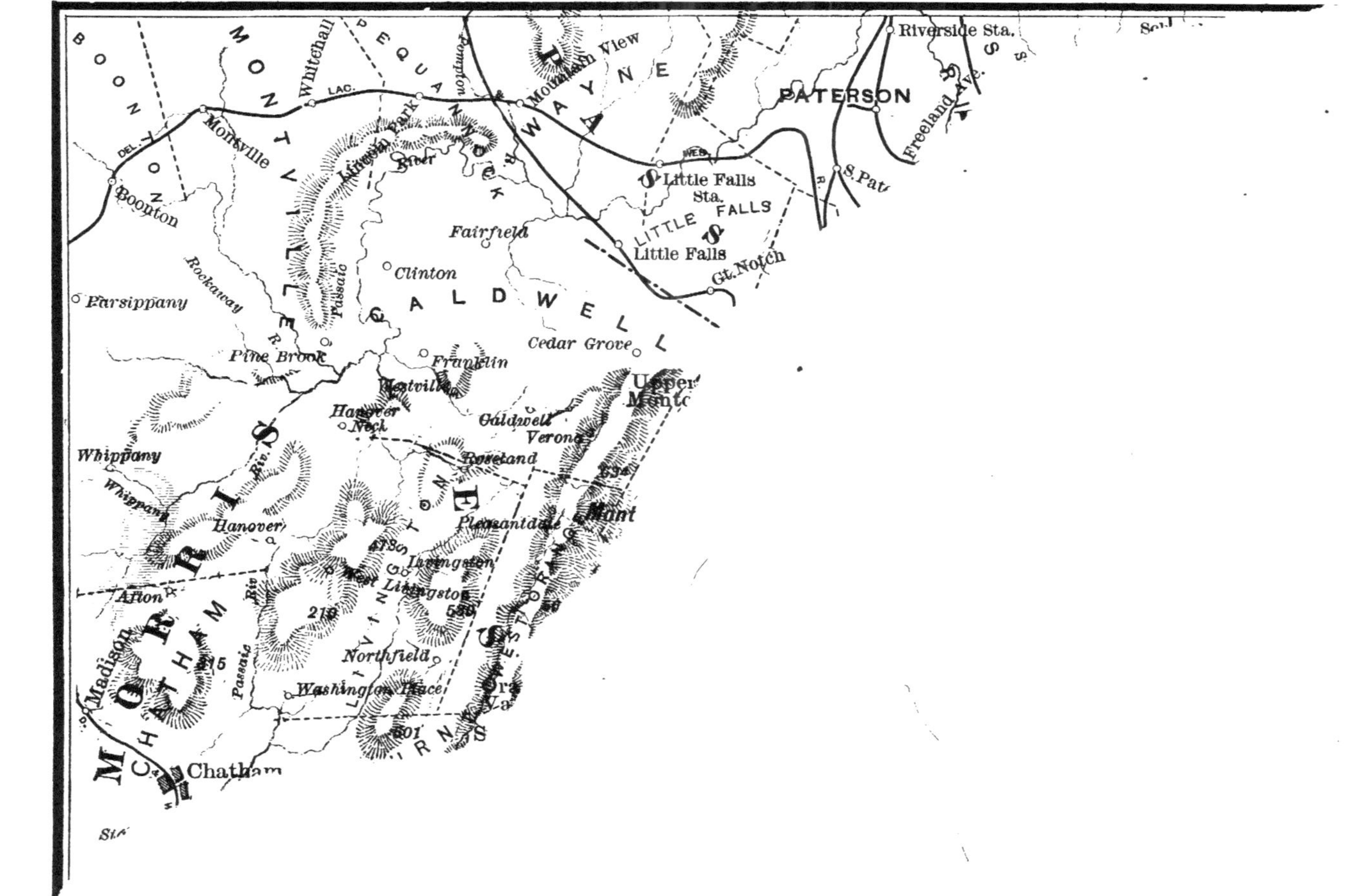
BOONTON
MONTVILLE
PEQUANNOCK
WAYNE
PASSAIC
PATERSON
Riverside Sta.
Freeland Ave.
Whitehall
Mountain View
Pompton
Montville
Boonton
Lincoln Park
Little Falls Sta.
LITTLE FALLS
Little Falls
Gt. Notch
S. Pat
Fairfield
Clinton
Rockaway
Parsippany
Passaic
CALDWELL
Cedar Grove
Pine Brook
Franklin
Hanover Neck
Caldwell
Verona
Roseland
Whippany
MORRIS
Hanover
ESSEX
LIVINGSTON
Livingston
West Livingston
Pleasantdale
Afton
CHATHAM
Madison
Northfield
Washington Place
Chatham
ORANGE
WEST ORANGE
Upper Montc
478
219
530
315
601
634

Perhaps even more interesting than these are the modern war vessels, one or several of which are usually moored here, and also the vessels upon which construction is in progress. The United States Naval Lyceum, founded in 1833, has besides an extensive library, collections of curiosities gathered during cruises in foreign seas, and fine geological and mineralogical cabinets. The 21 well kept acres surrounding the Naval Hospital form a pretty feature of the Yard.

Prospect Park, situated on high ground in the southwestern part of Brooklyn, commands a superb view of both the Upper and Lower Bays to the Atlantic Ocean. It is best reached by the Flatbush avenue cars from Fulton ferry. An excellent idea of the Park can be had by taking the Park carriages (25 cents), which convey the visitor to the highest point of the Park, Lookout Carriage Concourse, from which a fine view is to be had. The Ocean Parkway, a superb thoroughfare 210 feet wide, leads from Prospect Park to the ocean, six miles distant. At the principal entrance to the Park, the Plaza on Flatbush avenue, is a memorial arch to the soldiers and sailors of the Civil War and a statue of Lincoln.

Greenwood Cemetery, superbly located on a height overlooking New York Harbor, is reached by elevated railroad from the Brooklyn terminus of the East River Bridge.

Coney Island is the great seaside excursion resort for the populace of New York and Brooklyn and their suburbs, though the easterly part of the Island, known as Brighton Beach and Manhattan Beach are more exclusive. At West Brighton, where two iron piers extend 1,000 feet into the ocean, affording not only a landing for the boats of the Iron Steamboat Co., but also accommodations for restaurants, bath houses and promenades, are Cable's, Vanderveer's and the West Brighton hotels, where good, yet comparatively inexpensive accommodations may be had; the Elephant Hotel, built in the form of a mammoth pachyderm; an observatory 300 feet high, commanding a superb view; and untold numbers of small shows of all kinds, eating houses, and resorts of varied character. The Ocean Parkway, from Prospect Park, Brooklyn, ends at the more easterly of the two iron piers. The Concourse leads from West Brighton to Brighton Beach, where there is a spacious hotel, with large dining rooms and piazzas. Beyond it is Manhattan Beach, which, with its adjunct, the Oriental Hotel, forms the most exclusive resort on the Island. Music every day during the season at 2 and 7:30 P. M. Admission 10 cents and 25 cents. Fireworks every night; admission, with reserved seat, 50 cents. Strangers desiring to see Coney Island under the most favorable circumstances, are advised to stop either at the Manhattan or Oriental, and make detours from there.

Rockaway Beach.—Manhattan Beach is connected by a ferry, 10 cents, with Rockaway Beach, another great excursion resort, which a stranger desiring to study the characteristics of the populace will find interesting. It is reached from New York by the Long Island Railroad (Thirty-fourth street ferry), round trip 50 cents, and by steamboats (p. 30). The scene at Rockaway Beach resembles that on the popular portion of Coney Island.

Long Beach.—East of Rockaway Beach, 24 miles from New York, is Long Beach, reached by the Long Island Railroad. The beach here is one of the best on Long Island, for surf bathing and there are boating, yachting and fishing in Hempstead Bay. The Long Beach Hotel is large and well conducted. A railway leads to Point Lookout at the extreme eastern end of Long Beach, 4½ miles from the hotel. There are at Point Lookout a good hotel and a number of cottages.

Babylon and Fire Island.—Babylon, which lies on the mainland of the Great South Bay, affords excellent fishing, bathing and boating, and has an excellent hotel in the Argyle. Across the bay from Babylon is Fire Island, a long, narrow strip of sand, reached from Babylon by steamer. There are fine surf bathing, and in the bay still water bathing; and excellent blue fishing. The Surf House is a large, well-kept hotel.

JERSEY COAST.*—Those Jersey Coast resorts which may be properly classed as among the environs of New York—say to Elberon—are reached by the Jersey Southern route (boat from foot Rector street to Sandy

*Detailed accounts of the Jersey Coast resorts from Sandy Hook to Atlantic City and of Lakewood will be found in "Kobbé's Jersey Coast and Pines."

Hook) and by the New York and Long Branch R. R., operated by the Central R. R. of New Jersey (ferry from foot of Liberty street to Jersey City) and the Pennsylvania R. R. (ferry from foot of Cortlandt street). Of these the Jersey Southern is the most delightful, a fleet of fine steamers, including the two fast, twin-screw steamers *Sandy Hook* and *Monmouth* and the *St. Johns*, which, until the first two named were built, was the fastest boat on the bay, plying between the foot of Rector street and Atlantic Highlands. The train, after running for a short distance through the woods on Sandy Hook, emerges upon the beach, in full view of the ocean on one side and the Navesink river on the other, so that the railroad trip from the Hook is cool and refreshing.

From *Highland Beach*, the first stop, a bridge crosses the Navesink to the mainland, the *Highlands of Navesink*, among which Fenimore Cooper laid the scene of his romance, "The Water Witch."

Lighthouse Hill is named from the picturesque twin lighthouses, the "Highland Lights," which stand on its small, bare plateau, semi-encircled by thick woods.

Navesink Beach, adjoining Highland Beach, consists of cottages extending to *Normandie-by-the-Sea*, a first-class hotel (open June 15–October 1), capable of accommodating 300 guests. It commands a fine view of both ocean and river. Extending from this hotel to Seabright is *Rumson Beach* (formerly Stokem's), a line of pretty summer cottages.

Seabright is one of the gayest resorts on the coast. On the Rumson Road, not far from the Jumping Point Drawbridge, are the house and grounds of the Seabright Lawn-Tennis and Cricket Club. On *Rumson Neck* are some of the finest country residences in the United States. Hotels at Seabright: Octagon, $4; Hotel Shrewsbury, $3.50. A picturesque feature of Seabright is the fishing village of *Nauvoo*.

The great charms of *Monmouth Beach* are its privacy and refinement. The nearest approach to a hotel is the Club House, in which are a few sleeping apartments and a spacious dining-room, the latter for the use of the occupants of some 25 cottages, which are let to friends of the regular cottagers. There is a Casino, with hall and a stage for private theatricals, a bowling-alley and a billiard-room.

Long Branch is often spoken of as the "Brighton of America." It derives its name from the adjacent branch of the Shrewsbury river. It is known to have been in 1734 a camping ground of the Cranberry Indians. In 1753 a conference was held at Crosswicks between the Indians and four settlers from Rhode Island to arrange for the purchase by the latter of a portion of the State which now includes Long Branch. After much palaver, it was agreed that they should be allowed to buy as much land as a man could walk around in a day if one of them could throw an Indian champion in a wrestling match. John Slocum, a man of large size and athletic strength, was the white champion. After a long struggle he threw his man.

The Long Branch of to-day is a sea-shore cosmopolis. The features which attract the vast summer throng to it probably repel as many, if not more, from it, a circumstance to which the majority of the more rational resorts on the coast doubtless owe their origin. The leading characteristics of Long Branch may be described in one sentence: It supports numerous hotels, churches and a synagogue; the "tiger" has two superbly appointed jungles, in one of which at least one man is known to have left of a single night $25,000 for the voracious animal to paw over and devour; it is "fashionable" in the sense in which the word is used by those who fondly imagine that lavish display of wealth is evidence of high social position.

Yet, as there are islands in a rushing, roaring stream, so there are some spots in Long Branch where the noisy throng have not intruded. Besides many private cottages there are the fine hotel, cottages and grounds of Hollywood, near the West End station, a settlement within itself, under one management and including a huge bathing pavilion shut in by high walls from the gaze of the *ignobile vulgus* and for the use of the Hollywood guests only. Another pavilion is that of the West End Hotel, a first-class establishment.

Ocean avenue toward evening is probably the liveliest thoroughfare in the United States. Here one can see almost every kind of vehicle—stages crowded with excursionists, buggies drawn by swift roadsters, tandems, four-in-hands, T-carts, etc., many of them perfectly appointed and each interesting in its own way, as representing one of the many types of people to be found at this resort.

A short distance from Long Branch is the *Monmouth Park* race-track (p. 65).

Elberon, a continuation of Long Branch on the south, is one of the most complete and elegant resorts on the Jersey coast, with much the same refined and exclusive characteristics as Monmouth Beach. The Elberon Căsino was incorporated in 1882 with a capital of $50,000, and the company also erected the admirable hotel called the Elberon (from $4 upward). Among the handsome residences of this place is the Francklyn cottage, rendered famous as the refuge to which President Garfield was brought, and where he was lulled into his final sleep by the murmur of the sea. General Grant's former summer home is also at Elberon.

Among the resorts south of Elberon are *Asbury Park* and *Ocean Grove*, two populous summering places, largely dominated by the Methodist Episcopal Church, camp meetings and other religious exercises being a feature of life at the "Grove." *Seagirt*, still further south, is one of the most refined and delightful resorts on the coast, the Beach House being patronized by a number of refined New York and Philadelphia families.

From Long Branch to the south there runs back of the coast a section of New Jersey which is thickly wooded with pines. *Lakewood*, reached by fast trains of the Central R. R. of New Jersey, foot of Liberty street, is a charming winter resort in this balmy forest. (Laurel House and Hotel Lakewood.)

HUDSON RIVER.—For natural beauty there is no trip out of New York City comparable with a tour of the Hudson River by steamboat. The boats of the Albany Day Line leave the foot of Vestry street at 8:45 A. M., and foot of West Twenty-second street at 9 A. M., due at Albany at 6 P. M. Boats of this line leave Albany in the morning, and it is possible to take the morning boat from New York to *West Point*, which may properly be considered the extreme northern limit of the environs of New York as covered by this book, and return by a boat of the same line in the afternoon. Round trip, $1. Other boats by which the trip up the Hudson can be made, but without the facility for returning to New York the same day, are: *Mary Powell*, considered the swiftest steamboat in the world, entering the Highlands on the trip up the river about sunset, when the scene along this beautiful stretch of the Hudson is most inspiring. The Albany night boats leave foot of Canal street at 6 P. M., and the Troy night boats foot of Christopher at 6 P. M., both arriving at their destinations at 6 o'clock the next morning; fare $2, exclusive of meals. (See, also, p. 30).

Railroads which afford glimpses of the most beautiful points on the river are the New York Central and Hudson River R. R. along the east bank to Albany, and the New York, West Shore and Buffalo R. R. on the west shore to Albany (p 26).

The Trip by Steamboat.—Before the end of the Island of Manhattan is reached, the Palisades rise in sheer ascent to a height of 300 feet from the river's west bank, forming a columnar trap-rock precipice of unique grandeur 20 miles in length. The old Revolutionary fortification, *Fort Lee*, was on the brow of the Palisades at a point about opposite the present Fort Washington, (One Hundred and Eighty-first to One Hundred and Eighty-fifth streets) where the Revolutionary fort of that name stood. There are large excursion grounds at Fort Lee. Spuyten Duyvil Creek comes into the river at the end of the Island of Manhattan. Fifteen miles from New York, on the east shore, lies *Mt. St. Vincent*, the site of the convent in charge of the Ladies of the Sacred Heart. Two miles further up the river, on the same shore, is the city of *Yonkers*, and five miles beyond this, *Dobbs' Ferry*. At *Piermont*, twenty-two miles up the western shore, the river widens out and assumes a lake-like appearance, and is locally known as Tappan Zee, a reach of ten miles by four miles at its widest point. Washington had his headquarters at *Tappan*, about three miles southwest of Piermont, and here Major André was imprisoned and executed October 2, 1780. The headquarters still stands, and the site where André's execution took place is also pointed out. On the east shore of Tappan Zee, four miles above Dobbs' Ferry, is

Irvington, where Washington Irving resided in his pretty cottage, Sunnyside, which, though near the shore, cannot be seen from the river, because of the sheltering trees and shrubbery. The next settlement on the east shore is *Tarrytown*, which overlooks Tappan Zee at its widest point. All this region has been invested with a romantic interest by Irving's sketches. Irving's house at Irvington is the original of *Wolfert's Roost*. The valley of Sleepy Hollow lies along the course of Mill river, but a little way north of Tarrytown, and over the stream the traveler can still cross by the stone bridge made famous by Irving in his sketch of *Ichabod Crane*. Near the old Dutch Church in this valley, which is the oldest religious structure in this State (1699) is the spot where Andre was captured by three American minute-men while on his way to the British lines just after he had concluded the negotiation for the treason of Benedict Arnold. Opposite Tarrytown is the pretty suburban and summer residence place, *Nyack*. Just above is High Torn, a grand old headland, and near it Rockland Lake, which cannot, however, be seen from the river. About opposite Rockland Lake is *Sing Sing*, where one of the New York State prisons is situated, the great buildings having been constructed of marble and limestone from local quarries. Above Sing Sing is a prominent headland known as *Croton Point*, the Croton river here entering the Hudson (p. 11). At the foot of the northern slope of the Dunderberg on the west shore is *Haverstraw*. Here in a house then belonging to Joshua Hett Smith and still standing, Arnold and André met to arrange finally for the surrender of West Point, and it was after crossing the river from here that André was captured. The widening of the river is known as Haverstraw Bay, and as the boat enters this, the *Highlands* are seen in the distance above. *Stony Point*, on the western shore, at the northern end of Haverstraw Bay, is a rocky promontory marked by a light-house, and was, in the Revolution, the site of a fort captured by the British June 1, 1779, re-captured at the point of the bayonet in a brilliant charge up the declivity lead by Mad Anthony Wayne, midnight of July 15th, 1779, and abandoned for lack of the necessary force to hold it. *Peekskill*, on the east bank, not far above Stony Point, is the site of the State Militia Camp, which is located on what is known as Anthony's Nose, a short distance above the town. In the river-bed, near *Caldwell's Landing*, at the foot of Dunderberg Mountain, opposite Peekskill, Captain Kidd is supposed to have buried part of his treasure, and search for it has been made from time to time—once by a regularly organized company with extensive apparatus. Dunderberg Mountain, on the west shore, and Anthony's Nose, on the east, form the southern gates of the Highlands, the most beautiful passage of the river. The little island lying near the entrance is Iona Island, a picnic ground. Just above Anthony's Nose is *Sugar Loaf Mountain*, (865 feet), so called from its peculiar shape. It was while breakfasting with Col. Beverly Robinson in a house still standing at the foot of Sugar Loaf Mountain that Arnold received the news of Andre's arrest, and fled to the *Vulture*, a British vessel anchored down the river. At *Buttermilk Falls*, on the west bank, a series of cascades coming down from an elevation of 100 feet into the river, is Cranston's Hotel, and but a short distance above it, *West Point*. Opposite West Point is *Garrisons*. Those who desire to continue the trip through the Highlands to *Newburgh* will find on the west bank the superb headland of Crow Nest (1,428 feet) where J. Rodman Drake laid the scene of his "Culprit Fay," and above it the *Storm King* (1,529 feet). *Cold Spring*, above Garrisons, rests upon the slope of Mount Taurus. Nestling on the northern slope of the Storm King is the pretty village of *Cornwall*. Between it and Newburgh is *New Windsor*, and opposite Newburgh *Fishkill Landing*. *Newburgh* is not as interesting a place for a sojourn as West Point, but the visitor can while away an hour at Washington's headquarters, the old stone mansion south of the town built in 1750, where, June 23, 1783, the Revolutionary army was disbanded. The State, which owns the house, has gathered in it a collection of Revolutionary relics. The grounds about the house command a view of the superb entrance to the Highlands.

West Point.—At West Point is the United States Military Academy, whose buildings stand upon a beautiful plateau at the foot of Crow Nest, 157 feet above the river. The road leading from the landing is cut out of the cliff of solid rock. Among the buildings are the Cadets' Barracks, the Academic Building, both of stone, the latter containing class-rooms, laboratories and gymnasiums; the Mess Hall, the Chapel, and the Museum of Ordnance and Trophies. The low building on the terrace below the library is the Riding Hall. Beautiful views of the river are commanded from West Point, more especially, however, from Trophy Point to the north, which derives its name from the captured cannon to be seen there. Here is also a portion of the chain which the Americans stretched across the Hudson in 1778 to prevent the passage of British vessels up the river. At Fort Clinton, on the northeast angle of the plateau, is a monument to Kosciusko, which the cadets erected 1828. Flirtation Walk, where every cadet is supposed to lose his heart more or less frequently, is a path along the bank of the river sheltered from view by trees and shrubbery. On the parade ground is a bronze statue of Major-General Sedgwick, killed at the battle of Spottsylvania, May 9, 1864, and an obelisk to Lieut.-Col. Wood, who was killed at the head of a sortie from Fort Erie, Canada, in 1814. In the cemetery are, among other notable monuments, the Cadets' Monument, a castellated column surmounted by an urn and trophy, and a massive sarcophagus beneath which rest the remains of Gen. Winfield Scott. The best time to visit West Point is during June, July and August, but more especially at the time when the exercises and drills preparatory to graduation are taking place. These usually occur in June. Near West Point, 600 feet above the river, on Mount Independence, are the ruins of the Revolutionary Fort Putnam, from which a superb view is had. The West Point Hotel ($4.00 a day) is at the north of the plateau and Cranston's Hotel ($4.00 a day) the accommodations of which are unexceptionable, is near enough to enable its guests to enjoy all the varied sights of West Point.

STATEN ISLAND*.—*Sailors' Snug Harbor:* This is an institution with an annual income of about $100,000, situated on the north shore of Staten Island. It is reached by ferry from foot of Whitehall street to St.

*For description of Staten Island, see "Kobbé's Staten Island."

George and thence by train to Sailors' Snug Harbor station. (Fare 10 cents; time 30 min. from New York.) To the Harbor sailors of every nationality are admitted, the only requirement for admission being that they have had a five years' sea service under the Stars and Stripes, and are incapable of self-support. Here are blind sailors, lame sailors, sailors without legs, sailors without arms, and sailors physically and mentally sound, but perhaps too old to stand the exposure of a mariner's life. They have everything they need, including tobacco, and one of the forms of punishment is to deprive Jack of his pipe. On all secular days the visitor is welcomed and inmates of the institution are very glad to act as guides, for an optional fee, through the grounds and buildings.

GLEN ISLAND.—A popular excursion ground in Long Island Sound, near New Rochelle. Reached by steamboats making many trips daily. See advertisements in newspapers.

INDEX.

With the Nearest Elevated Railroad Stations to the Principal Points of Interest.

Electrotyped by De Leeuw & Oppenheimer, New York.

www.ingramcontent.com/pod-product-compliance
Lightning Source LLC
LaVergne TN
LVHW010543110826
845149LV00003B/545

* 9 7 8 1 4 1 8 1 8 7 8 1 1 *